IMMORTAL
HARLEQUIN

IMMORTAL HARLEQUIN

THE STORY OF ADRIAN STOOP

IAN COOPER

TEMPUS

Frontispiece: Stoop family coat of arms with motto *'Carpe Diem'* and three 'stoops' (tankards).

First published 2004

Tempus Publishing Limited
The Mill, Brimscombe Port,
Stroud, Gloucestershire, GL5 2QG
www.tempus-publishing.com

© Ian Cooper, 2004

The right of Ian Cooper to be identified as the Author
of this work has been asserted in accordance with the
Copyrights, Designs and Patents Act 1988.

British Library Cataloguing in Publication Data.
A catalogue record for this book is available from the British Library.

ISBN 0 7524 3180 3

Typesetting and origination by Tempus Publishing Limited
Printed and bound in Great Britain

CONTENTS

ACKNOWLEDGEMENTS

And on that cheek, and o'er that brow,
So soft, so calm, yet eloquent,
The smiles that win, the tints that glow
But tell of days in goodness spent,
A mind at peace with all below,
A heart whose love is innocent!

We were a gallant company,
Riding o'er land, and sailing o'er sea.
Oh! but we went merrily!

Prologue to *The Siege of Corinth*, Byron

This book owes much in the way of thanks to those that have provided inspiration and support along the way: to the working assistance and imagination provided by all at Birddog; to Basil Lambert and the Harlequins; to Jed, Ross and the crew at The Twickenham Museum of Rugby; David Ray and Rusty MacLean at Rugby School; Tessa Westlake and the Byfleet Heritage Society; David Chapman for his work on West Hall; Nick Cross for his research; Susie Dunn, Philip Hatt and David Hazell from Hartley Wintney for invaluable leads; Christopher Needham; St John the Evangelists (Hartley Wintney) for a sight of their special window; the National Archives, the Hampshire Records Office, The Liddell Hart Centre for Military Archives, The Queens Royal Surrey Regiment, The King's Royal Hussars and Dover College for valuable information and permission for the use of it.

To James, Holly, Wendy and Rob at Tempus.

To those from my own playing days at Churcher's College and with the teams of The Public Bar Wanderers, Tulse Hill & Dulwich and PWC Croydon who provided many lessons and memories.

To Véronique, Jon and Siobhan, Fernando, Steve and my family for pushing me 'over the line'.

And to Michael, thanks for the memories.

FOREWORDS

Foreword by Michael Stoop

Ian Cooper has skilfully chronicled passages of my father's life which took place a hundred years ago. The wealth of information and detail he has unearthed through his extensive research is most impressive, but as all this took place a quarter of a century before I ever really knew my father, my knowledge of them was scant.

Adrian was the son of a Dutch immigrant. I do not know why my grandfather elected to leave his Dordrecht where the Stoops were and had been of considerable influence for hundreds of years, but he decided to break with a thousand years of family history and come and live in England, where he bought West Hall, a large house in West Byfleet. Here he brought up his children, of whom my father was the firstborn.

At the age of fourteen Adrian was sent to Rugby School. With its strong religious culture and the lasting influence of Dr Arnold this did much to mode his character and outlook. After first excelling as a gymnast he was introduced to the game which was to influence his whole life. His outstanding performances on the rugby field at school were followed by more at Oxford, then with the Harlequins and finally as captain of England.

There followed the long years of the First World War, which Adrian spent mainly in Mesopotamia fighting the Turks, ironically the same theatre as today's infamous war in Iraq. My father never spoke about his war experiences, except to say that the Turks were fine fighters and that our troops made a hideous mess of the siege of Kut. Of his Military Cross, nothing.

On leaving India he met my mother, then a beautiful and ambitious eighteen-year-old staying with her tea-planter father. She may not have travelled 'port out' but having met my father, a rich man, she determined it would be 'starboard home'. And so it was, but no longer as Miss Needham from an impoverished Irish family, but as Mrs Adrian Stoop. She bore him four sons and they set up in a comfortable home in Hartley Wintney.

I later exchanged the disciplines of the nursery wing and its governesses for those of the private school. It was only during the holidays that I really got to know my father. Fanatic as he was about fitness he imposed upon us a daily routine of exercise, involving a cold bath, after which he would take us onto the lawn and teach us rugby skills such as running straight, swerving away when delivering a pass, how best to launch a tackle, to practise the iconic Poulton jink, and so on. Whether or not we benefited from this when we later took to the field, I am not sure.

He used to take us skiing and mountain climbing in Austria, fishing on his stretch of the Test, the occasional shoot and, whenever the occasion warranted, to Twickenham. Often he and I would sit alone behind the posts in the empty north stand from whence he considered he could best read the game. Woe betide the Harlequin guilty of running across! Many were the afternoons he would spend with the 'Quins – those who played for the club and those who played for the 'A' team – encouraging them and giving them the benefit of his advice and his experience.

Of course, as in any other sport, there can be no comparison made between the game at which my father excelled a hundred years ago and the one played today. My father would have applauded the skill of today's players, their astonishing speed and stamina, their slick and lightning-quick handling of the ball and the accuracy of their kicking. He would have applauded too the well-rehearsed tactics, strategies and cohesion of their teamwork. But sadly, I feel that with his Rugby School upbringing he might have enthused less about the spirit in which the game is played today.

Foreword by Jason Leonard

In finally drawing time on my own rugby-playing days I have been lucky to achieve all that I could have wanted with the Harlequins, Barbarians, England and the Lions. Big games have come and gone, and with them various milestones and records – records that will one day be broken. What will remain with me are the ideals that make rugby the great game that it is: the great friendships that it creates, the laughter and the cheers.

Reading *Immortal Harlequin* is to see how the game in England was brought along from its humble beginnings, the coming together of the nations and the development of their distinctive styles. Above all, however, it tells the story of a man for whom those same ideals were held as dear.

Adrian Stoop's standards of self-discipline and fitness a hundred years ago would not be out of place with the demands of the modern game. Most of us will be able to relate to the injuries that can hold us back. Few of us will experience the tremendous pride that comes in captaining our countries. All of us can live with the memories.

Adrian was a rugby man who never lost sight of the true spirit in which the great game should be played and as such his place in the history of game is assured, not just for his country but more specifically with his beloved Harlequins.

PREFACE

1966, 1977, 1981, 2000: On their own they are just years, but between them is a special bond, a bond that stands the test of time. Years when, just for a moment, a few sports personalities were peerless, and for which a mere date is not enough: 1966 – England's World Cup; 1977 – Red Rum's National; 1981 – Botham's Ashes; 2000 – Redgrave's Olympics. As we get older, the memories remain. We are always gently reminded of the casual brilliance by a news item, a television highlight or a video. Nobody could forget England's Rugby World Cup win in Australia in 2003. Pictures and images loomed large (and often).

Where all great sporting years, indeed all moments of sporting glory, can be joined is in their ability to be replayed over. In the mind, in conversation, on television. The further back we go, the less likely we are to be able to converse with those that were indeed there. A grainy newsreel may be all that remains. We live with what we can find, what we turn up.

With some degree of English World Cup relevance, I remember attending a sports club luncheon the day after Bobby Moore died. Jackie Charlton was the after-dinner speaker giving an amusing, but inwardly emotional, speech about the 1966 football team and the great man: to have played with these men, to have been inspired by their leader, to have experienced that powerful bond. The humility was there for all to see. I was too young to remember Wembley 1966, but I felt part of it because I have seen it a thousand times since. I could have been there. For ninety minutes I was there with Jackie and with Bobby. All so real. Shared experiences, shared grief.

I was there for the 1999 Rugby World Cup semi-final between France and New Zealand at that Englishman's castle, Twickenham. To everyone in the ground it was one of the greatest games of modern times. Certainly one of Twickenham's finest. The French were down at half time, but high up in the Twickenham stands one sensed something was about to happen. All through the first half the French had been throwing the ball about with apparent abandon. To the trained eye, however, there was definite method. The rub of the green and they would have gone in ahead. The second half is history. The French continued where they had left off, their passing awesome, their moves mesmeric, their purpose clear for all to see. The final result that day was a testimony to the great game of rugby itself. Passion, pride, skill and flair. And something else. To lose such a game, a semi-final at that, must have been shattering. As the victorious French team started out on a deserved lap of honour, the All Blacks retired to the sanctuary of the changing rooms. Except for one man. Jonah Lomu stood by the touchline. Stood and waited, alone in his thoughts. As the French returned, he applauded them, shook each and every hand and was last to leave the pitch. That something else. Sportsmanship of the highest order. Watch the video and feel humble.

Entertainers. Sportsmen. Gentlemen. Shades of yesteryear, and Sunday 9 May 1915 in particular, when back at the Rugby School chapel, the Reverend A.A. David gave a poignant and moving sermon, called simply *Counting the Cost*. Two great lives were mourned: Rupert Brooke and Ronald Poulton. The Reverend, speaking of his school's former pupils, drew from Luke, XIV 28-30:

For which of you desiring to build a tower, does not first sit down and count the cost, whether he hath the wherewithal to complete it? Lest haply, when he has laid a foundation, and is not able to finish it, all that behold it begin to mock him, saying: this man began to build, and was not able to finish.

We should confess I think to a certain sympathy with the man. It is not difficult to make out a good case for him. He saw that a tower was wanted. He could not wait to be sure that material was ready. So he began with what he had, sure that material enough was ready, and used it as far as it would go, hoping perhaps for some partnership which would help him to finish what he had begun, in a kind of faith, believing that he could not see.

Rupert Brooke and Ronald Poulton were geniuses of differing kinds, but they both played in the same Rugby School XV in 1905 as Freek Stoop. Adrian Stoop would often visit to watch a game, passing on advice to his younger brother and any other schoolboy who cared to listen. His motives, however, ran deeper. He had a greater cause for which he would not be disappointed. He was watching, thinking, planning ahead. 1910 was to be Stoop's year and he was already laying the foundations.

Within Twickenham Stadium lie ten years of newspaper cuttings. Four handsomely bound books of Adrian's career between 1903 and 1914 – not for him a video or a TV replay but the written memories, to learn from, to teach, wrapped up for all. To read them takes us back to the golden age of English rugby, before the First World War, when the people came to see the much-heralded Harlequins team, its individuals, its legends. They were a team who threw the ball about with seeming abandon, but actually with great method and purpose. Rugby players first and foremost, they were also entertainers, sportsmen, gentlemen one and all. One is humbled as the story unfolds, a living drama, one of incredible highs and lows. Their bond was strong, their fortunes differing, a band of brothers, under the leadership of the inspirational Stoop. He started with a blank canvas, but somehow painted a masterpiece. This is his story.

Ian Cooper

Trudging in the wind, a very small boy, on my way towards the fantastically muddy field where I was to play this rather terrifying game. How important it was, to be sure! Nothing else in life had any significance, though not so very far away the greatest of all wars was thundering itself to a close. Nothing else mattered; the world was bounded by the sagging ropes round that quagmire of a field, and the yelling boys who stood behind them.

(*What rugger means to me*, Howard Marshall)

—–m—

OLD SCHOOL
1823-1900

What we must look for here is: first, religious and moral principles;
secondly, gentlemanly conduct; thirdly intellectual ability.
(Thomas Arnold, Headmaster of Rugby School, 1827-1842)

The sixteenth century in Holland was a time of economic depression. Until then, Dordrecht, originally a small rural population that had been kept alive on farming, fishing and peat lands, had grown to be the first of Holland's eighteen cities, often being given preferential status over Amsterdam. Its position, on an island where the waters of the Rhine and Meuse met, was of singular strategic importance, controlling as it did the river ways to Germany. The sea port had become the main market for building materials, for hock from the Rhine, claret from Bordeaux and, significantly, British wool. With the depression, increased competition came from emerging new harbours at Bruges and Antwerp. Political disturbance saw Dordrecht, among other cities, rebelling against Philip, the Count of the day (who also happened to be the King of Spain). Safe amid the rivers, Dordrecht was a bastion of the new reformed religion. Chief among the agitators were the Stoops.

Prime among them was Dr Willem Stoop, Burgomaster of the city in 1535. In nearly every generation from the cities early days, one or more members of the Stoops held office in the city government, often related by marriage to families with similar positions. Willem commissioned a painting, the Stoop family triptych, depicting the Holy Family and that of himself with his wife and nineteen children. The work of art took years to complete and became a living tableau. Crosses above the heads of particular family members indicated those who had died before the painting was finished. Also depicted in the portrait was a monk carrying a palm leaf, representing the visit of an earlier forebear, Adriaan Stoop, to the Holy Land.

In England, some thirty years later in 1567, another legacy started. Under Lawrence Sheriff's intent, a small local grammar school was set up in Rugby to serve the needs of the small market town. Two and a half centuries later, William Webb Ellis ran himself into folklore during a game played at school, known then simply as 'football'. The 'rules', such as they were, had evolved through the schoolboy players, not through any outside body. Like any good boys' game, nothing was written down, everything was open to interpretation, and they learned by word of mouth. In fielding a kick, that should otherwise have been 'marked', Webb Ellis rushed forward to the astonishment of others, carrying the ball as he so did. Being a senior, and being armed with the element of complete surprise, probably saved him a trip to the sanatorium.

To his peers he may well have been deemed a cheat. Recognised as more of a cricketer, 'he was inclined to take unfair advantage in football'. Given that most of his contemporaries were even less sure of the rules themselves, whether he was the first to contravene the accepted conventions is open to doubt. With the passage of time, and only hearsay to go by, the matter was never going to be easy to prove.

In 1827, four years after Webb Ellis' application of 'independent thought', Thomas Arnold, educated at Winchester and Oxford, became headmaster of Rugby School. Immediately he set about reforming the education system there. While doing little to modernise the teaching methods and curriculum, he nevertheless widened it, and in so doing created a new learning culture, based on the pursuit of artistic and intellectual values and above all, the encouragement of genuine independent thought. At the root of this were the core values of principle, conduct and ability. Under his influence the school moved on from being the small local grammar school that Sheriff had devised. Arnold's genius lay in his power of infusing the school and his assistant masters with some of his own vigorous moral idealism. This was in turn imparted to the pupils, such as Rupert Brooke and Lewis Carroll, whose creative energies were to stand proud in future years.

Arnold had no coherent theory of sport. He valued exercise, but not necessarily in the form of sport. What he did, however, was to instil the discipline and fairness which allowed the boys to prosper if they too had the courage to foster their own principles, conduct and ability. His arrival signalled the replacement of gambling, drinking and other brutalities more commonly associated with days gone before, with sport.

As Arnold set about his own revolution, so the 'game' itself was revolutionised further by his pupils. The Close, a tract of land within the perimeters of the original school site, became the focal point for the boys' game. The pitches then had no boundaries and games could be contested by up to 200 people. With no touchlines in those early days, a player stood a reasonable chance of injury in a long scrum by being impaled against one of the trees, or more specifically one of the three great elms that encroached on to the playing surface. The gravel path running alongside became an awkward place to fall. But at least it was a ground of their own.

The ball was generally moved by 'hacking' (kicking). Handling of, but not running with it, was allowed, yielding another means by which to gain hard yards... from hand to hand, like some giant rolling maul. The aim of this game was to score 'goals', by one of two means. Firstly, if caught from an opposition kick, a player would earn the right to kick at goal. He would then attempt to place kick or drop kick the ball through one of a set of 'H' shaped posts. He could move backwards to ready himself for the kick, but could not cross the mark at which he caught the ball. Alternatively, any player handling the ball over the goal line on which the posts stood would earn the right for a 'try at goal'. Games could not be won unless a goal was actually scored. Due to tight scrummaging, games could last up to five days, at which time they would be considered draws.

Other schools took up a form of the game on their own playing surfaces (even cobbles), with their own interpretation of the rules. Common to all forms, however, were the rough handling of opponents, little carrying and much hacking. While not altogether banned, anyone running with the ball was likely to be 'hacked over', a crude attempt at tackling consisting of felling the runner by kicking out at their shins. Despite these painful obstacles, 'running, if taken on the bound', was legalised in 1842, Arnold's last year in charge. The option of running brought about the inclusion of specialist runners and place kickers, outside of the main scrum. The 'light brigade', smaller groups of swifter boys, were to play their part. The violence and injuries associated with hacking, however, remained.

Three years later, three senior pupils attempted to lay down 'The Laws of Football as Played at Rugby School': offside, fair catch, knock-on, touch and try at goal became more familiar terms. Despite this, variations of the game continued. The key debate, however, remained running with the ball. The 1845 rules were soon followed (and opposed) by the Cambridge rules, a compromise between differing schools. Particular to these were no charging, no handling of the ball and, almost in protest to its futility and barbarity, no hacking over. Rugby held its ground.

The next two decades saw the evolving games appreciated to wider audiences, passed on to further schools as teachers moved. With the moves, more variations appeared, the rules suitably adapted depending on school and circumstance.

Rugby continued to cement its own origins, sub-defining and clarifying its first set of principles. In an 1862 copy of 'The Laws of Football as played at Rugby School', Rule 20, went (quaintly) as far as to say:

Though it is lawful to hold any player in a maul, this holding does not include attempts to throttle or strangle, which are totally opposed to the principles of the game.

The following year saw the game's first crossroads. In order to codify and standardise the many hybrids of Rugby's original game that now existed into one, the Football Association was formed, deciding that the rules as followed by Cambridge were to prevail. Blackheath, supported by Richmond and others, withdrew from the London Association, preferring to continue playing Rugby's version of the game.

The school viewed the events with some indifference, stoically refusing to accept any version other than its own. In 1867 they played their first 'foreign' games at the school, against club sides and Old Rugbeians. The school magazine, the *Meteor*, passed its own statement on the split of its great game into Association Football and Rugby Football:

The old God of (Rugby) football is not yet tottering on his throne, and will probably bear sway in all his pristine glory and vigour over the heads of all true Rugbeians at least as long as the three trees and the goal posts last.

Rugby football outside of the school continued, but in order to flourish it would need a parent body. On 26 January 1871, the Rugby Football Union was formed, consisting of twenty member clubs, among them Harlequins and Blackheath. The first five presidents of the RFU were all Old Rugbeians. The rules as used by Rugby School were adopted except, most critically, with the abolishment of hacking. Rugby, as played under the 'Rugby rules' if not born, was at least now a recognised national sport with an identity of its own. However, once more, the school persisted in keeping with its old traditions and retained hacking.

The RFU set off promoting their sport at a pace. In March of 1871 England played Scotland in their first-ever international fixture. The pitch was 130 yards by 55 yards. Ten out of England's twenty players were Old Rugbeians and the school's original colours of red, white and blue were adopted for the national side. Reginald Birkett scored the game's, and England's, first international 'try'. Birkett was probably international rugby's first 'star'. A double international, being also capped for England at association football, he went on to earn four caps. A member of the original RFU, his brother Louis played with him in the three later internationals.

Further popularity came from the inaugural Oxford *v.* Cambridge Varsity game in 1872. Twenty-four of the forty participants were Old Rugbeians. Early days saw the teams changing in a pub and walking a mile to the ground, where the playing pitch was unenclosed and the handful of spectators would try to separate the players if things got out of hand. Pioneers instrumental in the game's development appeared: Vassall at Oxford perfected the Blackheath forward methods and proved that the senseless hacking and mauling of the early days were ultimately a waste of players; Arthur Rotherham started to develop passing by the backs, but even in these days of progressiveness, the passing of the ball out of the forwards was deemed to be somewhat akin to cowardice. In 1875, whether through injury or other availability, teams started to use fifteen players instead of the more customary twenty. The year also saw a fundamental change to the scoring, value being given to a touchdown in its own right (previously points were only awarded if the following try at goal was then successful).

The RFU had set out their statement of intent, and their desire to steal a march on the Association game and make their game of rugby the game for the public to watch.

At the same time as the game it had invented was becoming more organised and establishing its identity, the school was about to enter a period of crisis. *The Times* of the day had written of Rugby's rise from mediocrity:

Rugby was made not by endowments, but by its masters alone. Except for a succession of distinguished and powerful administrators, it would have been nothing but an ordinary grammar school.

It was then that the school trustees appointed Henry Hayman as head-master from a formidable field of candidates. Hayman's credentials, both academically and experience-wise were inferior to many of his opponents. Having entered the campaign late, with only old testimonials to support his case, his appointment seemed odd in the least. Such was the outburst of indignation at the selection that the press, both local and national, took sides. Hayman's failure to secure co-operation from staff or boys bedevilled the situation. Resignations of staff and subsequent appointments of Hayman aides followed. The whole miserable business was having a damaging effect on the reputation of the school, reflected in a sharp fall in numbers and income. In what should have been a great period in the history of Rugby School, it was instead in danger of imploding.

Like the school, the old city of Dordrecht was suffering from problems of its own. Economic disaster had followed the French supremacy of Napoleon's times. Recovery was very slow, and the surge of nearby Rotterdam left Dordrecht agape. The Stoop family continued their banking and legal practices, but needed to extend their influences and experience further afield in order to move with the times. In 1873, Frederick Cornelius Stoop decided to expand the family portfolio and options and moved to England. Initially resident in Surbiton, by 1878 he had passed his nationality and nationalisation test.

The game soon moved to other countries within the British Empire. Equally importantly, it was moving away from the privileged to the domain of the working classes. The codification of rules allowed what had been a mystery to many not afforded a public school education to understand the game. In the North and in Wales the game was to become as much to do with social integration of the community as it was a statement of manliness. The greater accessibility benefited the working man, who enjoyed the rough and tumble of hard exercise. In the North the game became a true spectator sport, with a community feel to it. While slow to take off in Wales, it was fast becoming the national sport. Trinity College, Dublin, took the lead in Ireland.

The game Rugby School had given to the world had changed from its humblest beginnings almost beyond recognition. Gone were the days of almost tribal warfare; in came a more sophisticated fifteen-a-side affair. While conservatives of each generation deplored the changes as they came, others appreciated them. An article in the *Meteor* suggested 'weight no longer to be the greatest asset... activity, pace and mind are now required'.

It had moved from an elephantine battle of brawn to one of wits and speed. The time had come for innovators to have their day, men who could see the possibilities of scientific open play, to see that the game had in it elements of chess as well as of mayhem.

Embracing the Union

The game, the school and those associated with 'rugby' had evolved through many guises over a short period of time. The 1880s were a period of quiet development for one and all.

The RFU consolidated its position, with the first home nations championship between England, Ireland, Scotland and Wales in 1882. Celebrated figures became attracted to some of the founder clubs. The Harlequins of the 1880s included W.A. Smith, Clifford Wells and Billy Williams, the MCC cricketer, on their committee. For them the burgeoning interest in rugby signalled promising times.

So too for Frederick Stoop, who had consolidated his legal practice in London, particularly in support of his brothers and their oil concerns out in the Dutch East Indies. His next objective was to find a suitable house for an ever-expanding family.

Hayman had long since resigned from his post at the school, and the school ambled along under the guidance of Jex-Blake. 1887 saw not only Queen Victoria's Golden Jubilee but also, for one of the school's housemasters, Mr Brooke, the birth of a son, Rupert. Jex-Blake gave way to John Percival:

He was a man of strong emotions and he was mortally afraid of them, bottled up and sealed with corks, and even so was afraid of the bottles bursting some day. His own will kept them in the bottle. He hungered for intimacy and companionship and feared it lest it should lead him from the path of duty.

He had infinite patience with anybody who tried, and infinite sympathy with people who had no chances; but no sympathy with people who had the chances but couldn't take them.

He also decided there was no time to waste and began making changes in all directions. He had intended to apply reform gently and progressively, but the school he found when he took up his duties bore little resemblance to the one he had left as a pupil in 1862. According to the poet T.E. Brown, Percival was: 'like an inspired demonic conductor of an orchestra'.

By sheer ability, indomitable industry and unwavering faith the new headmaster rose from humble beginnings to great eminence and restored the school's reputation. He set about widening his pupils' knowledge base. Guests invited to give lectures were renowned for their excellence in their fields. Professor E.B. Poulton, the renowned naturalist, was among the first. Percival could see the bigger picture: he saw what was needed and set about building it. The personality of the school's headmaster was having a great influence on its fortunes, but it was as a spiritual influence that he counted the most. Rugby the school was moving upwards again.

The school abandoned its old exclusiveness on its version of rugby and adopted the RFU rules. A committee set up by the Old Rugbeian Society further concluded that whether or not William Webb Ellis was the inventor of the game that had become 'rugby', it could be traced back to his time and his name was unequivocally associated with it. His and the school's would be the names forever linked to the legend.

In severing the final breaks with tradition, the last of the three great trees was felled in 1893. The goal posts remained, but the old god of rugby was about to totter.

By contrast to the school's increased standing, problems started to creep into the administration of the game, particularly over payments for loss of earnings. Time off, for what was basically an amateur pursuit, was hard to come by. The committee of the RFU were constantly hearing of illegal payments and of players returning to changing rooms to find money stuffed in their shoes. They declared that payments for 'broken time' (away from work) were contrary to the interests of the game and its spirit. The response was dramatic. In August 1895, twenty-two clubs from the Yorkshire and Leeds districts broke away to form the professional Northern Union (the forerunner of the Rugby League). With it came a drain of talent and a weakening of the amateur game's player base. As if to emphasise the changes in fortune, the time saw the early death of Reginald Birkett, a victim of poisoning, an industrial accident at his workplace. His young son John would have been proud of his father's sporting legacy, but saddened by his early death.

The breakaway had coincided with major changes in the fabric of English society. England was coming to the end of the Victorian era. A war was being fought with the Dutch in Africa. Transportation difficulties made it difficult to attract loyal followings. Changes in the social, industrial and economic environment had resulted in a warm embrace of the game everywhere but in England. For a sport invented by their public school-boys, the English were suddenly not very good at it.

The RFU became increasingly concerned with the organisation of the game in its minutiae, rather than the production of a consistently successful England XV. Problems were mounting and divisions were appearing: north and south; middle and upper class; public school and secondary modern. The professionalism debate became magnified and was symbolised by a testimonial to the great Welsh back, Arthur 'Monkey' Gould: the subsequent provision of a house to Gould caused such a furore that Wales withdrew temporarily from the international board. The game that had been evolving for over three-quarters of the century was in crisis.

Almost immediately the problems filtered down to the clubs. A stretched and understrength Harlequins team played the Rugby School XV. Their one side had just moved to Wimbledon Park. Their finances were on a downward spiral and it was felt that they would be lucky to see out the century.

Apart from picking up games against struggling club sides, the following year saw Rugby play their first foreign school game against Cheltenham. For the years to follow, the impressive, athletic Cheltenham side were to be Rugby's masters, emphasising a gap in fitness and standards that over the years had passed Rugby by. A.E. Donkin, one of Rugby's teachers, felt compelled to write in the December 1897 *Meteor*:

Among the reasons which may be given for our third successive defeat by the Cheltenham XV, there is one which should, emphatically, not be lost sight of. I refer to the great attention given by all Cheltenham boys to gymnastics. What are you to expect but good staying powers, lithe limbs, and great muscular strength, when bar and dumbbell are practised regularly four times a week and forty minutes each time? And this is precisely what several of their XV have been doing. Every one of them, moreover, is a gymnast, one or two quite in the first rank. You may tell me that Rugby has its gymnasium and that it is not neglected by our players, but there is all the world between occasionally going in for a casual bit of work, and that steady persevering practice which may add, even in one term, thirty to forty percent to your measurements.

Until some approach to such regular gymnastics as are in vogue at Cheltenham is made here, it seems probable they will continue to produce the better team.

On the Close, traditionally there had been no coaching, and a good side only came about by chance, or if an excellent individual appeared. Inspired by Donkin's criticisms, the various housemasters saw potential in developing their sides and their own reputations. To have one of their own house play in a foreign match was good advertisement enough. Out they came to 'coach' the smaller fellows in the Remnants, and referee the house matches.

Despite this, their 1899 season started to mixed fortunes. The school XV beat the Old Rugbeians 21-11 but lost against a strong Oxford University side 33-3 and by 10-6 to London Scottish 'A'. A 14-11 win against Cooper's Hill did little to suggest that anything other than another tough season loomed.

Weather claimed the match on 18 November against University College, Oxford. The expectant crowd could at least move inside as the same Saturday afternoon saw a gymnastics tournament against Harrow. Exercises comprised the horizontal bar, parallel bars, vaulting horse, vertical rope, pair of rings, and bridge ladder. That the school gym VIII had an overwhelming victory of 704 points to 585 was of moderate interest. The average per Harrow boy was 76, per Rugby boy 88. Of more significant interest was the Rugby schoolboy known only for spending most of his evenings after prep in the gym, practising his routines. The personal tally of 103 points by Adrian Stoop was both outstanding and astounding in equal measures. Prince Purachatra of the Harrow team (61 points) could only look on in awe at the sublime swings and upper body strength of a tremendous athlete. One of the judges stated: 'I think your instructor [Donkin] deserves great credit for the way the team was brought on.'

On 25 November 1899 the rugby XV played their inaugural match against Uppingham School, who had become part of the fixture list for the first time. The match resulted in an easy Rugby win 19-0. Their next game, against Oxford Old Rugbeians saw four of the XV scratch through injury. The replacements added little, the ORs cantering to a three goals, three tries 24-6 victory.

By means of respite, and in keeping with the thoughts of the day, the school debate for the month considered the hot topic of professionalism. The motion: the influence of professionalism on sports and games has been harmful. The addresses were varied, but while suggesting that other sports, namely horse racing, cricket and soccer had means for professionals, rugby had no place for it. For the motion:

Professionalism is but an instance of the modern tendency to specialism. Professionals are necessary to teach, but not to provide a spectacle to thousands, and then to retire as keepers of public houses.

Against:

Professionalism raises the standard of play all around.

The 'proposers' had not proved that 'soccer' was harmed by professionalism, only that it was harmed by something. Athletics was ruined by unfair play. Nevertheless, the motion was carried by two to one.

Outside of the formal debating chamber, the only debate of merit doing the rounds was whether the gym team should be worthy of cap ribbons as other recognised sports were. Adrian Stoop's performance was still being talked of, so brilliant had it been. He had set standards that the everyday fellow could never even hope to aspire to. However, while the gym team's performance in victory had been worthwhile, the purists still argued its greater exposure had come only as a result of the cancellation of the big rugby game of the day.

The next opponents for the XV were Cheltenham. The school knew the game would be tough: this year's opponents contained not only three from the previous year but also the not inconsiderable talents of arguably England's greatest-ever sportsman and Corinthian, C.B. Fry. To make matters worse, Lloyd, one of the school XV's half-backs, again scratched prior to the game due to injury.

The school needed a replacement. Almost as Donkin had demanded a year or so prior, a gymnast was offered up. Stoop had not only shown himself to be a finer gymnast than most, but had shown in the recent house matches he could also play a bit of rugby. The star of the recent gym tournament was to be the guinea pig and scapegoat: the anticipated loss to the fitter Cheltenham side would at least dull the gym's chorus. Like Lloyd, Stoop was playing a year before his finals; unlike Lloyd, who had made the exalted ranks of the XV for the year, Stoop had spent most of his time in the gym.

On Saturday 9 December Adrian Stoop played his first game at school level – his first Bigside. It was some introduction. Rugby scored three tries and Cheltenham were beaten 9-0. In the forwards there was little to choose between the two sides. Behind the scrum Cheltenham suffered from a lack of cohesion in their three-quarters, not unrelated to the pressure and passing from their opposite numbers. Adrian had had no practice with other members of the XV but the uniformity of the school's rules and the boys' approach to them allowed him to blend in from the start.

The match caused some consternation, not just in the result, but also in the unprecedented nature of the surging crowds, keen to witness an upset in the making. Adrian had caused a stir for the second time in a few weeks. In a letter to the *Meteor*, W. Temple wrote:

Several Old Rugbeians absolutely refused to move when asked by members of the Sixth to keep back, thus depriving many ladies of all view of the game.

The Editor replied:

We believe that a sufficient number of the Sixth were asked to carry canes, but the actions of several Old Rugbeians – among them we noticed more than one of last year's team – in absolutely refusing to keep back from the touchline prevented their efforts from being effective.

Lloyd was reinstated to his position in the school XV, but rued missing the laurels that had come to those who had played in *the* game.

The dawn of the new century was to be notable for several other events. Normal service was resumed internationally, with the adoption of a new set of laws bringing Wales' laws on professionalism in line with those of England. On paper at least the two countries were equal.

Under the stewardship of headmaster Herbert James, a stone was laid at Rugby School to celebrate the origins of the game. The tableau was short and to the point:

This stone commemorates the exploit of William Webb Ellis who with a fine disregard for the rules of football as played in his time first took the ball in his arms and ran with it thus originating the distinctive feature of the rugby game.

A simple historical statement of near fact. But what the stone could never describe were the monumental changes to the fabric of both the school and its game from the event it celebrated and the ensuing three-quarters of the century. The school and game in England had gone through tremendous highs and lows and opposing fortunes. Through sheer force of personality and the carefully laid plans of a few men the standards and expectations of the school had been taken to never-before-seen heights. By contrast, the reputation of the game in its native country had never been lower.

As 1900 closed, Adrian Stoop was in his last year at the school and had officially made the XV. Donkin rubbed his lapels and smiled a contended smile. His protestations had been vindicated. Little did he realise that in organising his one-off gymnastics competition he had set in place a chain of events that would lead rugby to an altogether higher plane.

two

THE PUPIL
1883-1904

When a boy goes to school, if he is big he is put in to the scrum, if small he plays half-back, if fast three-quarter, and if he has no particular characteristic beyond courage he is apt to find himself at full-back, and where he starts, there he generally remains for the whole of his school career.

(*Captaincy,* Adrian Stoop)

London of the late 1800s was a land of the Golden Jubilee, global imperialism and colonialism. Marcus Samuel, later to become First Viscount Bearsted, was one of the last of the great merchant adventurers. At the dawn of the technological revolution, which was to shape the twentieth century, he had a vision of oil as a global source of power. His journey took him from oil prospecting in malaria-infested jungles to the closed circles of high finance, from parliamentary lobbying to international intrigue, from triumphs of almost amateur improvisation to frustrating experiments with processes and engines, some of which were eventually to change the ways of life. In doing so he created the Shell Transport and Trading Company. He managed to turn the chain of Far Eastern connections established for his business into a commercial structure that which was ready to handle the sudden flood of trade between Britain and the Far East, to which lines of trade were newly opened. When oil emerged as a new and plentiful source of light and power, Marcus already had that system of worldwide distribution without which the young industry could not have survived. Faced at times with appalling obstacles, not excluding imminent ruin, sometimes fighting single-handed the whole world of oil, he lived to see his dream come true.

Frederick Cornelius Stoop, though of grand Dutch heritage, was actually born in Frankfurt. His more immediate ancestors were an old Netherlands-Indies family who had worked the plantations in Java, growing sugar, rice and tobacco, long before oil had been struck or even suspected. His mother was Cornelia Deking Dura, his father Adriaan Stoop. His eldest brother, also an Adriaan, followed the age-old naming tradition for first-born Stoop sons, a tradition stretching back beyond the Dordrecht Stoops of years gone by.

In 1879 the younger Adriaan had left for the Dutch East Indies as a mining engineer to discover oil for the Dutch government. After a study tour to the United States he decided to continue the search for oil on his own account. Taking unpaid leave, he enlisted the help of Frederick and a second brother, Jan, and between them they pulled in 150,000 Dutch guilders as capital for their exploration company, the 'Dordtsche Petroleum Maatschappij'. Adriaan was the managing director of the company in Java, and lived there. Jan, technical by trade, was the local manager in Java.

A legal stockbroker by trade, Frederick was the president of the Java Dordtsche. Having moved to England six years beforehand, he ran the London offices of Stoop & Co. with another of his brothers, Cornelius Francis. Outside of the day-to-day business of London city life, Cornelius' passion was art, knowing, as he did, Van Gogh, among others. Through the success of Stoop & Co. and his burgeoning relationships with influential contacts within the art world, his portfolio of new paintings increased.

Frederick's ideals were pride and honour among friends. Those who knew him knew that while he could be gruff on occasions, he was unbelievably kind. And while he never lost his Dutch accent, he had become a nationalised Englishman after falling in love with his adopted country. Frederick soon met and also fell in love with Agnes MacFarlane Clark, the daughter of Robert Clark of Paisley and Ellen Corry of Belfast. They were married on 1 June 1882.

Their first son was born ten months later on 27 March 1883 at 5 Collingham Gardens, near the Cromwell Road, London. Christened after his grandparents, Adrian Dura Stoop came into the world half Dutch/German, a quarter Scottish and a quarter Irish.

Frederick's family, not untypical of the Stoops and not untypical of the day, was to be a large one: Ellen Corry (Nellie) born in 1885, Jane Corry (Janey) in 1887, Frederick MacFarlane (Freek, often also Tim) on 17 September 1888, and Agnes MacFarlane (Nesta) in 1892. Like most, the family were a close one, and Frederick's vast fortune allowed them to be indulged.

Frederick decided that with an ever-increasing family, there was a need for a big enough house, in the country, to bring them all up in. After a long search, they rounded in on Byfleet, Surrey. On the western side of the village, shielded from the main Parvis Road, West Hall stood at the end of a half-mile tree-lined drive. The great house had evolved over time, as each new owner had tried to give it an identity of his or her own. By 1893 it bore little resemblance to that originally built by the West family in the 1700s. Frederick decided to make this home for his young, but increasing, family. While they would want for nothing, the house and gardens would be rebuilt in a style that would always remind them of their great heritage: a family coat of arms hanging in the Great Hall, Dutch and Italian gardens, underground vaults full of family secrets, tended walled fruit and vegetable gardens, colourful herbaceous walks, spacious lawns and shrubs and a boathouse down by the river. All were built from scratch, reflective of both Frederick's great wealth and status. As works commenced, Frederick and Agnes had another daughter, Cornelie Dura (Cora). Four years on in 1898, Mina Kathleen (Khe), the last of his children, was born.

Schooling became the next problem. Having been educated initially at Lockers Park in Hemel Hempstead, where cricket was his strength, Adrian was sent on to Dover College in January 1896. The school had established a good reputation for sport and, while on the young side, he played in their rugby under-16 side as a half-back, also helping his house win the junior house cup in both rugby and cricket.

With a new house in Surrey, Frederick changed his perspective on schooling, having read much about the changes going on at Rugby. Percival had restored the school's image to its former glories and put it back at the top of the pile. Before he had time to find his feet on the south-east coast, Adrian was relocated once more. By September 1897, now aged fourteen, he was up at Rugby. Frederick hoped that one day Adrian would follow in his own distinguished legal footsteps, and nothing but the best education would do.

The move to West Hall had meant changes elsewhere. Frederick and his brothers had oilfields not in Sumatra like most of the Dutch producers but in Java. Here they found themselves alongside and in direct competition with both Standard Oil and Samuel's Shell, which also had its tanks and agents there. Shrewd investment in equipment and an uncanny ability to attract the best personnel allowed the Stoops to prosper. Their oil source was so great that they built a refinery. Once Royal Dutch oilfields in Sumatra had run dry, their firm became the largest producer in the Dutch East Indies. Being able to work from raw through to finished product aided their growth yet further. Their biggest concern however was that of transportation. The further investment for that and the corresponding steps into the unknown were risky in the extreme.

By the mid-nineties Adriaan had become the first prospector to acquire an area bordering on Samuel's in the Kutei Lama, where the Stoop brothers formed an exploratory concern called the East Borneo Company. In August 1899, when Samuel was considering whether to prospect or not in Kutei Lama, he sought the further advice of Frederick, the two men having already corresponded with each other on the subject of the Java market. Samuel wrote:

As verbally agreed this morning, we confirm our willingness, in the event of our purchasing Kutei Lama to make arrangements with you for the marketing of this oil in Java, upon terms which shall prevent undue competition between us, by local agreements between our respective agents… as to selling prices, it being understood that neither of us will, by cutting against each other, bring rates down below the price necessary to compete with oil imported from Russia and America. I renew the assurance that I gave you that it is not part of our policy to inflict either loss or annoyance upon friendly competitors, but that our aim would be to certainly act in accord with them.

Frederick's response explained that unless the Dordtsche could market all its oil in Java they would be forced to export a certain proportion where it would inevitably find itself competing with Shell. Samuel responded:

Naturally I can understand that you wish to market the whole of your own products in Java and we shall do our utmost to facilitate this process. When you have any residuals to dispose of, we should be very glad if you would let us know.

Frederick handwrote on the letter itself by way of confirmation: 'This is a true and proper reply. FCS.' Respect between two proud gentlemen.

Samuel had alleviated the Stoops' transport problem. Frederick was seen to pay several visits to Samuel's Leadenhall Street offices. Forging an agreement with Shell meant they would be able to sell the whole of their product in their local markets. And if the Stoops could sell all their oil in Java, they would have no need to send it elsewhere to compete with Shell. Frederick and his Dordtsche found themselves both powerbrokers and kingmakers in the early days of oil exploration.

The relative, if qualified, affection for the British on the part of the Dutch had been gradually eroded by the friction in South Africa between the British Government and the Boers, which had led to the outbreak of war in October 1899. Nevertheless there were many Dutchmen who liked Samuel and whom Samuel liked. In Frederick he found a man he could respect for his mutual integrity, a man of both word and deed. Above all Samuel found a Dutch gentleman who was so fond of England that he was almost anglicised.

The Stoops had shown themselves to be singularly focused. They knew what was required, they knew the path needing to be followed, and they had set off down it. More significantly, in the cut-throat world of big business, they carried out their actions with the highest degree of integrity and unflinching purpose.

The goodwill of the Stoops was worth a small sacrifice, by Samuels, of part of his Java trade. Samuel now had unlimited sources of oil in the Dutch East Indies at his disposal. With the largest tanker fleet in the world, and with his unique system of halving transportation costs by carrying return cargoes, he could take on his competitors in the European market with a product similar in quality to American kerosene, better in quality than the Russian equivalent and sold at more competitive prices. Two years later, when J.B. August Kessler's Royal Dutch had won over all the Dutch East Indies producers to a union, it was the Stoops who stayed loyal to Samuel. Failure to get the Stoops into the union of Netherland-Indies producers considerably weakened Royal Dutch's position in future negotiations with Samuel's Shell.

As the century closed, Leadenhall Street remained busy, progressive partnerships being forged and honed by the two men setting their respective concerns up for the future. Across town, in their unpretentious offices in Surrey Street, off the Strand, the RFU officials met to discuss the start of another season and potential lambs for their now-customary spring slaughtering. England had lost all three of their games of early 1899, scoring but three points in total in the process. Progressive they hoped to be, but given the state of their team, standing still would be an achievement.

Bigside

Far out of London, past the sprawling new towns of Clapham and Wandsworth, and the river towns of Kingston and Richmond, lay the countryside and with it typically quaint little English villages like Twickenham and Byfleet. Out in the sticks, everyday life was bathed in peace and tranquillity and the pace very much sedate. West Hall had become a prime example of the quintessential English retreat. Perfect for entertaining, and the Stoops liked their parties, introducing Adrian to all forms of higher society.

The tennis and croquet lawns to one side of the great house provided an idyllic setting. To the rear the lawns sloped down to a private mooring on the river Wey, where the punt, dinghy and Canadian canoe were moored. There was plenty to keep young boys entertained: swimming down the river from Dodds Bridge and under the West Hall Bridge; in winter sometimes skating on Dutch skates across the frozen water meadows. The gardens provided an oasis of further pleasure and games. The walk through the Old Wood was magnificent and there was a moat for fishing. At the right time of the year, when the cowslips and bluebells were out, it was the picture of English country life. A local observer once claimed: 'West Hall is paradise that has been resurrected in the grounds of the original Garden of Eden.'

The house was situated at the end of the appropriately named Parvis (from the Latin *Paradisum*) Road. Paradise needs upkeep, and West Hall, not unlike the larger houses of the time, had a large staff: Mr White the carpenter, Mr Carpenter the head gardener, Miss Peacock the cook, Parsons the head maid, Wilson and Gorringe the chauffeurs of two magnificent Daimlers, and Cooper the assistant head gardener and handyman. The Stoop boys would often get up to mischief, but the staff enjoyed their company and particularly enjoyed joining in their games on the lawns. It was at a game of football there that young Cooper broke his leg.

The generosity and indulgence of Frederick spread further than his family, and was renowned throughout the Byfleet community. The Stoops ensured Cooper did not want for whatever he needed while recovering. It was Adrian, however, who seemed to show the greatest concern, visiting Cooper as often as he could to hear about his progress to better health and to cheer him up. The concerns were well received and fondly remembered.

Back at Rugby school Adrian immersed himself in the school's activities: the cadet corps, some studies, a bit of debating, and a little chess. But only one thing was to consume his mind. He had no real time for the usual public and boarding school attitudes and behaviour. All he had time for was sport, and more specifically the gym. Typically those that avoided the gym by day tended to be the extra big and the extra thin. The big avoided it because they found their place on the rugby field; the thin just avoided it. For Adrian, the gym was a continuation of the all-day-long activities and exercise that surrounded West Hall. All he did in the long school evenings was practise. Saturday morning lectures were almost a waste of time, most thoughts being on the big rugby match to follow in the afternoon.

The rules of the game were simple. No kicking in your own half of the field, tackle hard, run low and straight. The scrum was first up, first down and there were no tactical manoeuvres of note. Traditionally, practice had not been deemed necessary, the game being so uniform, any coaching being carried by the captain of the team, time and desire permitting. The only coaching that Adrian had ever had was how to throw the ball in back at Dover, one of his jobs in those days being to inject to the line-outs. Being of relatively small build, he found himself a half-back, chief further requisites of whom were ability to dribble the ball, a skill at which he had become particularly adept, and speed off the mark, to be able to be first to the ball, subsequently falling on it to stop opposition forward rushes. In those days half-backs were also picked dependant upon whether their hand strength lay to the left or right. One half-back played closest to the scrum if a left put-in, the other closest if a right put-in. The rest of the backs simply made up the numbers.

Adrian's developed and further developing upper-body strength meant he could play either side of the scrum, making him a most useful stand-in if either of the normal halves scratched before a game. The victorious game against Cheltenham of December 1899 proved that point.

For the rest of that month, the celebrations magnified as everyone's thoughts were drawn to the approaching new century. Following the promise he had shown as Lloyd's stand-in in the victorious XV, Adrian's thoughts were solely on proving that he should have been in the official XV from the start of the year. For the next round of house games, Adrian's house, Steel's, were to play the formidable Collin's, who featured three of the regular XV, the feared and formidable Cartwright brothers and the unfortunate Lloyd.

The game provided another reminder of a burgeoning talent. Steel's kicked off. Cartwright caught and returned a kick back. Adrian caught, marked and returned to touch: early jousting and playing for territory as were the accepted tactics of that and any other day. For Collin's, Lloyd and the brothers Cartwright (contributing a try each) did everything. With three tries to his name, Adrian did more, leading his side to an 18-11 victory. The gym team had never had it so proud. Neither had the school when early the next year the heritage plaque was laid.

On Saturday 24 February 1900, the XV played Cambridge Old Rugbeians. The OR's turned up short. A willing volunteer needed to be found and Adrian stepped in. The school won 13-11 but, once again, Stoop had come to the rescue of a fair and even game, and acquitted himself well. Adrian was a must for the first XV next season.

Adrian had always been a good learner, although only in the areas that interested him. At school he showed an interest in military history and he learned of the great leaders, such as Wellington and his refusal to obey the principles of the time. His greatest test, his Waterloo, might have had some luck attached, but careful consideration of the elements of surprise, of changing the direction of attack and of attacking with his cavalry at pace from the flanks, was to win the day. Such leadership success could only have been achieved with the full respect and support of his troops. These lessons were taken on board, as were the rest of Adrian's studies. The July certificate examinations saw him pass French, German, elementary maths, scripture knowledge and Greek text, and English. Nothing spectacular, no distinctions, very much middle of the pack sandwiched as he was between Professor Poulton's eldest son, Edward, at the lower end and W. Spens, distinctions and all, at the top end. Like Saturday mornings, the summer and the exams were but a distraction from the real business of playing rugby again.

On 1 November 1900, Adrian won his colours, being made an official member of the XV for the year. Under Vincent Henry 'Lump' Cartwright's imposing, from-the-front leadership, the school XV had for the first time a collective sense of spirit and ethics, ideals not lost on Adrian. The successes of the year before, chiefly in the game against Cheltenham, had stemmed from the discipline and sense of learning developed by a succession of the old school masters, culminating in Percival's single-minded focus. The boys became better for the training and coaching that the masters had started to offer in their spare time, and with this came a better understanding and appreciation of the developing rules and a sense of teamwork. Above and beyond this, and no small thanks to the perceptiveness of Donkin, something far greater: fitness and agility.

The first fixture of the season, and Adrian's first official fixture in the top flight, was Oxford University. Having played for the XV before, he was now experienced enough to not be nervous. Now, however, his name was in lights and expectations were far greater. Collecting boots from the old boot room, changing up, putting liniment on, all gave a newfound sense of pride. Then it was out on to the pitch in front of fellow pupils and excited parents. Tossing balls around, they warmed up. With final words from Cartwright, they lined up ready for the kick-off. In strong winds the game went to and fro:

After the resumption, Stoop and Lloyd, who were playing an excellent game, made several good openings… a dash by the Varsity forwards compelled the school forwards to touch down, and Schultz bungling badly from the drop out, Stoop kicked the ball away from him and Lloyd put in an unconverted try.

The school won 19-8, the *Meteor* going on to describe Adrian as: 'a tricky half-back; very smart, cool-headed, full of resource, picks up well and makes good openings; safe tackler.'

Other representative matches followed against University College, Oxford (a loss), Corpus Christi, Oxford (a win) and London Scottish.

By 24 November the team had clicked into gear. Following a morning lecture from Professor Poulton on 'Uses of Colours of Animals for Purposes of Concealment', Uppingham never saw what hit them and were summarily dispatched 58-0, an absolutely unheard-of scoreline which Adrian contributed to by scoring twice. The *Meteor* reported:

In the scrum Rugby were much heavier and quicker than their opponents, and so were able to get the ball whenever they liked. Being content simply to let it out, the outsides were given every opportunity, and the score shows how they made use of them. Their passing was really magnificent, very few mistakes indeed being made, while what tackling they had to do was quite satisfactory.

Sandwiched in between the two inter-school fixtures were a game against Balliol College, Oxford – the school winning with Adrian scoring one of the many tries – and a defeat to Oxford Old Rugbeians.

The second inter-school fixture, against Cheltenham Grammar School, was scheduled for 8 December. The exploits of exactly a year previous were now in the past. This time Rugby had a daunting away visit to contend with, the inaugural victory of last season coming as it had done on Bigside. Cartwright lost the toss, and taking account of the conditions, Fry elected to defend their chapel goal. The *Cheltenham Echo* remarked of the game:

Individually the Rugby halves stood out most prominently. They were simply irresistible behind a good pack of forwards, and besides making many fine runs themselves, they fed their three-quarters in the best style, making their play almost perfect... it is many a long day since a more evenly balanced team was seen on the College enclosure.

By half-time Rugby had blown Cheltenham away, scoring five tries in the process. Crossing another four times to Cheltenham's two in the second half, they romped home peerlessly 29-8.

Winning both the school games by such huge margins emphasised how a well-prepared team could come together and challenge even the best of opponents. Traditionally there had been a noted difference in playing for the school, rather than just your house. That, in essence, was not knowing your teammates, not getting the chance to practise. The new learning culture and Lump's excellent leadership had changed all that.

The successes on the pitch had raised the bar and were rich reward for this, but the school principles knew that two school games a year were not enough to keep their profile raised: Clifton played four times a week; at Wellington coaching was on a school, not a house, basis. Realising this to be the way forward, two men were sought to coach the XV on a regular, rather than ad hoc, basis. Independent thought, self-discipline and artistic expression were back in vogue and being applied to the fundamentals of rugby the game, as well as Rugby the school. Arnold would have been proud.

So too would Frederick and Agnes. As indulgent as they were, and with high hopes that their son would follow in his father's footsteps, by now they could see what rugby meant to their son. Seeing Adrian practise swerves in and out of lines of chairs on the West Hall lawns was just the beginning. His gifts as a player were starting to shine through: great speed off the mark; an elusive and quick runner; and the ability to play in several different positions. What was not seen by most, however, was that he was starting to think about the game. Others were starting to think about him.

The London rugby clubs had already seen the value in playing games against the school XVs. Having made it to the twentieth century, so impressed were Harlequins on their visit by the gifted young half opposing them that they invited him to join. Blackheath, much the bigger of the senior clubs then, also started knocking at his door. These were early days, however, and the schoolboy was not ready to commit, despite the temptations that were put his way.

Gifts of a different kind went the way of Byfleet. In commemoration of the Diamond Jubilee of Queen Victoria's reign, Frederick had a village hall and village club built for his beloved hometown. He became president of the trustees of the hall and first president of the club in the process. Taking his son's lead, there was not a sports organisation to which he was not associated, and this included being president of the tennis club, golf club and bowling club. Not content with that, he then saved the cricket club from the builders. The Stoops' kindliness and intense interest in the lives of those they came in contact with became renowned throughout the area. They always saw the best in people rather than the worst and their lives became a shining example of how to give pleasure and happiness to those with whom they lived.

Queen's

The turn of the century had heralded a dynamic, new and exciting world. The French were showing the way forward, the Great Exposition in Paris attracting thirty-nine million visitors, reviewing the past but allowing glimpses of the future. The end of one era was the start of another.

From school, Adrian moved to University College, Oxford, to study law. Unfortunately, nothing for Adrian could beat the smell of an autumn day. Studies again came second to rugby, as the sport consumed even more of Adrian's thoughts. At school he had practised hard; at University College with a place in the Varsity at stake, he practised harder. He immediately became secretary of the university rugby team, carefully logging reports of the matches, studying the games with a rare intensity. His old friend and school playing captain Lump Cartwright had gone to Oxford, and Adrian valued his opinion. Like his father before him, Adrian would never forget the value of friendship, and often sought Lump's advice. Adrian's main difficulty, however, lay in finding someone outside of the forwards who played on his wavelength. Most of his colleagues found him a little too radical for their tastes, preferring as they did the relative safety of conformity to the norm. In realising that much could be done to improve the game further by intelligent and constructive thought, Adrian started to take matters into his own hands, introducing several unorthodox schemes of midfield attack.

Adrian's thoughts drifted to the club scene, recognising as he did that greater experience would come from further exposure and an expanded fixture list. Blackheath, the most famous club of the day, were knocking ever louder, and seemed the obvious choice. By now the Harlequins were a team with no permanent ground and no finances. Playing for them would mean waiting for trains, far-distant opponents' grounds and cold water (if any) to clean up in. With no support and close to folding, the light-blue, magenta, chocolate, French grey and black pastel colours of their shirts had become dulled in recent years. Cartwright, however, already on the Harlequins books as student representative, persuaded Adrian to join him. A different turn in the road, a different story. A bold decision in the circumstances, but only to be the first of many.

Despite their lack of a place to call their own and their limited finances, the Harlequins were attempting to expand their fixture list, which at the time contained Old Merchant Taylors, Richmond, Cambridge, London Irish, Catford Bridge, Barts Hospital, Rosslyn Park, London Scottish, Old Alleynians, Surbiton, Kensington and Blackheath. Games outside London were about to be arranged, particularly Northampton, with Coventry and Leicester possibilities. At least they couldn't be faulted for effort.

On 16 October 1901, Adrian played his first game for the Harlequins, actually against the university, scoring his side's only try. His only comment on his new side was that the back play was very poor indeed. The problems encountered while playing for the school, as opposed to house, before the system was changed, were readily apparent elsewhere in the game. And not just at club level. The game in England was starting to stagnate. In the twenty-first century players seem to be able to choose any country for whom to play. 100 years ago they could have been forgiven for wanting to.

Lump was selected for the 1901 Varsity but Adrian was not, his ideas on the game not reaching a listening audience. He trained even harder and the Harlequins were more than happy to make best use of his enthusiasm.

In April 1902 the Harlequins arranged a lease from the Heathfield Cricket club to use their facilities at Wandsworth Common for the sum of £35 a year. Finances were hard and the club, such as it was, had to conform to its limited means, which meant no more than £10 to be spent on hot-water arrangements and no more than £25 on a stand. At their AGM the committee was raised to twelve and included some of the clubs greatest stalwarts: W.A. Smith the president, C.M. Wells, Cipriani, Surtees and Curly Hammond, the club captain. The twelve also included Lump Cartwright and Adrian Stoop.

The new season at the end of 1902 started well for Adrian. Tempering his excessiveness slightly he pulled the best out of his backline and they notched up some creditable results.

In November, in the hope that the Harlequins might attract more than the two they already had, the club decided to organise a dinner for Oxford students. Wishful thinking, but positive action nonetheless. Later that month they received a letter asking if they would care to make provision for a game against a New Zealand XV if they were to tour the following season. Fulfilling the fixtures they had would be difficult enough, but a game against a touring side would at least help the coffers.

Freek Stoop, who had started at Rugby, had something of a legacy to live up to, one which was about to gain greater focus. On 11 December Adrian sent a hastily written letter to his parents following their visit:

My dear mother and father

Just after you left I received a note asking me to play v. Cambridge.

Your loving son,

Adrian.

Simple. Short. He was in the Varsity. A proud father, a proud son.

Many believed the 1902 Varsity game would go to Oxford, judgement being based on the relative strength of their dynamic back division. With a brilliant newcomer at half-back in Stoop, they said, the superior Oxford backs would carry the day if only the forwards could rise to the occasion. As it was, the ground at the Queens Club was heavy, the weather was cold and grey and a forwards' game. The result ended up a reflection of the respective qualities of the sides. Had the Cambridge backs and their attacks been better, they would probably have won. Had the Oxford forwards been better, then they would have won by a landslide. It was noted that the young Stoop, and his partner Lyle, did well in checking the Cambridge rushes, and in kicking to touch. Some said the two halves saved the day. Snapping the ball from the feet of the clumsy Cambridge forwards, time and again they converted defence into attack by clever running. Having gone two tries ahead, Oxford spent the last twenty minutes in desperate defence. The swarming Cambridge forwards pulled out two tries to even up the match. Heroic defence by the half-back pairing ensured the draw resulted. Few who watched the game thought they saw some greats in the making, although in winning his first Blue, Adrian had done enough to make it clear that at least he would be heard of again.

The *Athletic Review* of 15 December 1902 report on the game was cut out and filed away. The first record of many, perhaps for posterity, but more importantly for critical review later on.

Further favourable reviews got him into the 1902 England trials. Playing for the South, his side lost 11-0 to the North, and he was not considered further. Adrian's season finished as it had started: some solid performances, some spectacular ones and, with no great responsibility hanging around his shoulders, a general enjoyment of the game itself.

Into Adrian's next year at Oxford, Lump was made university captain. More significant, however, was the arrival of a young Scotsman, Pat Munro, from Leeds Grammar. In him Adrian almost immediately found someone who shared his ideas of creativity and who, like Adrian, was full of resource and energy. At last Adrian had found a kindred spirit who cared little for convention and more for invention. Many a combination and variation was tried and the two were forever testing out 'alternatives to the alternative'. Poor Lump knew he had his hands full keeping his young impresarios on the straight and narrow, not least with the 1903 Varsity looming.

That game became a desperately close affair, which turned on the excellent work of Stoop, Munro and surprisingly, given the previous year, the scrummaging of their forwards under Lump. It was thought that the Cambridge pack would again neutralise the Oxford brilliance behind. The Oxford pack entered at their lightest ever, three members being under eleven stone. Despite the weight disparity, they held their own by exercising admirable control in the tight and cohesion in the loose. Frequently the Oxford half-backs found the ball in their hands. Their instinctiveness and quick thinking, using cross-kicks and punts ahead, often caught Cambridge on the wrong foot. Tries were traded evenly, Adrian securing the third for Oxford with a finely judged cross-kick to his wing. They snatched victory with a try in the final minute.

According to *The Sportsman* of 16 December: 'Oxford *v*. Cambridge. A splendid struggle at the Queens Club. Superior tactics win the day.' Adrian had found his first great playing partner, Lump another great team.

The plaudits coming to the Stoop family became greater. Everyone in Byfleet was proud of their famous resident. The family remained close, proud at the exploits of Adrian, but without losing their sense of community – Frederick built the village a boat club, on the west bank of the Wey navigation canal. He could see the professional and middle classes moving into the new housing being built on Agnes' estate at Dartnell Park. More land was later acquired from Hugh Locke-King, who himself went on to build the racing circuit at Brooklands.

Despite the critical acclaim that had come by way of the Varsity, the international team remained out of Adrian's reach. His only admission to those games came by ticket along with the rest of the paying public.

Despite England's less than impressive record over the past few years, there was always something he could learn from watching them, even if the selectors seemingly could not. On 13 February 1904 he went to see England play Ireland at Blackheath. The English had not won a game for four matches, all of which had featured the unfortunate Lump. John Daniell had played in his team's last victory two years previous, and having returned from injury, was made captain. Little was expected.

The first scrum of the game happened very early on, near to the Irish left corner flag, far from where Adrian sat, but he said of what he saw:

Every word of his [Daniell's] *pungent exhortation was plainly audible. In five minutes the English eight were playing together like a club scrum, and the issue of the match was never in doubt, thanks to a few well-chosen words from a leader of men.*

England won 19-0. The complete domination by the English forwards prevented the Irish halves from giving their three-quarters any reasonable scoring opportunities. Adrian could see that the sphere of a captain's responsibility extended beyond the choice of ends, should he be lucky enough to win the toss, and included the initial measured violence of his conduct and outbursts. He would remember it well.

A month later saw Adrian's twenty-first birthday. To mark the occasion he was given a marble mine by his father. Situated in the Sea of Mamara, an enclosed body of water bounded by Turkey on both sides, its only entrances were the Gallipoli peninsula and the Dardanelles to the west, Constantinople and the Bosporus to the east. Marmara Ltd was set up as a company to run the prosperous concern, generating an income that would set Adrian up for life.

Prosperity was something the Harlequins were not used to. Their finances were under threat from the increased rent charged by Heathfield at Wandsworth, on justification of the ground having been drained. In June the Queens Club sent a letter to the Harlequins offering them terms for tenancy. The downside to Queens, who were looking to promote their ground outside of the Varsity, was that only the First XV would be able to play there. The offer was declined. Approaches to Tripp and Roberts, who had played for the Rugby School XV, were accepted. Good players, good club men. At least the Harlequins now had better numbers.

If the Harlequins ship looked to have been partly stabilised, it was just about to hit the rocks. On 12 September 1904 it was noted at their AGM that many subscriptions remained unpaid. This was not surprising as the treasurer of fifteen years, the careful Surtees, had retired exactly a year before. The club was staring at financial ruin and it seemed that officership was something of a poisoned chalice. Poor Ward had been elected honorary secretary for the coming season. Adrian had crossed swords with Robert Oscar Cyril Ward in the Varsity of 1902. 'Roc' to his friends, he had been a club member for a few seasons. Formerly of Clifton College, and now living in Kensington, he was a man of large build: his greatest claim to fame lay in holding the great boxer John Hopley to three rounds while at Cambridge. Roc would need to find a greater sense of conviction and courage than he had ever known before.

Roc's first task was to arrange a club dinner for 1 November. Given the general malaise that seemed to be going around, this was almost as formidable a task as facing Hopley. At the dinner itself most of the talk centred around one of their own. Following in Cartwright's great footsteps, Adrian was to be the new Oxford captain for the Varsity.

Before that main event, however, came the side show. In early December 1904, Oxford met London Scottish. The *Morning Post* reported: 'Dark Blues surprise London Scots. Stoop and Munro. Sheer brilliance.'

Munro was by his side again and the Varsity was set for a cracker as a record crowd attended. Adrian lost the toss and his side were made to kick off. Cambridge collected the kick and returned it back, hoping to keep the ball in Oxford's half.

All the scoring came in the first period. Hearson put Cambridge ahead early but, playing a captain's innings, Adrian's response was quick. The crowd were on their feet as he jinked and swerved through the entire Cambridge side. To general surprise he held the ball and ran half the length of the pitch to score under the posts, a try that would live long in the memories of those that saw it. Oxford were to lose the game, but Adrian's confidence in his own abilities was growing and his audacity becoming renowned.

Adrian left university with a lesser degree in his chosen subject. His Oxford playing career ended after forty-three games, of which thirty-three were won. Scores and records of all the games were again recorded for posterity and reason, not least since many a player playing in these games would, like Lump and Roc, likely be seen again at some stage, in some other competitive guise, in the future. Hearson, Raphael, Maclear and Pat Munro stood out from the crowd.

For the present, however, Christmas 1904 at West Hall was fabulous. All the Stoops cared to do was look forward to the New Year.

three

NEW SCHOOL
1905

*No man's judgement is infallible, but the greater the captain's knowledge,
the less will his judgement be at fault. And a team will gladly follow any
captain whose knowledge is greater than their own.*

(*Captaincy*, Adrian Stoop)

Times were changing. With the advent of the 'motor', people were
starting to find greater flexibility to their travel. Moving pictures
provided a new outlet for the use of spare time. People's lives and habits
were gradually being altered.

The week after the Varsity Adrian was picked for the South in the international trial, partnering Butcher. But again, his services were not required
any further, as he was still considered too unconventional for the selectors'
liking. A general reluctance to fall down on the ball should have been the
least of their worries. The selectors had been having a difficult time trying
to find a competitive XV for some years, being continually beset by the
same old problems: trying to be too representative to all the regions, little
opportunity to see quality matches to assess ability and form, and a single
trial in the hope that one game might solve those faults. The internationals
themselves were characterised by no shortage of effort, but a general lack
of cohesiveness and fitness and a woeful shortage of skill on England's part.
Any player offering up a modicum of talent, flair or skill saw better than
to play for England. MacLear was the supreme case in point: as good as
any, born in Hampshire, English through and through – and playing for
Ireland. Daniell's great game as captain had been a one-off.

The steady decline in England's fortunes saw an embarrassing 25-0
defeat to Wales on 14 January, the Welshmen crossing the line seven times.
The result was standard fare, as Ireland demonstrated by crossing five times
the next month. England were in despair.

The debates raged as to who would form the next English line-up
against Scotland. A letter to *The Sportsman* homed in on one of the hotter
topics of the day:

*There is one man who seems to me to merit especial consideration, and that is
A.D. Stoop. The better the class of his opponents, the better he plays. In college*

matches at Oxford he is said to be of no special brilliancy, but against Cambridge he is a holy terror. Against Scotland he would be better still. He seems to reserve his best efforts for great occasions and a large and enthusiastic crowd evidently inspires him.

All other options exhausted, a month later, Adrian received a handwritten note from the RFU:

Dear Sir,

You have been chosen to play for England against Scotland at Richmond on Saturday March 18th.

Kindly let me know at once by enclosed telegram if you can play.

Yours truly,

Percival Coates

Short and to the point. He had to bring his own socks and shorts, the shirt was to be provided, travelling expenses would be paid. Ever proud, Adrian wrote to his parents, abroad in North Africa: 'I have been chosen to play *v*. Scotland. ADS.' Having proved difficult to locate, they eventually received a simple telex in Algiers: 'Adrian got his international.' The selectors had gone for the last throw of the dice in the last-chance saloon, having seen little value in the young Oxford star until now. Ever pessimistic about all things English, the papers had their say under the banner 'Stoops to Conquer':

… thoroughly well merited is the cap that has at last come the way of certainly one of the fastest half-backs in the Four Unions, the Oxford and Old Rugbeian captain A.D. Stoop. When he can cure himself of his only fault of not getting down to the ball in stopping a forward rush, he must join the ranks of great half-backs, as a surer tackler we have not, and he does not neglect his backline. His selection, and that of C.E.L. Hammond, forward, will be the most popular of all.

The game was played at Athletic Park, Richmond, on 18 March 1905. Adrian was in good company: playing with him were Cartwright and Raphael, who had centered for Oxford in all three of Adrian's Varsities, as well as Curly Hammond, his Harlequins captain. Opposing Adrian's left half, Pat Munro was at right. Both international teams had already played two and lost two that season. This game was for either the Calcutta Cup or the wooden spoon. The press had already taken their somewhat negative guess as to which would be England's.

Adrian woke on the morning of the game with a heavy cold. 20,000 people came to witness Scotland record a convincing victory. Analysing the game after his own fashion, he wrote in a letter to his father:

As you will have seen no doubt, England was beaten in a poor game in which I played worse. My cough took it out of me very much and I hadn't the energy to do anything up to form.

I did not let the side down, that was done by our full-back and left wing, but if I had been fit I am almost sure we would have won. Munro saved his side more than once; once I ran through their three-quarters, but Munro was on the look out and collared me.

Confidence in his own (fully fit) abilities, problems in his team's defensive and attacking lines, and shackled by someone who knew his game so well. Points readily taken on board.

The newspapers told it as they saw it. Stoop, on his debut, showed signs of early promise, creating openings for Brettargh. Brettargh, like many Englishmen on the day, had a nightmare, spoiling chances, his second with a dreadful knock-on. The visiting forwards carried all before them and the English halves had a torrid time. Munro had a great afternoon at the heels of his pack and bested Adrian throughout. The papers had the final say: 'There is no doubt that on his day Stoop is the finest half-back in England, but he is a man of moods and can play moderately at times.' Thus ended another disappointing season for the followers of English rugby.

Munro had come out on top in his first international game against Adrian. There were those, however, who still saw the value in keeping them together. In 1890 W.P. Carpmael had founded the Barbarians, a rugby football club without fixed abode or subscriptions, but upheld by honourable associations and the desire to entertain. Carpmael had led such a successful invasion of the powerful rugby territories of Yorkshire and the Midlands that immediately afterwards it was decided to form a representative touring club, named after the legendary marauding warriors of two thousand years before. Carpmael recognised that running tours on any extensive scale demanded a different organisation to that of the ordinary club. He conceived the idea of a powerful band of players drawn from anywhere in the British Isles and capable of playing rugby, as it ought to be played, on the grounds of great but outlying clubs. Their flag held the simplest of mottos: 'Rugby football is a game for gentlemen in all classes but never for a bad sportsman in any.' The Order of the

Barbarians could be conferred upon any rugby-playing citizen of the Empire, if he were good enough and 'not lacking in manners and sportsmanship'. In April 1905, the Barbarians committee knew that Stoop and Munro were the perfect players to uphold Carpmael's traditions. Selected to tour, the two friends played together against Swansea on 22 April, Cardiff on the 23rd and Devonport Albion on the 25th. Three games in four days. Open, fast rugby with Oxford's finest furthering their educations. Adrian was clearly enjoying his rugby. So too were the crowds who came to watch.

The Harlequins closed their season with the election of two new members to the club: Roc's brother Holly and, at Adrian's insistence, Kenneth Powell, rugby's latest athletic prodigy. At their AGM on 25 July, H.J.H. Sibree was elected a new member. Born in Madagascar on 9 May 1885, Herbert John Hyde Sibree had attended the School for Sons of Missionaries in Blackheath. Living at 88 Bishopsgate, his 'Old Kensington' club had ceased to be – another casualty of the state of rugby in England. He hoped the Harlequins would be able to accommodate him in his chosen position of full-back. Great as it was to have a few new members, attentions were swiftly refocused on the reported serious deficit in the club's balance sheet. Given the poor attendance at the meeting, however, the AGM was adjourned until September, the start of the following season.

The summer saw further touches being made to West Hall. The timbered boathouse, with its thatched roof of Norfolk reeds, was completed. The glass conservatory was transformed in to a 'winter wonderland', the internal walls of which were a mass of ferns, hydrangeas, climbing plants and palms. The tranquillity inside complemented the serenity of the Dutch gardens outside. West Hall had become a pleasure palace providing a warm welcome for friends and family alike.

Back in Holland the remainder of the Stoop dynasty looked forward to the visits of their cousins. The great success of their oil and financial concerns allowed all of Frederick's brothers and sisters to indulge their respective families. Cornelius' contacts, particularly in the art world, allowed his nephews and nieces to be spoiled in their greater understandings of fine art. The interest of one in particular, Anne, was to be advanced by the greater purchasing power that came her way when she married J.B. August Kessler. The family's attention to the art world met with great favour in their part of Holland, where Pablo Picasso had become friends with several Dutch writers and painters, particularly Tom Schilperoort and Otto Van Rees. In the summer of 1905 Picasso spent six weeks in Schoorl and Schoorldam, at the invite of Schilperoort, producing several paintings as he did so. Cornelius in particular liked what he saw.

Picasso had been born into an artistic environment in 1881, two years before Adrian. Like Adrian his achievements in formal schooling were negligible and like Adrian there was also no doubt as to his rapid and astonishing progress in his chosen field. What stood Picasso apart from his peers was his awareness of the infinite possibilities of using every conceivable material for his art. His lack of money on his initial forays to Paris, coming on the back of scepticism about his works, left him struggling. The cold winters he experienced led to his self-styled 'Blue Period', where the general gloominess of the canvases made them difficult to sell. Needing stimulation, he returned to his spiritual home, Barcelona. The ensuing years saw him flitting between both bases, and also saw a wider appreciation of his works. His subjects took on a more delicate touch. One such, *Woman in a Chemise*, (also known as *Madeleine*), was a picture that Cornelius was quick to acquire. Picasso's newfound fondness for all things Dutch and English had seen him pass out of the 'Blue' and through the softer colours of his 'Rose Period'. This was followed by three of his more famed works, the *Saltimbanques* – the family of Harlequins. The mythical symbolism of the Harlequin's power over life and death greatly interested him. A sponsored collection of his Harlequin paintings allowed him time to consolidate. And so 1905 became a pivotal year for the artist as he found a new audience.

As years go, 1905 had already been a pivotal one for Adrian too. He had already played some stages: Bigside, Wandsworth Common, Richmond, Queens. He too had had his Oxford 'Blue' period, taken in the Rose of England, and was about to expand his own Harlequin theories.

Pastel shades

Autumn came and with it a new season.

Saturday 16 September 1905 was a fine, sunny afternoon and the newly arrived New Zealand tourists, under Dave Gallaher, were playing their first game. Down in Devon the county champions of the previous season were beaten 55-4, an unheard-of score in those days. The rugby world was stunned. Five days later the Cornish team were dispatched 41-0. Over the following week came the turns of Bristol (41-0), Northampton (32-0) and Leicester (28-0), to be led to the altar. No ground was sacred to the all-conquering visitors.

Seemingly penniless, the Harlequins had at least gained (or regained) a ground of their own by retaining the lease on Wandsworth Common. Their held-over AGM finally took place on 29 September. Sixteen people made it. Rent at Wandsworth of £35 represented the largest outflow for the coming season, followed by player expenses, Lewins' shirt account, stationary and postage. Total outflows in the region of £120 were unlikely to be matched by subscriptions and shares of gate monies. Such was the state of the club finances, those present were asked to make a voluntary subscription to wipe out the balance sheet deficit. The amount of £23 13s raised represented half of the club's funds at that date. The AGM closed with Curly Hammond elected captain for the fourth successive year. Adrian's enthusiasm and growing reputation contributed significantly to his own election as vice-captain, honorary secretary of the First XV and club secretary.

The best teachers pass on their wisdom, which is then widely accepted by pupils willing to learn. At Rugby the development of the game, and its organisation, came from the boys, and as a member of the school XV, Adrian would have been instrumental not only in arranging house games, but also in training and refereeing. If Adrian had already learned much, he now had a plan, a long-sighted vision. He knew exactly what the club needed. His first task in his new club capacity was to tear up the rulebook.

The start had to be new players – players willing to learn. Roc, Holly and Curly Hammond were already the backbone of a big pack. Donkeys they might have been called, but Adrian knew their worth. Get the ball and heel it back as quickly as possible, and while they were never the most skilful, they followed orders. And they could look after themselves. The problem, as Adrian knew from earlier experience, was a lack of any balance and cohesiveness in the backline. His ideas were already taking him away from the mundane duties of a normal half, those of falling and dribbling with the ball. This was a ball-in-hand sport after all, not just 'foot' ball. All he needed was a few like-minded individuals.

Harlequins' traditional source of recruits was Dulwich College, just as Blackheath's was Marlborough. Adrian knew they needed to go further, having already picked up some of Rugby School's talent in prior years, including Roberts and Tripp. In Kenneth Powell, they had a fine athlete who had won the school high jump and hurdles in 1902, 1903 and 1904, the broad jump, the 100 yards and quarter-mile in 1903 and 1904, and the half-mile and 150 yards in 1904.

Trials were arranged for the start of the new season. If Adrian was to find his men, the net would have to be cast wide. At the same time as Gallaher's tourists were trampling all over English rugby, a motley band of would-be rugby players turned up from all walks of life to a scratch pitch in a South London park. The simple session on Wandsworth Common on a sunny September afternoon in 1905 was to change the course of English rugby forever.

Herbert Sibree was there. Traditionally, the half's role had been to fall on the ball to stop forward rushes. Almost immediately Adrian labelled

Herbert a 'scrum' half, because while he dribbled well, he also had a strong, accurate pass. Adrian knew that was what he wanted from a scrum-half. 'No Sibree, no me' was his only take on the matter.

John Birkett was invited to come to the trials by Holly Ward. Born on 27 December 1884 in Richmond, and now living in Burgess Hill, he had been an old playing colleague of Holly's in Brighton. Formerly of Haileybury College, he was a big man. He had come to the trials hoping to get in to the Harlequins, and maybe even one day to be able to emulate his late father Reginald, scorer of England's first-ever international try. John's chosen position was that of half, but Adrian had already found his new scrum-half. He saw in John a right-hand man and, as such, someone who should play outside him. When John was to be selected for the first game of the season, he was somewhat concerned to hear Adrian tell him he would be playing three-quarter:

I could have cried, in fact I think I did, for I was terribly keen and anxious to please and convinced that I should not in this strange position. I was much too young and nervous to argue and so it was forever after.

Douglas (Danny) Lambert had been playing, unnoticed, as a forward in the Harlequin 'A' team for a few years. Born on 14 October 1883, he lived in South Kensington. He had played football at school in Eastbourne, but when the school changed over to rugby in 1900, Danny went with them. A big man like John Birkett, the key facet of his armoury was a long deceptive stride. To see him running you might have thought he was going slowly, until it became obvious everyone else was being left behind. At the trials, Adrian produced one of his own trademark runs, ending up show-boating down the wing as he neared the try-line. As he went to cross it, he was suddenly bulldozed into touch by a blur that had sped across the pitch to cut him down. Enquiring what it was that had hit him as he picked himself up from the ground, he was told it was a forward from the 'A' team. Adrian had found a wing three-quarter for the Firsts.

Sibree, Birkett, Lambert. All players with potential. But they had more than that. Adrian knew only too well that the problem with 'sports masters' was that they could only teach the game one way and as such the pupils would only learn one way. The ideal had to be to teach two or three ways, then allow the pupils to think of another – making choices as needs demanded. Adrian's new-found recruits were not ready-made rugby players, and certainly not stars. But they could run, kick, and tackle in more than ordinary fashion. They had natural football ability, speed, strength and good handling skills, but perhaps above all, they had the intelligence to make the most of these qualities. Given the way they were all about to adapt from their preferred to Adrian's preferred positions, they would show they were willing to learn second and third ways – and that they were willing to follow a leader.

The Harlequins were not the only English club fighting to survive. The crisis in the game was reaching a head as the national team's run of losses continued and several of the RFU's founder clubs folded. Over at the small market town of Northampton the problems were as great as any. Being closer to the Midlands and the North, the Northern agents were rife, forever looking for conscripts to join the professional game. However, Northampton were also lucky enough to find an individual for whom second and third ways were second nature.

Edgar Mobbs came late to the game. Born 29 June 1882, a public schoolboy he most definitely was not. A 'busboy' at Bedford Modern, he was a keen hockey and cricket player. It was only after joining his local village rugby side in 1905, five years from leaving school, that he was spotted by Northampton. Despite not having a great schooling in the game, his character and demeanour stood him out as a man to be respected. It was just two seasons before he was made captain of Northampton. His leadership qualities were second to none, but it was his personable approach and love of life that earned him the nickname 'Great Heart'.

As the new season progressed, the Harlequins were having a modicum of success playing the Stoop way. Their forwards were doing their job: winning the ball and releasing the backs. Herbert to Adrian, Adrian to John, John to Danny. Practice makes perfect. And so the backs caught and passed, caught and passed. Over the remaining games, the basics of their running, handling and passing started to be elaborated on. Movement became instinctive. The way Herbert played was allowing Adrian to define the flying-half position as one in its own right – unorthodox for the day but, as Wales and the All Blacks had shown, innovate and others have to follow.

While Adrian knew that initial success would be good for the fortunes of the club, there was still much to do. He also knew that the jigsaw was not yet complete. Surrounded by a good and supportive family, life was good, but he had also long since learned that there was as much to be gained from giving as there was from receiving. It was time to go back to school, having already pencilled in another name in the club's address book, just before that of Lancelot Sweetlove of East Moseley: 'F.M. Stoop, West Hall'.

Over at Rugby Freek had made the XV for 1905, five years after his brother. The outside world showed more than a passing interest, seizing on any opportunity. Curtis & Evans of Leicester, makers of football and cricket boots and shoes 'with impenetrable protectors against knobs and spikes bedding into the feet of players (patent applied for)' wrote to Adrian:

Dear Sir,

Enclosed comments from the Leicester paper about match. As an old Rugby follower your brother has the making of a fine half-back, he had an advantage over the others with his boots gripping the sticky ground... that's what the three's [three-quarters] *wanted on Sat so more could stand up. If you can recommend them we shall esteem it a great favour.*

Yours sincerely,

Curtis & Evans.

And to Freek:

Dear Sir,

Enclosed find receipt for your football boots at same time allow me to congratulate you on your play at Leicester and the way you kept your feet in comparison to the others, if you can recommend our boots to others at school then we shall be greatly esteemed.

Yours sincerely,

Curtis & Evans

Ringing endorsements, not that Adrian needed any prompting to return to Rugby to watch the school games and see his brother play. Having already captured Kenneth Powell, as well as another Stoop, there might be other athletic gems on show – maybe even another Adrian. On one particular visit he was not to be disappointed.

The school XV for 1905 made for interesting reading. Alongside Freek, Rupert Brooke. In Brooke's own words regarding his brief playing days: 'I used to run around a bit.' Brooke was destined for other glories: rugby was of but passing interest for him. Far greater was Adrian's interest in a sixteen-year-old, playing for the XV, quite exceptionally, two years before his time. The young Ronald Poulton had attracted many further admirers, some of whom wrote offering gifts:

Sir,

Will you kindly accept the accompanying case [what this refers to is unknown] *from one who has seen and very much appreciated your play on the football field this season. Your clever attack v. defence, also sporting all round play has had such an influence upon the other players that it has raised the School fortunes from above the average. Wishing you still greater success, both in schoolwork and on other playing fields.*

Ronald Poulton was born on 12 September 1889, at Wykeham House in Oxford, to Edward Bagnall Poulton the renowned zoologist. At 5ft 11½ins he was built perfectly for sports, particularly athletics and hockey. What stood him apart from his school and his teammates, however, were his rugby skills: a run that had to be seen to be believed, head held far back, swinging the ball from side to side in outstretched hands, mesmerisingly crossing his legs as he ran. Top that off with a swerve that could not be seen coming, and many a defender was left all ends up before they had realised he was long gone. There had been suggestions that he was difficult to play with because he played his own game. Freek knew better because he had spent many a day chasing his brother at West Hall. The game was about anticipation, both of opponents and teammates.

Four years earlier, Adrian had marked a future spot in his team-building for Freek. Almost at once he knew that the young Poulton would complete the picture. Adrian had once been asked by the Harlequins 'A' whether he would like to join but had taken his time before deciding, originally declining as being too young. Ronnie was given a personal invite in a letter from Adrian. He too recognised he was too young.

Adrian would have to try again later, but not before the winter of 1905 – the New Zealand tourists, despite having been in town for but a short while, had knocked rugby all out of shape.

All Black

The press went wild. Never before had they seen the like. In their first five games Gallaher's men were 190 points for to 4 against. English rugby had fallen so low it would not have recognised a lesson if it had seen one. Until perhaps now. The New Zealanders were sensational. Their passing, team organisation, moves, handling and lines of running were incredible. They would strike fast and keep the ball alive. A specialist hooker threw the ball in to line-outs, not one of the halves, freeing up men outside. Gallaher himself played as a roving wing forward, detached from the scrum, acting as an extra scrum-half and with the function of destroying opposition attacks. He was swiftly nicknamed 'the Holy Terror', seemingly fearless as he dropped down to stop rushes, his fierce tackling and pace standing out. Very much the man for the big occasion, his captain's game was played as much in his head as his feet. His backs deliberately altered their positions, rarely playing in the same place in consecutive matches, partly to ward against any staleness, partly to give the players a greater perception of another's game, and partly to allow interchanging in the event of casualty. At times it seemed as if the New Zealanders were playing with fifteen backs. 'All backs' or not, it was as much as the press could do to keep up. Dressed in black, they were like a tornado, enveloping all in their path. Almost at once the 'all backs' became the 'All Blacks'.

The tourists' sixth game was to be played in London. Interest had risen exponentially as each game had been played, and there was no rugby ground in London large enough to meet public demand. An association football ground had to be chosen and Chelsea's Stamford Bridge got the nod, Middlesex being the sacrificial lambs. Adrian played as one of their half-backs, his side losing 34-0. He had never played in such a one-sided game in his life. Given the points tally to date this was not unexpected, but all of a sudden the capital had awoken to a new game, a new spectator sport, the like of which they had not seen before.

The All Blacks' game against Surrey proved interesting on two accounts. Adrian went along to see John Birkett play in a match refereed by one of their more esteemed Harlequin old boys, Billy Williams. A fine cricketer, particularly behind the wicket, and an MCC member, Billy had stood by the Harlequins in their earlier years. Strong of mind and character, his more active years were behind him but he still enjoyed pottering about the park, dispensing his own brand of justice. Gallaher, the scourge of all England in his roving role, stood down for the game. His replacement, Gillett, might have wished he hadn't. Billy whistled Gillett and the All Blacks off the park, rarely a minute going by without him adjudicating their style of play to be contrary to his steadfast inter-pretation of the rules (as played in his day). Twelve penalties were given against the tourists in the first half. Gallaher's men won 9-0 but it seemed that the best England could find to temporarily slow them down was an old man and his whistle. Billy Williams had had his eighty minutes of infamy and his (first) fifteen of fame.

A further trip to Oxford saw Munro's university team meet a similar fate. The New Zealanders were unstoppable.

When their test with England loomed up on 2 December 1905, the All Blacks' unbeaten record boosted the crowd at Crystal Palace to 50,000. The conditions were swamp-like, not surprising since the pitch had been laid out on the infilled site of a former artificial lake. After an inauspicious start to his international career earlier that year, Adrian had lost his place for this, England's next international, despite being the star of the show in the recent South and Universities 35-3 thrashing of the West in a trial game. Maybe this was a blessing. Braithwaite and Dai Gent came in as two of the eight new caps and had the honours at half-back. Cartwright was the new captain and had Curly Hammond by his side. In a bid to counter Gallaher, Raphael was played as a rover. Perhaps due to the conditions, the All Blacks' margin of victory, 15-0, was not as great as recorded in other matches, but Gallaher's men still managed to record five tries to nil. Outplayed up front, the mud had saved England from a pasting. The only positive aspect to the game was a profit of over £1,000.

Two weeks later the tourists took their game to Wales for the match everyone wanted to see, perhaps the first unofficial world championship. In the red corner, Wales, in their pomp, recognised as the greatest team around: Gwyn Nicholls, Rees Gabe, Dicky Owen, Dicky Jones, Teddy Morgan et al. In the black corner, New Zealand. The Welsh had led a revolution in rugby in the 1890s, replacing one of the then nine scrum players to release an extra back almost by default due to the unavailability of an opposition player. As a concept it worked, and the rest of Britain had to follow suit, if only to counter with a defence of at least equal numbers to the attack. The All Blacks were different. They were not merely tinkering with positions. They had a complete change to all facets of the game. Rugby had experienced upheavals in its time, but the All Blacks were far ahead of theirs. They played a different ball game. This match was to be a firecracker.

The referee, Scotsman John Dewar Dallas, was to be forever linked to one of rugby's greatest controversies. Wales scored first with a try hatched days beforehand by their half, Dicky Owen. A wily character, he had spent days practising set moves behind closed doors. Set moves? In those days? The try came quite spectacularly from a blindside dummy and a reverse pass to Pritchard who fed the alert Morgan to score. Wales went on to win 3-0, but the result hinged on the 'try' that never was. The All Black Bob Deans was pulled down close to the corner flag by two Welshman. Over the line or not? Dallas was perhaps too far behind to get a clear view. Deans was to later telegram him: 'Ball grounded six inches over the line. Some Welsh players admit try.' Either way, Wales had won, and the All Blacks were to lose their only game on the tour. The New Zealanders went on to total 730 points for to 47 against in their thirty-two matches. Gallaher's men left with a reputation above all others, then or since. And for Wales? Of as much note were the tourists' scores against their own club sides: Newport, Cardiff, and Swansea only going down 6-3, 10-8, and 4-3 respectively. This unarguably was the start of their golden period, under-pinned by the overwhelming superiority of their club sides. The financial prosperity of their game stemmed from playing the rugby that spectators wanted to see. Theirs was the standard to which the rest of British rugby would have to measure up.

The New Zealand shock treatment left rugby, particularly in England, in a state of bewilderment. Quite apart from the way the game was being played on the pitch, other cracks were appearing. The administrative power base, in trying to define and redefine laws, was ruling to the letter of them and a power game was emerging. The clubs had created the RFU, but the emphasis had shifted to the counties to look after the organisation of the game. The counties would then become represented on the RFU's laws, grounds and selection committees: a democratic but cumbersome decision-making process. In England, sport was seen as recreation and fun, and had never been taken as seriously as in New Zealand or Wales. At the root of the game in those countries were principles that had long since been neglected in England.

The messages were not lost on Adrian. His days at Rugby and Oxford had led him to be a keen spectator and student of the game. He fully appreciated what Wales had achieved and New Zealand had evidenced further. The most significant entries in his cuttings were not the records of his own games, but the several versions of events on the day the English had faced the All Blacks. Underpinning the analysis thereof were the clear facts: a team beaten by its own lack of understanding in the three-quarters and, in the way the New Zealanders played their own game, an ability to alter positions and change direction of play. A full-back could be a wing or a centre, which did not happen by chance. The players needed to understand each other perfectly to be able to execute their moves and the whole style of play.

Following England's spirited but nonetheless hollow performance against the All Blacks at the end of 1905, the selectors turned to trials for the home internationals of the next spring. With a new partner at half, Adrian played for the South against the North, his side winning 35-0. It was written that 'Stoop was the master and eased the new boy in.' For Adrian, 1905 had started inauspiciously and gathered momentum as it had gone. Despite this, he was not selected for the first international of 1906. His partner in the trial was.

—~m~—

THE PUPIL'S PUPILS
1906-1907

*We were willing to cut down smoking, especially cigarettes, and to confine
ourselves to drinking only beer, with an occasional sherry and bitters.*
(John Birkett, as recorded by H.B.T. Wakelam)

As 1905 closed, it had become clear to Adrian from all he had seen that valuable as the work of a captain in the field might be, this was but a small part of his duties. Watching Daniell, Gallaher and even Cartwright served only to prove that the captain needed to be a master of not only the game in general, but his own in particular, from its basic principles to its smallest detail, and to be a wise strategist and a skilful tactician to boot. To attain these qualities, not only was considerable study required but, in a game of infinite possibilities, so too was a far greater degree of original thought – more than was on show in England at the time, where confusion reigned.

As Adrian knew, the English were accustomed to only playing left-half/right-half. In trying to get 'noticed', typically the senior partner would often opt to play, increasingly, both sides of the scrum. Unfortunately, with no one having the necessary ability to fill the skill gap between the self-appointed 'scrum-half' and the backs, the junior half often looked ineffective and the backs became worthless.

Dai Gent had learned his rugby in Wales, where it had become more the vogue for one half-back to work the scrum and one to stand off and provide a link with the three-quarters – teamwork subordinated individual preference. In his first England trial, Dai was partnered by Jago. A dispute arose as to who should play where, Jago fancying the scrum-half role in its entirety. With the help of mediation, Jago offered a compromise: he play the scrum first and switch with Dai at half time. Come half-time however, he suggested that as they had played so well in the first half then he, Jago, should stay put for the second.

England's first outing of 1906 was yet another defeat to the newly exalted legends of Wales, and their team which seemingly had the monopoly on skilled backs in the land. Playing at the Athletic Ground in Richmond, Wales romped to a four-tries-to-one victory with a controlled and carefully planned performance. Much of the game was spent in the English half, the Welsh technique in the scrum pinning the English forwards back, which allowed their backs to run the English ragged. Ireland added insult to injury by putting another four past them in the next game. Including the match against New Zealand, poor old Dai had found himself playing the outside of the two halves on all three of his outings for England, the most recent two being with Jago. England in general, and Dai in particular, seemed unable to progress.

Overall, the international season had been a topsy-turvy affair, with no real domination by any side. Scotland had beaten Ireland, Ireland had beaten Wales, and everyone had beaten England, who had now endured seven losses on the trot. As if any further confirmation of their position at the bottom of the pile were necessary, they had not beaten Scotland, their last opponents of the season, for four years. These were desperate times. Even the press were getting bored.

Unsurprisingly, Dai Gent was cast into the wilderness leaving the remaining incumbent, Jago, requiring yet another partner. John Birkett was one of four new caps selected for the game, but not before an extraordinary debate had raged over the selection of James Peters as the new half-back. If the papers ever needed an opportunity to awaken from their slumber, then now they had it. Playing down in Plymouth, Peters' father was of West Indian descent: James was about to become the first black player ever to play for England. Not only were England without direction and enduring their worst run in history, they had used forty-four players in six games in a mere season and a half. The colour of a man's skin should have been the least of their concerns.

The Scottish game was played on 17 March 1906 at Inverleith Park in Edinburgh, the then home of Scottish rugby. England's fortunes, limited as they were, scraped the bottom of the barrel when Jago pulled out at the eleventh hour. Adrian was summoned as his replacement, almost a year to the day from his fateful first cap. Back then Adrian had boldly proclaimed that both he and England had been robbed of victory by his cold. Now he had to stand by that statement and prove otherwise. A sense of déjà vu must have pervaded, as once again Pat Munro was in opposition.

Captain once more, Cartwright assembled his team at their hotel the night before the game and discussed in detail the team they were to meet the next day. Many of the Scottish players were familiar to them. Cartwright, Adrian and Raphael had all played for Oxford in the 1904 Varsity against MacLeod and Monteith. Pat Munro's play was a given. Those in the English team that knew the opposition only by their sufficiently alarming newspaper reputations came away from the fairly frank discussions in high hope. Lump had got his team to believe that the

Scottish pack were not nearly as fearsome as their reputations held out, and that hard work could win the day.

John Birkett found it hard work trying to get some sleep on the overnight train up from London – not the best of preparations for his debut international. The press were well prepared for theirs. On the Saturday morning of the game, Cartwright's men opened the English papers to be met with the less-than-inspirational headline: 'England goes north to her third defeat.' No one believed in them except themselves, the team still feeling sufficiently heartened by their captain's rousing of the night before. They would go in to the game evens, if only in their own minds.

England's win was as convincing as it was unexpected. Not only was the victory richly deserved, but it came in one of Scotland's better years. The *Westminster Gazette* reported:

Scotland had a slight advantage in the pack, and Munro was at his best behind the forwards; but Munro and Simson did not work quite so well as usual as a pair, probably because Stoop, who worked the scrum for England, proved to be absolutely at the top of his form and made himself a serious obstacle to their combination. His spoiling was magnificent, and he never missed the slightest opportunity of making openings for his own three-quarters. It was not at half-back, however, but in the three-quarter line that Scotland were completely beaten, though, of course, Stoop's success was to some extent responsible for this. The Scottish threes never got together and they failed quite as badly as they did against Wales. The English threes in consequence, though they never looked by any means to be a great line, were easily the better of the two. Birkett, the new international, played a splendid game in the centre and so did Simpson on the wing; Shewring was sound enough, and very clever play between him and Raphael produced the first try; and Raphael, on the wing, played a great defensive game, but was too slow to be very prominent in attack. Jackett began badly, but as soon as he settled down showed his best form. The whole side, in fact, played well, with Stoop and Birkett as the 'stars'; but it was the ineffectiveness of the Scottish threes that gave England the victory by three tries to one.

For John, the pride at winning his first cap could only have been tempered by the fact his father was never able to see him play. He had however responded in more than kind for the faith in him and positional perceptiveness that his club vice-captain had shown at the Harlequin trials just six months before.

For Adrian, knuckling down to servitude and giving the selectors what they wanted, stood him in good stead for now. Playing against his natural instincts, his quick service had continued to threaten the opposition line, and kept the Scots constantly on the back foot. His triumphant return to the international arena had set a new standard:

We won by three tries to one, but it was certainly one of the hardest matches in which I have taken part. There was an English regiment stationed at the castle, and at the end of the game one of the Tommies was so overwrought that he flung his arms around my neck and kissed me. I had not the strength to raise a hand against him.

After the unexpected result of the game, people started to talk in a more optimistic light about England's fortunes and the successes that had come from the game. The *Westminster Gazette* report was cut out and again filed away for future reference.

The last international of the season was to be a friendly, England's first encounter with France in a test match. Played at the Parc des Princes five days after the Scotland game, the English team showed only two changes, and those due only to an inability to make the trip. England won the game convincingly 35-8, Adrian scoring his first international try. That trip, in the late spring of 1906, allowed the players to relax and take in the Parisian sights. In the critical spotlight, the star pupil could now develop his Harlequin theories further. Up in Montmatre, Picasso was already moving forward from his.

Adrian knew that to gain further momentum his own Harlequins would have to set up an infrastructure capable of dealing with the game as it had become. And he set about doing it. The fixture with Racing Club of Paris was reinstated; annual dinners were held at Simpson's-in-the-Strand; Preece's riding school was hired for an evening during the week at £2 a time for training sessions (unheard of then, for the Harlequins or any other club).

The significance of his hard work was not lost on those around him. They did as they were told and, starting to reap the benefits themselves, were happy to do so. If improvement meant cutting down on the alcohol and the cigarettes, then so be it. Having benefited more than most, John was one of the first to recognise how and where the improvements in standards were coming from. Drawing on his own experiences he was to say that those up and coming were:

Selected by Adrian who was pretty good at spotting a likely player; keen and fit, with a real club spirit, this latter being greatly helped by the constant hospitality and parties given to us all at West Hall by Mr and Mrs F.C. Stoop; ready to fall in with Adrian's ideas and so to exploit his methods; helped considerably by the training evenings in the riding school; very particular about our boots, not always an easy matter in those days, before 'Cotton Oxfords' or similar types were on the market.

As Adrian led by example, nothing escaped his attention to detail: drinking a minimum of four pints of water a day; breathing through the nose; and of course proper boots, which became his pet subject: 'Some players will not even take the trouble to tie their laces securely before a match, but special institutions are provided for such as they.' Seeing Ronald Poulton up at Rugby merely enhanced his views thereon. To be able to twist and turn, to change direction at will as Ronnie did required boots that were not going to slip on the predominately greasy surfaces. Proper studs were needed, as opposed to the bladed variety common to all at the time. Next to that came cleaning. If boots needed to be as strong, but as lightweight as possible a week's worth of mud countered any benefits they might have. Two or three used sets allowed remedial repairs to one without the pain that came with having to use a new set.

As the club started to have a buzz about it, Adrian knew he had to keep it moving forwards. Elsewhere, others were generating momentum of their own.

Over at Rugby, the year's results in the Athletics cup were both convincing and expected. Everyone waited to see the young Poulton live up to the promise he had shown the year before, when he had won the 150 yards in 16⅔ seconds. This year's heats were run in snowstorms, eventually giving way to clear blue sky for the two days of main competition. Ronnie, still in his penultimate year, quite literally ran away with the honours. He won the broad jump with 19ft 6in, the 150 yards, the quarter mile, and the hurdles. His 'lesser' placings included second in the 100 yards, fourth in the half-mile and second to Freek in the high jump. Both jumped 5ft 1½ins, Freek clearing on the second to Ronnie's third – a triumph for the smaller man, at 5ft 8¾in, who also came third in putting the weight. As if their athletic dominance were not enough, Freek came third in the gymnasium cup with a score of 80 while a week later Ronnie won the racquets cup. The two schoolboys were keeping themselves busy and fit out of season.

Adrian's mind was already running ahead to the start of the next. Before that, however, he had to complete studies of his own. Between 28 May and 1 June he sat his law exams at Lincoln's Inn Halls. Two weeks later, the published results told of a Class II pass for his Inner Temple finals. He had become a barrister, much as his father had hoped for.

When the new season came, there was further good news at the Harlequins AGM. Their balance sheet for the close of 1905/06 showed total outgoings of £125 13s 8d. Gate share of £77 10s and that year's subscriptions of £49 3s actually yielded a profit. The prior year's voluntary donations of £48 17s 6d, not ultimately required, were held over and with subscription arrears from prior years of £11 4s, a healthy bank balance existed. The balance sheet was duly approved, with a note that monies would not be recklessly spent. The only caution noted was that the HCC, from whom Wandsworth was leased, was starting to make more demands of the club, requesting, for one thing, the installation of automatic ticket turnstiles and shares of gate monies.

Financial matters dealt with, it came as no surprise that after his efforts of the previous year, Adrian was elected Harlequins captain for the season to come, a role he took up in conjunction with the secretaryship. Roc was appointed vice-captain. Adrian took it in his stride: 'Somehow I was shouldered with the complete responsibility of the club.' He was not alone. Over at Northampton, Edgar Mobbs found himself in much the same position. Little did the two new chiefs realise what the future would hold for them. Their paths would cross many a time, and not just on the field.

A Crisp Autumn Day

At the end of 1906, a new group of tourists arrived on Britain's shores.

The South Africans' approach to the game, while not as revolutionary as that of the All Blacks, stirred up the interest factor in much the same fashion. Their forwards were good and big, although not superstars. Where they and their backs stood out, however, was in their athleticism, a fact the press could not fail to pick up on. They also had fine wings and they used them. Their sole game plan appeared to be centred on their desire to attack. Their first three tour games were won on aggregate 87 points to 0, the victims being the East Midlands, Middlesex and Kent. Like the All Blacks, all of England sat up and took notice. Close games against Ireland and Scotland resulted in a win and a defeat for the tourists. Beating the unbeatables of Wales 11-0, however, was the biggest shock of all. How could England ever achieve what Morgan, Gabe, Bush, Owen and Nicholls had failed to do? Two victories at the end of the previous season might not have been enough to erase the misery of seasons past, but to their success-starved supporters it was at least a start. All of England suddenly wanted to see how good England might now be. But not just any old England – Stoop's England.

In the run up to the game, the press were full of their would-be saviour. For them there was only one name guaranteed to be on the team sheet and only one the public wanted to see. The only question of concern on their lips was who, of the many who had played in the position, would partner Stoop?

The Peters row continued, the South Africans initially refusing to play against him at Plymouth. As it was he was not picked for the international and Jago had the honour, with John once again at centre. The roles were now reversed. From being Jago's substitute against Scotland, Adrian was now the undisputed number one in a position where traditionally two shared the duties. England went into the game with only two new caps which, like the recent French game, ushered in a feeling of continuity not seen too many times in the past. Normality was upheld in part, however, as due to a clerical error, Dr A. Alcock, of Guys, gained his one and only cap at the expense of the intended L.A.N. Slocock.

Forty thousand came to Crystal Palace on 8 December. Not as big a crowd as for New Zealand, but enough to suggest the public appreciated the relative importance of the game. Light rain had been falling and once again the pitch resembled a quagmire. Almost immediately from the start the ball became difficult to handle, and the game suffered as a result. The South Africans scored the only points of the first half through an unconverted try. As the second half wore on, England got themselves more into the game. Then Adrian set up an opportunity down the blind side, allowing the English forwards to rush the ball over the line. A mistimed clearance hack by the South Africans' centre sent the ball straight to Brooks on the English wing, who touched down to level the game. The match finished an honourable draw, but the reputation of English rugby's newly crowned king was being further inflated.

The next international against France again heralded in the New Year. The game, on 5 January 1907, resulted in a nine-try thrashing. John scored one, but the star of the show this time was Danny Lambert. Coming in as a late replacement for his first international, he ran away with the plaudits, scoring five tries. This being the first visit by a side from France, great interest was shown – the performance of the Harlequins on display attracted most. None took greater note than the referee, Billy Williams. The English were not alone in their celebrations, having not lost now for four games – the Harlequins had also shown further improvement, paralleling the fortunes of their country. Neither team had anywhere to call their own, but everyone seemed to want to watch them.

Rugby School's XV had a home and also continued to pull out impressive results. The *Meteor* remarked on two of its returning pupils:

R.W. Poulton: a really good centre three-quarter, with plenty of pace; has an excellent swerving run and makes good openings, but is sometimes inclined to pass rather wildly; a good tackle and fair kick.

F.M. Stoop: a very fast half-back with plenty of originality; takes his passes at full speed, and makes splendid openings; a good tackle.

Life in rugby circles was indeed rich for the Stoops. Frederick would do anything to support his sons' causes but, again, his labours did not stop there. Coming up to his silver wedding anniversary, he funded the new 'Stoop Ward' at the local Pyrford orthopaedic hospital he had helped to purchase and set up a few years before. Whenever funds were needed for a building venture, be it repairs to the old church or organising a Dutch fair in aid of the building fund of the new church, he was always to be found with his chequebook open.

The chequebook was about to be opened at the RFU. It had long been recognised that until now the national team, quite apart from its poor but improving form, had little else to pride itself on. The recent visit of both the All Blacks and the South Africans had shown that, when public interest was sufficiently stoked, seats would be filled. And while 40,000 people would turn up to the Palace to watch a match of great significance, inevitably any match would suffer from the bog-like conditions there. Blackheath and Richmond were also venues that had staged internationals in the past, but the rotation of grounds and their lack of intimacy were problems that were all too readily apparent. It had also long been realised that the RFU offices in London were themselves a world away from the many venues that England were forced to play in. In response to this, the RFU charged Billy Williams, the ex-Harlequin and whistling star of the All Black tour, with the responsibility of finding some land fit for developing into a fortress for the national team.

Everyone's gardens looked rosy. Then disaster struck.

Wales had beaten New Zealand but had come unstuck against South Africa and England were, remarkably, in danger of reclaiming the rugby high ground after their draw with the latest tourists. Bizarrely, however, the English selectors chose the January 1907 game against Wales to put out an experimental English pack. Adrian and John played, but mystifyingly Danny was dropped, despite his heroics in the game before. Realising England's folly of playing with an untried pack, Wales sacrificed one of their own to employ an extra back. Wales duly swamped the English both up front and behind. A stiff wind in their faces in the first half all but disappeared by half-time. The Welsh won 22-0 scoring three tries in each half.

Time for scapegoats. The newly crowned king of English rugby was dropped from the international side for the next game, along with John and five others. The selectors were back in panic mode. England fared as poorly against Ireland, and another five changes were made for the last game of the season. They lost that too. From a position of mini-recovery in the wake of ten years of Rugby League fallout, selectorial incompetence for one game had rocked the foundations sufficiently to put all the good work to waste.

Adrian licked his wounds and thought long and hard. He would never be able to change the mindset of the selectors on his own. There was clearly much more work to be done but England would have to wait. Embittered as he might have been about his treatment, his Harlequin jigsaw needed finishing and he still needed to get his pivotal piece.

On 20 March 1907 Rugby School held its athletic cup. The *Meteor* said of its favourite son: 'Once again, as we did last year, and as we seem likely to repeat next year, we have to chronicle the phenomenal success of Poulton.' Almost as predicted, he won the half-mile, the quarter-mile, the 150 yards, the 100 yards, the hurdles and the high jump, with a second in the broad jump topped off by winning the double racquets. He could only look innocently forward to the summer and cricket for the XI. Adrian looked on, ever the interested bystander.

As the summer progressed, Frederick looked on as an interested bystander as the Shell Group decided a merger with the Royal Dutch was in the best interests of both companies. The Dutch and British companies had been in competition for some time but clearly decided it was in the interests of both to incorporate their worldwide activities. He too now had to think long and hard about the future and the direction of his company.

Summer over and, as if proving a point, the Harlequins season in September 1907 started to great acclaim. The scores for their first two games backed up an attacking game plan, winning as they did 42-0 against Richmond and 49-8 against Bath. At the 18 September AGM, sanction was given to buying £50 of East India stock, care of a balance sheet for the previous season that was the best the club had ever had. In two years the club had moved from having to get the cap out to being able to invest sizeable sums. The club spirit was good, with the continued dinners at Simpson's and Thursday evening training sessions at Preece's.

Following the international debacle at the end of the previous season, the press needed something more positive to analyse and started to take a greater interest in what was happening down at Wandsworth in general, and Adrian in particular. His leadership and his excellent judgement during games were obvious. What they could also not fail to see was the perfect harmony that existed between Adrian and Herbert. Unlike the squabbling for best position that existed at international half-back, these two stuck to their own more favoured positions, and each seemed to work as an extension of the other. Herbert fired the balls out quickly from the base of the scrum, and Adrian provided a dynamic link to his backs.

Comparisons were readily drawn against the All Blacks and their methods of attack. It had long been thought that Englishmen were incapable of replicating such strategies. Yet down on a Wandsworth park pitch, evidence to the contrary was abounding. Adrian was testing out theories, putting into practice schemes he had dreamt up. His disciples, Herbert, John, Danny and the newly joined Freek, were more than happy to play ball.

They were not content in merely throwing the ball along the line until it reached the wing, who might find himself marked by two or three players and out of space in which to run as everyone drifted across (assuming of course the ball had in fact been passed anywhere in his general space to start with). The Harlequins were being radical, using a variety of methods to change the point of attack: changes of direction, reverse passes, cross kicks. Each man knew his exact duties, both in attack and defence, and each could cover for another in the event of a mistake. Where they took a lead from the South Africans was in the athleticism with which they carried it out.

The press christened Adrian's methods the 'Stoop system'. Adrian maintained it was Clifford Wells, the old Harlequin, who had sowed the seeds. There is little doubt that the Welsh, the All Blacks and the South Africans had all played a part in the learning process. What was important was being able to see the possibilities and to have the courage and conviction to realise them.

For their third game of the new season, the Harlequins came up against the United Services. Adrian wanted to continue with his 'box' line-up, consisting of two fly halves, employed so successfully against Bath the previous week . The idea had caused a stir in the papers, but he was unable to see it through. The headlines in the *Sportsman* of 28 October 1907 had only one significance to report: 'United Services *v*. Harlequins. Adrian Stoop breaks his collarbone.' His gradual rise and rise in rugby circles had come to an abrupt halt. Once again he had to nurse his wounds, only this time they were physical rather than mental. He was not alone in having to take the knocks.

Billy Williams was coming up against his own obstacles and (yet more) fierce criticism in his quest for an English fortress. The critics were by no means convinced that 'a field of their own' was necessary or even desirable, arguing that international fixtures should be spread around the country's grounds to avoid disunion and discontent. Even if a field were to be purchased, it should be a good one. As it was, a twenty-one-year lease could have been secured on Richmond, with provision of a new stand only costing £3,000.

As 1907 drew to a close Billy persuaded his paymasters to purchase a ten-acre plot of land out in the sleepy village of Twickenham, giving reasoned and sound argument along the way. The ground itself was little more than a market garden, full of cabbages, turnips and other vegetables, twelve miles out in the country. Seizing the opportunity, the critics were even fiercer in their opposition. Transportation would clearly be a problem, being as 'far out' as it was. Even after its initial clearing it resembled what it was, a cabbage patch. Being in close proximity to the River Crane, a Thames tributary, the ground was prone to flooding, which would yield a heavy and holding ground in wet weather. 'Penny wise, pound foolish,' they cried. To the critics, Williams and the committee had embarked on a project that was ill-conceived, unbusinesslike and financially unsound: in short they had shown the same incapacity, nay stupidity, that they traditionally showed in their administration and secretaryship of the game itself.

The critical attacks were met with dignified silence from the RFU. A stubborn man, Billy believed that what he was doing was fundamentally right and in the best interests of the game. What he had the foresight to see, which others perhaps could not, was the potential of a permanent home, as both a commercial venture and as a symbol. The petty hair-splitters were not party to both an exhaustive search and detailed surveys of the lot. Rail and transport facilities were in fact one of the main consid-erations in selecting the ground. The South Western served Twickenham by train, and with extra services on match days could accommodate the influx of people. A tram link from Shepherd's Bush served Hampton Court, via Twickenham – better transportation links than for either Blackheath or Crystal Palace. Motor vehicles, an unheard-of invention a few years before, were suddenly opening up different routes of accessibility. The local authority had indicated that they would take on the responsi-bility of widening and improving the roads. Of greater significance was the drainage, deeds of contract being signed only once a contract for clearing and drainage had been negotiated. In addition to draining, the pitch would be raised eighteen inches. Of the ten acres, eight were to be used for the football ground, the remaining two to be sold for building purposes. An initial freehold outlay of £4,500 was thus immediately offset by offers of £3,000 for the additional space. The issue of debentures would meet the balance of costs for equipment. Contrary to popular opinion, Billy had been busy and had done his homework.

Picasso had also been busy and had left his doubters behind. Having completed his Harlequin series, he was searching for something new. He withdrew into himself. He had been a success at what he had done, but it was not enough. He needed to break out of the traditional mould, and so he entered a period of self-examination. Without the joy and exuberance of his youth, he needed to examine the values of his past, those of his present, and what he wanted for the future. He needed to break new ground. In 1907 Picasso painted *Les Demoiselles D'Avignon*, one of the most significant and revolutionary paintings of modern art. It was not a likeness, it was not a copy, and it was not a faithful representation. The initial reaction from the art world was one of shock and revulsion. Its capital importance, however, was its daring in breaking away from the past. Its distorted images opened up new ways of expressing emotion.

Adrian's emotions at his own inactivity were bottled up and sealed with corks. His dynamism, youth and enthusiasm were not things to be held in check. He too was in a period of self-examination. He needed to be active, to be breathing rugby, pursuing dreams. He too had to examine the values he held dear and think about what he wanted for the future. He was desperate to break new ground and he had to hang his hat on something. Just as triumph and disaster are two sides of the same coin, remedy of sorts was about to come to hand.

Ronnie was still at school and the XV for his last year, for which he was joint captain, had totalled 250 points for to 59 against. In December 1907 he wrote to his family at Wykeham House in Oxford, enclosing Adrian's original letter inviting him to join the Harlequins:

Of course it is quite an exception, and I certainly should not suggest doing it again. It only means half a day away. I should be back by dinner… it would be awfully good fun playing.

Adrian had got his man. Despite his own problems, the news put a renewed spring in his step. Looking ahead again, on 17 December a tour to Frankfurt, Frederick's birthplace, was sanctioned. Of far greater significance was the Harlequin committee agreeing to Adrian writing a letter to the RFU to enquire about the letting of the Twickenham project, once completed, on a permanent basis.

On New Years Day 1908 England entertained France for the first international of the season. After the abject failure of the previous one, John and Danny were restored and Herbert came in for his first cap. G.D. Roberts in the scrum took the number of Harlequins in the game to four. A snowstorm on the morning of the game made conditions tricky: England played without any rhythm, their overall display unconvincing and, but for the loss of two Frenchmen to injury, may well have been in trouble. Herbert was dropped two weeks later for the game against Wales who, as expected, maintained their supremacy over England.

Danny was then dropped for the Ireland game of February. Henry Vassall, the latest star of Oxford University, came in for his debut alongside John in the centre. Acclaimed by the press as possibly the best centre pairing in England, the side still failed to impress in the backs. Poor alignment and over-running wasted several opportunities and Portus, tried at fly-half, was anything but a success. Williamson at scrum-half was a success, and he paved the way for both an eventual English victory and, for himself, an extended stay in the side. The topsy-turvy world that was

English selection saw Danny return to support John for the last international against Scotland in March. Having won their one game for the season, nobody expected England to pick up another. They didn't.

With his shoulder eventually healed, Adrian was back for the end of the season, but too late for any international consideration. His inactivity had been more painful than the injury itself. In the months that followed he was called to the Bar by the Inner Temple, and carried out one case. One case too many, as it proved to be. Having missed much of the previous season, he knew he had to make up for lost time. Taking a huge leap of faith in his rugby-playing abilities and what he thought he still had to achieve, he 'retired' himself from law. His marble mine provided a sure enough income. Rugby and the Harlequins were to be his career from there on in.

The new season was ushered in at the club's AGM. Generally, finances were healthy, but the books showed a considerable increase in expenses due to the number of players who had 'disabled' themselves over the past year. As a workout for the games to come, the club took on the German national side in Frankfurt. The Germans, new to the game, knew their rugby and knew their players, and were more than happy to put themselves up against some of the best. For Adrian the trip allowed him to test out new ideas away from prying eyes.

Their home fixtures started much as they had in the previous season, except that this year Ronnie, who was now up at Oxford having gained an exhibition in science at Balliol, was also playing. He had done little to diminish his reputation to close out his school career over the early summer, once again winning the broad jump, the 150 yards, the quarter-mile, the high jump, the 100 yards, the hurdles and unsurprisingly the overall cup for the third time in three years. Cricket for the XI merely confirmed his status as the greatest all-rounder the school had ever had.

Edward Poulton knew the influence that Adrian was starting to have at Harlequins, but he also knew of the regard in which Adrian was held at Rugby and at Oxford. He professed of his son: 'He was fitted by knowledge as well as by nature to be the Oxford exponent of his mentor's teaching.' On Ronnie's debut in September 1908, the club president, W.A. Smith, stated:

Come and see a future international. Young Poulton of Rugby is playing today. Adrian is trying him in a number of positions. He is the greatest 'find' that we have had for years.

In his first game Ronnie scored from under his own posts, the Harlequins beating Old Merchant Taylor's 53-3. Once again Adrian had an abundance of riches at his disposal: Herbert, himself, John, Freek, Danny, and now

Ronnie. It was a backline of raw talent that was the envy of many clubs. The results started to match this promise.

And then déjà vu. With but a few games gone, while playing London Scottish, Adrian broke his shoulder again. Worse still, in the same game, John broke his too. Two breaks in one match, and Adrian's second in two years. The disappointment was there for all to see.

This time, Adrian's did not heal well. Doubts about whether he would play again crept in and he had to dig deep. His faith in himself was being sorely tested. Once more his canvas had dulled and, like Picasso, he had to believe deeply in himself.

five

TRIALS
1907-1909

*As I lay in bed at night, before going to sleep, the best time of all to make
plans, I mapped out my ideas, and then tried them out on the field.*
(Adrian Stoop, as recorded by H.B.T. Wakelam)

Bitterness and anger are energies better applied to turning a situation
around… and to influence what might happen next.

Adrian pretty much knew the side he wanted as his First XV, particularly
in the backs. In trying to foster an early enthusiasm, however, he had to mix
and match his players, knowing as he did that the fringe players were the
bedrock of the club. As captain he could not be seen to show any suspicion
of favouritism. It was a fine balancing act between success on and off the field.
Building up a team at the start of the season on a principle not unlike that of
the old school XV, that would be playing, irrespective of form, for the whole
season, would not take the club forward. To set aside a place for star players
in matches of special importance would certainly have a detrimental effect
on the club as a whole a few seasons down the line. As captain he had to
convince his fellow members that the club held the first place in his thoughts
and that those on the fringe of the first XV should not feel disheartened.

On the pitch his men were coping. They had been moulded into a
formidable unit, even if their leader was absent. Ronald Poulton was taking
the reins and most of the plaudits. Ronnie could have read all he needed to
know about Adrian, but playing alongside Freek, he could see first hand the
impact Adrian had on his brother's play. Ronnie too was a studier, noting:

*Fast running is not as important as people believed. Adrian Stoop is not a fast
runner, but extremely successful in getting through. Often achieved by a deceptive
pace that was slower than it seemed to be, so that an opponent running to intercept,
overshot the mark and crossed Stoop's tracks at a point he had not yet reached.*

Adrian Stoop – guileless, yet full of guile. His antics, his tricks, his sleight
of hand, just like the Harlequin of the *commedia dell'arte* of old Italian
history that had so entranced Picasso.

Edward Bagnall Poulton took a higher view:

A Stoop or a Ranji will find at Oxford a general readiness to test their innovations
by experiment, and no obstinate conservatism will hinder their adoption if they pass
that test. Poulton provided a unique opportunity for such experiment in 1908. He
came up a Harlequin born and made. If there had been no Stoop to start the New
Football he would most certainly have taken on the job.

Adrian had realised that the successes of Wales, New Zealand and South
Africa were largely due to the perfection of their handling and backing up,
the giving and taking of properly delivered passes at the right moment (after
a defender had been drawn), and carefully worked running lines. Quick
thinking and an offensive spirit, allied to team-work, speed, rhythm and a
certain amount of thought and practice all added to the pot. What his
Harlequins were adding to this mixture, in the way they passed, was spacing,
and hence simplicity. The Welsh were more accustomed to wet and muddier
pitches and stood closer. The New Zealanders specialised in swift, intensive
backing up on both sides of the man with the ball. Like the South Africans,
Adrian's men also had athleticism. The press had the final word: 'The
Harlequins slowly but surely made progress.' To those up with the pace, the
new football revolution had already begun. Those behind it were still
occupied in analysing Adrian's methods and not agreed as to their value.
What they were confusing themselves with was an inability to split the
basics from tactics, and it was tactics that won games. The selectors dawdled.

Notwithstanding the injuries just recently suffered by Adrian and John,
The Observer of 18 October 1908 hit a rusty nail firmly on the head:
'Choosing the London fifteen. Ignoring form. Methods of selection criticised.' To the disbelief of most, Ronnie would be left out of the 1908
Varsity, care of a bad game against Blackheath. Vassall was preferred instead,
the Oxford selectors deciding, like others before, that the young Poulton
was too much of an individual.

While Adrian's own playing career stalled, his foresight grew. He had to
keep moving forward. With the men he had handpicked reasonably established, in local and national thought, the second part of his grand plan
was about to take shape: Billy Williams' market garden. Following the
purchase of the ground in 1907, £1,606 9s 4d had been spent in the first
year, a further £8,000 in 1908, largely on drainage, road improvements,
entrances, mounds and terraces.

Adrian knew Billy Williams of old and had been seen in several conver-
sations with him recently. On 27 November 1908, the RFU received the
formal letter on behalf of the Harlequins about sharing the new ground at
Twickenham. A representative was scheduled to meet them at the start of
the following season. Ever canny, Billy knew that England should not share
a club ground. He was not averse, however, to the letting of his ground the

other way. Billy knew that only two games a year would not keep any new stadium in the public eye. It would need exposure and he liked what he had seen of Adrian's men. Billy had already taken one shrewd gamble on the site itself. Adrian's men were starting to produce results. The two men believed in themselves enough to gamble on each other.

Not without personal assurances, Adrian's application was accepted. In January 1909, the Harlequin committee discussed the terms of a draft agreement, especially the point regarding reservation of seats by the RFU. Adrian signed the agreement, on his club's behalf, as head lessee of the new ground, for the princely sum of £100 a season. Knowing only too well that a successful strike is best followed up by a swift second, with a foot in the door, Adrian took another bold step. He immediately sent a letter to the RFU Finance Committee asking for a further three years at the end of the first two, along with a suggestion that season tickets be divided with the club. This was tough talking, needing to be supported by action. Adrian knew both what was needed and what was possible.

The internationals kicked off in January 1909 with an English defeat to the touring Australians. With the erratic form of England, anyone was up for a cap. Edgar Mobbs, who had been fighting more than enough battles with the Union and Northern agents over amateurism, was selected along with nine others for their first internationals, with not a Harlequin in sight. Williamson, at half, who had played in the three previous internationals, had retained his place and finally looked set for the sort of lengthy run not normally associated with the position. Edgar scored his side's only try and did enough to be selected for the game the following week which, predictably, Wales won.

Two weeks later came the friendly against France. Not unexpectedly, given the Wales loss, the selectors saw a need for changes. Ronnie played for Harlequins against London Scottish knowing that he had been picked reserve for England, again behind Vassall. Vassall scratched. Ronnie's inclusion would depend on his play in the London Scottish game. No incentive was needed and after that game Adrian said to him: 'We have to congratulate you, I think.' Edward Bagnall Poulton commented:

Adrian Stoop's influence had much to do with the selection; it was a bold act to recommend, or pick a man whose physical strength had not fully matured, and who had been left out of the Inter-Varsity match shortly before. But Stoop is a remarkable judge, and an equally remarkable trainer of footballers, and Ronnie completely justified his selection.

England had gambled where Oxford dared not, and put the youngster in their side. The papers were quick to comment: '... the persistence of Adrian

Stoop won in the end… what Adrian Stoop thinks today, England think tomorrow.'

After Ronnie's debut, his mother merely said: 'he felt nervous… he got a big knock on his nose which bled.' England won, Edgar scoring again. Almost immediately, he struck up a great rapport with the younger Poulton, their shared interests of cricket, hockey and rugby standing them in good stead. The two also starred in the East Midlands victory over the touring Australians, cementing them in the national side for the immediate future. They both played in the February and March games against Ireland (a victory) and Scotland (a loss). Unfortunately for Williamson, having played himself in, with no real reason he had now played himself out. Herbert replaced him for both games, Edgar collecting a try in each.

The international promise of 1908 and 1909, scarce though it was, manifested itself chiefly in a new spirit and sense of attack. Teamwork, however, generally remained poor, particularly at half-back. Peters, Williamson, Davey, Hutchinson and even Gent and Jago of old were all clever scrum-halves, but were often wasted by being incorrectly paired. They had their strengths, which were to be found close to the scrum. With the general sluggishness of English forward play, that is where they found themselves most. Adrian's early international career had stagnated for both these reasons: lack of a decent partner, and the forwards. Birkett and Lambert had been associated with him, but it had all too frequently been a broken association. Building English back play had proved to be hard work.

Men in the Beauty of Movement

With another £20,000 expenditure in 1909, funded by the RFU, the ground at Twickenham was ready. Two single-deck stands ran the length of the two sides of the ground. Originally named 'A' and 'B', they soon became known as East and West, each with 3,000 capacity. The south terrace would hold another 7,000, with a total of 17,000 in front of the terraces and on the mound at the north end.

Everyone has their own mounds to climb. At the age of twenty-six, Picasso had matured into the greatest and most daring painter of his time. The single work that was his *Les Demoiselles D'Avignon* had changed the course of art history forever, laying as it did the foundations for a complete revolution in the world of art. In the two years since that canvas, Twickenham's foundations had been well and truly laid and rugby was about to reach a wider audience. Adrian's field was now set. At the age of twenty-six, the rest was down to him.

If the ground was ready, so too were the Harlequins. With £25 for the stock and posts, the start of the 1909/10 season saw Wandsworth Common left behind. Playing at the new ground would take money and planning. London Society referees needed to be booked, balls ordered from Grandridge & Sons, payments for the inflation thereof, quarterly rent to the RFU of £25, brushes and soaps, advertising from Williams & Walker, billposting from Hannams, gatemen, straw layers and removers to protect the ground from frost, Vaseline, stationery from W. Straker Ltd, programme boys, ladies to clean the stands after games, and shandy and lemons for refreshments. The fixture list was extended to include Cardiff and Newport at the end of the season. As a further ploy to increase the exposure of the sport and/or the ground and/or the club, each club member was allowed to introduce two ladies to the members' enclosure free of charge. Dinner dances held at the Empress ballrooms reinforced the club spirit of unity.

The first ever game at Twickenham was scheduled for 2 October 1909, between Harlequins and Richmond. All of Adrian's carefully laid preparations were in place.

The opening was kept a relatively low-key affair. No great announcements were made by the RFU. The papers merely indicated that the fixture existed and had little to say about the ground, it being something of a novelty, stuck out in the sticks. Comments that were made were relatively cheap, doubting that it could be an international success. What they hadn't considered and couldn't fail to report on were the Harlequins. Two years of relative inactivity had left Adrian tightly wound. Everything had been primed for this moment.

A big pack of forwards, for no other reason than to get the ball to the backs, and a set of backs that read, as he would have wanted: Sibree, A. Stoop, Poulton, Birkett, F. Stoop and Lambert, backed up by the ever-dependable Maxwell-Dove. The gauntlet had been thrown down for the 2,000 present to see, and the rest of England to ponder on.

Carey had the honour of taking the first kick. The Harlequins put four tries past Richmond. Twickenham's first was scored by John, a feat comparable to his father Reginald's first-ever try for England back in 1871. Tries that followed came from Danny, Adrian and Freek. The field of dreams was now complete.

Or at least it should have been.

Monday's *Times* gave up 3½ column inches to the ground and a brief report of the match itself. Alongside, the opening of the lacrosse season at Lords attracted 15 inches. Only the local papers carried any reports of weight. Among the tomes, the *Thames Valley Times* stated:

The ground and its appointments are good one must admit. The hypercritical will doubtless find some points to grumble about… one objection to the ground has been its distance from the station. One scribe said it took him twelve minutes to do the walk. All we can say is that he would stand a poor chance in the Marathon.

The *Richmond and Twickenham Times* followed suit:

Opinions as to the ground itself seem to be somewhat divided, but the general impression certainly seems to be in its favour. As to the distance from the railway station, that should mean little to Rugby enthusiasts, though it may be a little uncomfortable on wet days.

Those that commented on the match were to the point: 'Harlequins beat Richmond. Genius at half-back.' The style and panache by which the first match was won fuelled the debates. The battle was over but the war had not been won.

The result was not a freak. As the weeks rolled by, so did the victories. And not small ones at that. The Harlequins demolished every team they came up against. All of England had to sit up and take notice as they had done four years beforehand with the All Blacks and the South Africans. The only difference this time was that these were Englishmen. The Harlequins played as if each were an extension of the others, with their running lines and outrageous moves. They were almost having a laugh. And how the public warmed to it. The people came and the gate receipts soared.

By November the Harlequins were unbeaten and could not find a side to match them. On the 6th they faced Poulton's Oxford University. The resultant draw, while a small candle to the usual fireworks, served to add only one further dimension to the bag of tricks that had become the Harlequins: the reputation of Poulton, who, almost single-handedly, carried the students to be their equal.

The early prognosis on Billy William's judgement in both his project and its protectors was happily a good one. The *Morning Post* and *Sportsman* could not get their superlatives out quick enough: 'Bristol *v*. Harlequins. Londoners win a brilliant match'; 'Stoop "single handed"'; 'Poulton and A.D. Stoop in great form'; 'Harlequins *v*. Rosslyn Park: heavy scoring'. After a 27-11 thrashing of Mobbs' Northampton, the papers said of the side:

> *Wether the Saints adnt better av a shaperone,*
> *Nekst tyme tha visit Lundun,*
> *Wich was the mowst bewylderin,*
> *The Toob trayns or the Arlyquins passin.*

The *Athletic News* of 15 November 1909 narrowed the source of the inspiration down in their ode *En Passant*:

> *A 'half' should be the perfect blend*
> *Of weasel and of fox:*
> *Like a stag to dart,*
> *With a lions' heart,*
> *To face the rugged shocks*
> *Which would affright a timid youth*
> *Considering his skin:*
> *These virtues group*
> *Themselves in Stoop*
> *That agile Harlequin.*
>
> *Just see him hov'ring near the pack,*
> *And darting round the scrums*
> *Swiftly to nip*
> *With eager grip*
> *The ball when out it comes.*
> *Note, too, with what elusiveness.*
> *Away he'll gaily spin*
> *Both in and out*
> *And round about*
> *This tricky Harlequin*
>
> *He cogs not with black selfishness*
> *That most unpleasant vice*
> *But hands the sphere,*
> *With words of cheer,*
> *To someone in a thrice.*
> *'Well passed!' 'Well run!' 'Well passed again!'*
> *That wing three-quarters in:*
> *'A rattling try!'*
> *Spectators cry:*
> *Stoop-endous Harlequin.*

Next up, the press coined the phrase 'the Harlequin bubble' – getting bigger the more they played, the more they won, enveloping all with it. There was nothing slow about their progress now. They were running riot. And if the reborn Adrian was the lion of the press, then Ronnie was their darling. As if he still had any critics to impress, Ronnie now left no one in doubt, in one game doubling back yet again behind his posts at one end and delivering a try at the other. Stoop and Poulton. One name had become synonymous with the other. This was rugby: their rugby.

Come late November, as the team racked up further big victories, the preoccupation of all started to centre on the forthcoming international season in January. This season was to be special for several reasons. England's first opponents were Wales, both welcome and worthy for what would be Twickenham's first-ever international. But the internationals had another, more far-reaching significance. France had entered the English arena in 1906. The Welsh had acknowledged them in 1908 and the Irish in 1909. Having found themselves left out in the cold with only three internationals to the others four, Scotland could only follow suit, and had now arranged for their inaugural game against France. The series of games this season were the first 'Five Nations'.

Billy Williams' vision was coming to fruition. The new ground might not have had a fanfare of trumpets to herald it in, but a crescendo of noise was building. Fuelling the prophecy were the Harlequins and their spectacular rugby, delivering just as Adrian had said they would. Twickenham's inaugural international was a little over six weeks away, but somehow old Billy knew the day itself would run smoothly: for he knew Adrian had the balls – and the ball boys, and the ground staff and the programme and ticket men. If only England could find fifteen players to do the whole set-up justice.

As always the press felt they had the answer:

So far as three-quarters are concerned, indeed, there seems little room to speculate on probabilities. Birkett, Poulton and Mobbs should already be certainties, leaving only one place to fill. Whether Lambert will get it will doubtless depend on his play during the next few weeks.

A.D. Stoop is a cast-iron certainty: his play on Wednesday puts him in a class of his own. He is by himself among English halves and at the present moment he is probably the best half in all four countries. He has in fact passed from the stage of being a good player to that of being a great player.

Who to partner him? Who but Sibree. There are others possibly as good as Sibree, possibly there may be some a little better. But there is no better partner for Stoop.

Shades of Seasons Past

Three years previous, Stoop had been trumpeted as king: back then the Welsh had spoiled the coronation. Once again they stood in the way. Only this time Adrian had an army modelled in his own guise in support.

The selectors decided on a series of trials as a means by which to achieve a winning formula. Previously selection had turned on perform-ances in the one game between the North and the South. The theory this time was that by playing an England possible XV against first the North and secondly the South, they would be able to play England Probables against the Rest in final confirmation of the best XV. At least this time they would be able to assess form and adaptability over a number of games. All England expected to see the Harlequins backs heavily involved.

As a precursor to the trials, the Combined Universities (old and new) played the Army and Navy on 27 November – the first real test of the season outside of club circles. No one needed to have followed rugby that closely to know where form lay: 'The Services routed. Stoop's great game.' The match merely confirmed what everyone already knew. The Varsities, containing both Poulton and Stoop, crossed the line seven times to record a 29-0 victory. Enough had already been said, yet still they wrote:

Stoop's praises have been so loudly and so frequently sung of late that there is nothing further to add to them except to say that he played if anything better than ever, taking a prominent part in every attacking movement and gaining a try which will be long remembered by those who saw it… he picked up the ball in the thick of his opponents and looked round to pass. The Service forwards hesitated. In a moment Stoop flashed past them, swerved out and swerved in again scoring close to the posts. In his run of thirty yards, although he had to go through nearly all his opponents, he was hardly ten yards out of the straight all the way. It was brilliant…

… in Poulton, Stoop found a player well worthy of him…

… as a match it was absorbing; as a trial I do not think that the Selection Committee, who were there in force, can have learned much except that Stoop and Poulton are essential to the England side…

… it was a treat to see how these men combined; and it was both a surprise and a pleasure to realise that they were not Welshmen but Englishmen.

No doubt the reasoning to the trials was a good one, particularly as over the years the ability to pick fifteen consistently, let alone the best fifteen, had been a challenge. Adrian and Edgar both played in the first game, held on 11 December, versus the North, which 'England' won.

Ronnie took the greater exposure all in his deceptive stride. His half-day journeying encroached heavily on his studying time, so much so that a lecture he gave at Rugby School had to be changed from its original title of 'Reinforced Concrete' to 'Maps in the Making', owing to a lack of time available to carry out experiments. Partly responsible for his lack of time was his selection for the year's Varsity, correcting the oversight of the previous season. Oxford walked away with the game. The young Oxford half Gotley played a good game, but like his teammates he was completely overshadowed by one name in particular. If the name had not caused enough of a stir in the papers in the months beforehand, incredibly Ronnie Poulton scored five tries. He could do no wrong. He too should have been a cast-iron certainty to play Wales.

Injuries to key players, however, were about to hamper the trials process, Adrian and Edgar both having slight knocks to get over. Keeping an eye on the future, Adrian used his spare time beneficially and on 17 December invited the young Henry Brougham down from Wellington to see the Harlequins set-up. Nothing for the future, as far as he was concerned, was being left to chance.

Without some of its recognised players, England's second trial the next day, against the South, was a more difficult affair. Ronnie played, but with much on his mind and without either Edgar or any of his Harlequin colleagues, seemed to struggle. Two games down, and the selectors were also struggling, with no idea of the shape of their side. They approached the last of their trials with no better plans than in any season previous.

On 8 January 1910 there was less than a week until the Wales game. The English players went to their final trial at Twickenham having played their customary three games in four days over Christmas. All the selectors could do was bow to public pressure. England's 'Probables' contained John, Ronnie, Freek, Adrian and Herbert. The 'Rest', a team of hopefuls. Such was the interest, 5,000 people came to watch. Sadly, one fundamental problem was left exposed. The Harlequin backs were tried and tested – the forwards they played with in this trial were not. Behind a very poor scrum, the Harlequins struggled and their side were losing at half-time. Time for drastic measures. Herbert was replaced with Dai Gent, whose last cap had been well before Adrian's, and Freek was swapped with Bert Solomon, the big Cornishman. Chapman also came into the line, and half the pack were changed. The Probables played better in the second half, but still lost 19-9.

Adrian's only real contribution, although a fine one, had been a cross punt for Hudson to score. John did not play like the Birkett of two seasons before and his general form could hardly justify another cap.

The press headlines, '"England" defeat: surprising trial at Twickenham. Harlequins fail', did not highlight the underlying problem, that of a 'Probables' pack of inexperienced forwards who had failed to secure any ball. The selectors were as clueless as ever and had failed quite spectacularly in their stated aim. To them, the Harlequin experiment had not come off, and no one was any the wiser as to who should, or would, play against Wales. With no time to play around, the remnants of the second half 'Probables' were picked. Adrian, Ronnie and John were the residue of the bold experimentation. Into the backline to support them came Dai Gent, Solomon and Chapman.

Dai Gent at least could feel comfortable. Recalled to the fold from the wilderness of 1906, he at least this time had a partner who wanted to play outside of him and he could play for the first time in his preferred position. His partnership with Adrian however would be as much an experiment as actually playing international rugby at Twickenham.

Dai was not alone in the comfort zone. Wales had got used to a habit of winning, England of losing. As a result England sides had traditionally been selected with defence foremost – this time they had no strategy at all. Wales, if they could ever have been nervous beforehand, could on this occasion go into battle with real confidence.

At the eleventh hour, Adrian was selected as captain. From the selectors' point of view, the trust and the rugby legacy of a nation had been placed in the hands of a flawed entertainer. At least he would be the obvious scapegoat come Sunday morning. It was left to the press to have the final word: 'All depends on the forwards and the type of game they play. Wales generally find their game at once and have won many a game by the excellence of their starts.' Adrian was left to take in his newly exalted position. He lived for his Harlequins. He would die for them. Dedicated, tireless and fearless, and they the same to him. But he knew nothing of his new side and how they would respond, save for Ronnie and John.

Entering his fiftieth year, Billy Williams' hopes of a fitting celebration for his half-century were receding fast.

six

THE MATCH
1910

They that wait upon the Lord shall renew their strength. They shall mount up with wings as eagles. They shall run and not be weary. They shall walk and not faint.

(Wavell Wakefield, eulogy to Adrian Stoop)

Friday 14 January 1910, the night before the biggest game in history: a night of differing reflections and considerations.

In London, the Welsh team of legends under Billy Trew had chosen to stay at the Waldorf: Owen, Jones, Bancroft, Morgan and the rest. Considered the greatest side of the past – or indeed any – decade, they had beaten New Zealand five years before and had not lost an international since the start of 1907 – ten games in a row. For Wales, the years had indeed been golden, which meant the best of preparations now. Staying in a nice hotel, just near Drury Lane and St Martin-in-the-Fields, they could see the sights and relax – except that they were kept up late that night by the noise of all the revellers in the Strand. People had come from all over to see the big game, and they were making a capital night of it.

Adrian lay awake in bed too, thinking. Thinking of this Welsh side, one whom England had not beaten in twelve years; one containing most of the men who had humiliated his England three years before, consigning him to the international wilderness. For Adrian it had been three years to think, to plot, to scheme, to rebuild body and mind. He thought also of his England side for the next day. It was to be a side containing a backline of Dai Gent, Adrian and John, none of whom had played an international in years; three new caps in Johnston, Chapman and Solomon; and the twenty-one-year-old darling of the crowds, Ronnie. Adrian had played just half a match with Gent before, and that the losing second half of the last trial. At least he knew John and Ronnie's games inside out. Five of his pack were new caps. Of the other three, Morton and Chambers were winning only their second. Johns alone could have been considered a regular and his first cap had been in the corresponding fixture the season before. England would need a man above all men to carry the day. Adrian knew this would be his Waterloo. When he eventually got to sleep he slept well, master of his own soul, master of his own destiny.

The selectors would have been sleepless throughout. They had gambled heavily for this one. Bereft of ideas, short on positive thought, they had again taken a soft route after so many years of indecision, too many wasted talents. Their reputations were on the line. Again. At worst, a bad result could be excused on the grounds that it was an experimental side. But this was Twickenham, the former cabbage patch, the new home of English rugby. It would be the first game at the Promised Land. Defeat would fall heavy. But then Stoop was there again, being lauded to the heights once more, just like three years previous: the perfect scapegoat. There was consistency there at least.

Back at Bigside they would have been praying. The closing of an old chapter had come with the death of Brooke Senior earlier that month. But with two of their old favourites up for the game, possibly a new one about to open.

Wales' mental and physical superiority played heavily on the thoughts of everyone. It would be a long night for one and all.

The day itself saw early rain – not that that would deter the crowds thronging around Waterloo station. Extra trains took them out to the picturesque village of Twickenham. They were all in a hurry and there were ugly rushes at the small station, but no one was hurt. They were coming to see Stoop's England again. They had been before, years earlier, but had not been satiated. The old walls had come down then, but had since been carefully reconstructed. The public hoped they would stand the test once more. Every seat in the new stands had been booked weeks beforehand; every space in the village's inns was taken now. Serving wines, spirits and tea, the Railway Tavern, with its billiards tables and skittle saloon, had never had it so good. People spilled out onto the streets, soaking up this wonderful new experience.

The crowd started to fill the gleaming new ground and the tension started to build. George, the Prince of Wales, was in the royal box. Having a keen interest in rugby, he had become the patron of the RFU. This was one match he was not going to miss. The programmes on sale gave a slight hint at the haste with which the English team had been put together, their captain not even being referenced.

In the bowels of the stadium the changing rooms were claustrophobic. The muffled noise of the crowd gave but a small indication of what awaited the gladiators outside.

The band started with a German march. There was little singing until they played 'Reminiscences of Wales'. Suddenly, Welshmen resplendent in caps, waving the leek, their weapon of choice, were in full cry. This was an unnatural experience for the sleepy village. Loud Welsh hwyls started to win the battle with the band, drowning it out. First blood to the Welsh.

As kick-off time approached, matters were running far from smoothly. The crowd were still arriving. A possible excuse for them was that a general election was on, and they had been delayed by voting. Adrian was informed that the start would be delayed by fifteen minutes due to congestion outside the ground. This would stretch the nerves of his inexperienced men. Worse still, Solomon had not arrived, having been delayed on his journey up from Cornwall on the milk train in the early morning.

In the Welsh changing room, the experienced players talked of what they had to do. They had not lost in the championship for three years. Clutching his lucky shilling, Billy Trew, the Welsh captain, briefed his men: start with their usual dynamic, muscular pace, take the game to England, stifle Stoop and the brilliant Poulton, and the game would be won. In the English changing room, brave men pondered their fate.

Just in time, Solomon arrived. At last England had their fifteen men, anxious, nervous, adrenaline starting to flow. Alone with them in the confined space, eight new caps and all, the captain delivered the speech of all speeches to fire their souls. And then they were ready.

Everyman: I Will Go With Thee and Be Thy Guide

Out of the sanctuary of the changing rooms and along the narrow corridor, there were faint strains of the two-step 'Dreams of Ragtime' as the bandleader attempted to restore musical parity with the Welsh chorus. The green of the turf at the end of the tunnel grew larger, the noise louder, until it surrounded the players. The crowd, standing ten deep on the earth banks behind the goalposts, put an almost gladiatorial slant on the arena. For Adrian it was déjà vu. His last international was against Wales, three years ago to the day. Were the ghosts of seasons past coming back to haunt him? It had been a desperate result then. Five thousand and fifteen Welsh hearts and voices were ahead of him now.

Amid the confusion and lateness of start, there were no team photographs taken. The referee for the day, John Dewar Dallas, would have hoped for a match devoid of incident. Wales would have been happy to see him, Dallas having booked his place in their rugby folklore back in that infamous 1905 match with New Zealand. He called the captains over. Adrian and Trew had been through this many a time before, but this was the first time as opposing captains at national level. A healthy respect existed between the two men. Adrian won the toss and elected to defend the south end. Wales would have the honour of kicking off and charging into their opponents. As the English lined up in preparation for receiving the kick, Adrian walked slowly back through his nervous pack and staked his ground just behind them.

Ben Gronow, the Welsh kicker, walked to the halfway line. Slowly he kicked up the turf around the centre spot. Kneeling, he shaped the earth into a small mound on which to place the ball. He stood up and checked the readiness of his team. As one they bristled with anticipation, ready for the charge, ready for the off. The game that had been debated for months beforehand was ready to go. In the stands the crowd were still settling, with so much to take in: the excitement at the beginning of a big match; interest in the new ground; endeavouring to identify the unnumbered players; annoyance at the latecomers trying to push past into their places. On the pitch too, both sides were hyped up. This one would take time to settle.

Gronow stood silently over the ball on the centre spot. His kick of choice would land deep, force a return and allow the Welsh forwards to seize the day from the off. Dallas checked his watch and blew a shrill blast on his whistle. Red shirt resplendent, Gronow launched the ball into the air. Blazing red forwards followed up.

Adrian, eye on the ball, called 'Mine'. If Stoop could be unpredictable at times, the one surety for the English in the crowd, and more significantly the selectors, was the knowledge that he could kick supremely off either foot and would return the ball back with interest.

A *Times* correspondent of the day wrote:

The only new principle they [the Harlequins] *have set up is the value of unorthodoxy per se, the intrinsic worth of the unexpected move as an attacking factor, simply because it is unexpected.*

Adrian's catch, followed by a shuffle of the feet, and he was in position to hoof the ball back down the line. No one expected what happened next.

The kick never came. A quick feint, a turn of direction, and he was off, running diagonally to his left back up the field. As Welsh defenders hurried across to close him down, he picked up speed. The English cavalry followed in surprised but hot pursuit. Reaching the Welsh twenty-five yard line, Adrian put in a well-judged cross-kick that dropped behind the retreating Welshmen, just in front of their posts. First there, Gent retrieved and passed back to Adrian, still at speed, from whence it went to John, to Solomon and to Chapman for a try in the corner. Thirty seconds, no Welsh hands. Three-nil. Those that saw it were the lucky ones. Those who missed it because they were still sitting down could at least say, 'I was there'.

John Daniell's leadership lesson back in 1904 had now been put to best effect.

The first minute of Twickenham's first international was to change the course of England's rugby heritage forever. Reports vary in exact details. So stunned were twenty-nine players and 20,000 in the crowd that the future tales of those there took on legendary proportions. Who exactly passed to whom as the move progressed mattered little. What was beyond doubt was the identity of the perpetrator of the crime, the man who had robbed Wales blind when they were least expecting it. Three long years of disappointment had been erased in an instant. The fire so near to being extinguished was still burning bright. The king was back from the wilderness.

Gronow remembered long afterwards the words he used to his team as they stood under the posts and watched the conversion go over. Having to kick-off again so abruptly was such a big dent to the Welsh mental superiority as to completely nullify and reverse its direction. Wales were rocked and immediately playing off the back foot. Adrian's planning of the night before was coming to ready fruition. Part one had been executed to perfection. He had been around long enough, however, to know that one minute does not a victory make. Seventy-nine were left.

Part two. With Wales on the back foot he had to keep them there. With light drizzle and a greasy pitch, the old leather ball would become heavy and slippery as the game wore on. He had made the most of the only time that it would have been dry. What he now had to do was play his other trump card: the latent threat of the mercurial Poulton on the wing.

Organising his lines of running superbly, Adrian immediately took the game back to Wales. He did not pass for passing's sake. His primary idea was to push on. He looked to run down the yards whenever he could using his pace, his swerve and the greater respect now afforded him by Wales. He masked his game and the Welsh centres were bewildered. His quick doubles kept his opponents in the dark. And then it came: Wales in too close, the ball out to Ronnie on his wing, Ronnie's strong run, chip and chase, and England were back in the Welsh twenty-five. The yards that Ronnie made were not important in the overall context of the battle. What was important was the casual reminder that whatever Stoop could do from fly-half, Poulton could do even better from the wing. Wales' backline would spend the rest of the half unsure of their own positioning in terms of how best to defend, and so were often out of position when coming to attack.

Another swift move resulted in a line-out, and an infringement by the Welsh. Penalty to England, duly kicked by Chapman. Two scores to none in the opening quarter of the game. The home team were flying, if not on air, at least over the ever-muddying surface.

Gradually the Welsh forwards played their way back into the game, but efforts were thwarted as the ball stuck in the ground. The slow ball meant slow attacks. The pace of Pillman as the flying forward, Gent at scrum-half and Adrian at fly were able to disrupt the Welsh moves before they could start. That much could have been expected. The real revelation of the half was the dashing energy of the English forwards. Tails up from the first minute, their inexperience was trampled all over by their adrenaline. And if the ball ever looked like leaving the pack on the other side, they quickly broke up and charged on.

The half wore on. Wales managed to gain some territory and were eventually rewarded with a scrappy push-over try of their own, which went unconverted. 8-3. The next score would be vital. Knowing that he had to keep the ball alive, Adrian busied himself everywhere.

Following his standard, the English forwards rushed the ball to the Welsh twenty-five. Adrian sized up the position and immediately pushed John out further towards Ronnie, calling Solomon in close. The desperate Welsh knew there and then to expect the might of Birkett and the genius of Poulton to be set upon them once more. They had read about the Harlequins and their tricks week in week out for the entire season to date, and they prepared themselves in anticipation. The ball came to Dai Gent. At the last, knowing that Gibbs, the Welsh wing, would be tighter on Ronnie than the shirt on his back, Adrian waved Solomon around behind him. Dai passed to Adrian who sent a bullet of a pass to Solomon. Suddenly a two-on-one on the reverse side existed. A feint to Chapman on the wing and big Bert was off. The Cornishman had a clear run to the posts for England's second try.

For those that had spent too much money at the Railway Tavern, the need to spend a penny more was pressing. But the pace was breathless, and they were not going to miss this. Chapman too must have felt uncomfortable as he missed the simple conversion.

Wales responded once more from the off. Ball in hand, they were driven across the pitch. With nowhere to go they tried to double back inside, but the pass was dropped. Hopkins, the Welsh wing, was quick to show his frustration. More dropped passes, poor positioning and the tackling of the English backs, taking the lead from their rampaging forwards, kept them out. Wales were sorely rattled.

With no clear openings and the half drawing to a close, Wales attempted a drop at goal. It narrowly missed. Then came the whistle. Half-time. Respite. 11-3 to England.

The break gave the Welsh time to regroup and the crowd time to take their leaks. The one tea shop in the ground was besieged. Trew kept his men out on the pitch for their talk. His lucky shilling was suddenly feeling a little spent – an unusual position for them, but one they were capable of redressing. For England it was a different story. Adrian took them straight back to the pavilion. They had already run their legs off. It was time to find some more. Their captain would again have to rally his men to keep them going forward. They had realised their opportunities, something they had not always done in the past, but this was now dig deep time. What they had, they had forty minutes to hold. He had to inspire inexperience to greater heights. This was now about not letting one's country down, not letting one's team down, but most importantly not letting oneself down. The men would now have to respond to their own abilities rather than their captain's lead.

He Who Would Valiant Be

Second half. Having had time to take stock, Wales played with more control. Early on they scored their second try, Gibbs on the wing rounding Poulton to score, again unconverted. 11-6. Now there was little more than a converted try in it. The pressure was back on. England were up against it and every Englishman looked deep inside himself. John Birkett gave his captain everything, even the shirt off his back: stampeding around in the thick of it, his shirt was literally torn from him. With no immediate replacement he played on, torn fabric flapping in the wind. He alone knew what this game meant to Adrian, and he knew the debt he owed for the faith Adrian had shown in him five years previously. Now was the time to honour it. He tackled like a demon. When he ran with the ball he handed off as Mobbs had done so many times to him. Hard yards were good yards. He made them.

Playing almost solely in the English half, the Welsh created opportunities to win the game, but the defence was superb. A penalty kick was missed, the ball now taking on the expected leaden qualities. The Welsh crossed the line only to be called back for a forward pass. Adrian stopped a certain try when, instead of falling on the ball, he swept in front of the dribbling Welsh forwards, picked the ball up as they were about to cross, darted behind the posts and kicked back upfield. Gent hurried and harried. Time after time the English forwards assisted with relief rushes from defence.

With the game at boiling point, the Welsh attacked again. The ball came out wide to Trew. From experience he knew that cutting inside would open up the line. Off he went. A try seemed certain. The ground underneath him gave way and he and his shilling slipped to the mud – another opportunity gone.

And then finally Dallas blew for the end of the game. England had won. The players embraced, knowing they had all contributed to an epic victory. The crowd rampaged across the pitch with wild abandon, much as their darlings the Harlequins had been doing all season. Perhaps they sought the magic dust that Stoop had left all over it. Adrian left the field, carried shoulder-high by the crowd, still in his and their dreams from the night before.

Back in the changing rooms the English XV were silent. If a man hasn't given everything, he has given nothing. They had given their all.

The post-match dinner was held at Richmond, where Adrian would sit with his opposing halves, the dancing Dicks, Owen and Jones. The Welshmen could only admit that England deserved their win and that tactically they themselves had been out-thought. These older Welshmen had not lasted the course on the day. They still had the skill, but not the speed and energy. They had had their time, their great seasons, and now was not the time to be sore losers. Never had they faced so crafty and vigorous an opposition. In their own words, the English XV were one of the best sides they had played against. Billy Trew recognised the decisive factor: a grand opening plan and the personal triumph of his opposite captain, who had taken the lead and got his untried men to follow. In that ever-modest captain's own words:

At the very kick-off the Good Fairy of Twickenham asserted herself. Ben Gronow miskicked into the middle of the field, with the Welsh forwards bunched on the touchline. The immediate details are vague, but within half a minute Chapman had scored in the right corner, and I was bringing out the ball from the most depressed fifteen I had ever seen. I knew at once that we had won the match.

He graciously followed by saying that England were lucky to win. He had received a blow on the back of his neck with ten minutes to go and did not recall what had happened thereafter. It must have been some blow. In paying his tributes he had to acknowledge the game played by his forwards. History, however, belongs to the victors. For Adrian the night before had been long. This one promised to be longer.

John Birkett knew he had given of his best when his captain needed it. Dai Gent slept happy. He had finally found the perfect partner, and Adrian too had found another who wanted to play it his way. Billy Williams was happy counting the £2,000 profit on the gate money.

England's latest season had started to acclaim like no other and the papers of the next few days were unbounded in their praise: 'Wales surprised at Twickenham. A sensational start by the Saxons. First victory v. Wales for twelve years.' The public knew that Stoop was back. The selectors, however, were not yet finished. It was left to the boy wonder, Ronnie, to recount his start to 1910 thus:

I had to come back after a week [at Wengen] *to play in a trial match in London. We were badly beaten, but I succeeded in staying for the Welsh match a week later. After that they had no further use for me.*

The season had only just begun.

seven

THE SEASON
1910

They were doing very badly but they feared to be bold. They looked
askance at genius and declined to pay the price for it.
(Major Philip Trevor, referring to English rugby,
Daily Telegraph, 21 February 1910)

The press, both Welsh and English, were generous in their tributes.
The big game had had the best of everything: it had been close, with
little to choose between the sides; great drama had been conducted on
the best of sporting lines; and heroes had been found, with the two full-
backs, Bancroft of Wales and Johnson of England excelling. It had been a
great day for English rugby, but there were still three more international
games to be played that season. Was the result a one-off? For a short while
nobody cared. 'The Stoop Opening' entered legend and the waves of
euphoria surrounding the result would have lasted the season. It was left
to the public to sum up:

Letter to the *Times*, 5 February 1910

My dear Stoop,

If history should describe you as the saviour of your country, history will not lie, for
that rare flash of genius which gave England a try in the first minute of the recent
international with Wales undoubtedly turned the fortunes of the game.

'Apparently guileless yet full of guile' is how I heard a man describe you the
other day. He had just seen you put into successful operation one of those seemingly
simple ruses which are so terribly hard to frustrate.

As in racing circles the year is known by the name of the horse that wins the
Derby, so, surely, shall 1910 be hallmarked as 'Stoop's year'. I would willingly
surrender a seat in the 'Babble Shop' at Westminster to know and understand
exactly how you felt on the night that Wales was beaten.

Captain of England, and redeemer of the laurels that had been lost to her for
twelve years! That is how the future biographers of the game will describe you.
Personally I shall always think of you as the great leader of a great side, for in spite
of all the hair-splitting faultfinders can say, your men were truly great against Wales.

Sir, you are in my humble opinion a fixed star of the very first magnitude. I raise my glass to you.

Penanon.

Adrian had laid the foundations for victory in the first minute of the game, and as much as anything else it was a win for mind over body in the most physical of sports. In the cold, clear light of a new day, however, few doubted that Wales would win a rematch. With a few exceptions, considered opinion had Wales better man for man. The general surprise on the day had been the inability of the Welsh backs to get going. Wales had had no luck; Stoop had had all of it. Maybe, but he had also had a plan which had prevented the Welsh backs from settling. He had made the best of the resources he had available and crafted a result. And with backs to the wall for much of the second half, the result had come down to how much something was wanted. Adrian had wanted it. His side had come to want it. On the English side the forwards, particularly Pillman, had indeed exceeded expectation. Their footwork in the loose and work at the line-out were second to those of Wales, but their pace, stamina and strength had been just enough to carry them through. The half-backs had performed as one. Where faults could be found, and someone would go looking for them, was in the general attacking play of the residual English backs. Solomon had tended to hold onto the ball too long. Poulton, except for his one run, was out of the game on the wing and had been given the runaround by Gibbs for Wales' second try.

Despite the hair-splitting, the selectors should have had their easiest selection meeting in years. But would they accept the result as accurate in every sense, or would they consider much of the form as false? The players who had performed so admirably against Wales would, surely, be able to continue for the season, starting with the next game against Ireland. But alas, life, and indeed selectorial judgement, is often a mystery. In the end they compromised and 'evolved' the XV who beat Wales.

The selectors' first problem to address was replacing Bert Solomon. The big Cornishman had left his butcher's shop for his big day out, and how he had starred. He had returned back home immediately after the game, vowing never to play again, quitting while ahead. Not for him the long haul up – he had had his fifteen minutes of fame. Even then the solution should have been an easy one. Ronnie could drop into his normal outside centre position, moving from the wing, which he clearly did not favour. Mobbs would take over there. These two had played together in this combination for the three international games at the end of the previous season, one of which was a victory against the Irish in Dublin. The selectors got the Edgar bit right. Unfortunately they dropped Ronnie and replaced him with Hayward, the Gloucester man, for his one (and only) cap.

The selection was mystifying to say the least. Why change what you don't need to? Perhaps, as his father Edward Poulton was to say, Ronnie hadn't seen enough of the ball against Wales playing in an unaccustomed wing position. This should hardly have been of concern, because the Wales game was his fourth international on the trot. He had never let England down, and the whole of England knew what he was capable of when playing in position. Indeed, perhaps the pivotal moment of the Wales game was not the early try but the one inspired move Ronnie had been able to make. The value of that move in keeping the Wales backs stretched and out of line should not have been underestimated. Perhaps the selectors were aiming to nullify the Irish strengths. Theirs would be an aggressive, forward-dominated approach to the game, and England would need a strong defence, allegedly not one of Poulton's better qualities. Gibbs had passed him easily for the second try. In fact his defending was as good as anyone's, it just so happened his attacking was better than everyone's. Perhaps there was a political element to the team selection. With Solomon, a Cornishman, having departed, was there a conscious effort to cap people from various places around the country to spread the message that international rugby was a game for all of England? And perhaps also Adrian had taken one too many plaudits for the current state of national euphoria. Had not the selectors chosen the team? Adrian's standing had never been higher in the eyes of the public and his Harlequins were sweeping all before them. But his dogmatic refusal to play the game the old-fashioned way had upset a few people in upper quarters, and the non-selection of Poulton would temper the spirit.

Whatever the reason was, and there may have been some truth in all of these, Adrian was angered and spoke his mind where he felt it appropriate. Poulton was the player people came to see. More importantly, he could play Adrian's game and the two thought alike. Against Wales he had had a foil in Poulton to back up his own carefully laid plans, enabling him to carry them through with conviction.

Adrian's backline for the forthcoming Ireland game would now consist of a West Country man, a northerner, a midlander and a metropolitan. At least the counties would have been pleased at the division of labour. Adrian was not. This was the first time he had faced Ireland, and he had no plan.

Déjà Vu

It was 12 February, Twickenham, one month later, and the day of the Ireland game. Much had been said of the congestion at the start of the previous game and the muddy state of the approaches and paths. The old school of supporters had found it difficult to go to pastures new. They were more comfortable with the grounds at Blackheath and Richmond, where the railway station was at their gates. Having been at the game, however, the paying public had soon realised that the best way to enjoy the experience was not to rush down and be first away, but to savour the day, the atmosphere, the bonhomie. And, if it turned out like the Welsh game, the result.

As it turned out, there was little difference from the momentous game of four weeks previously. The start was again held up for fifteen minutes, this time due to the Irish charter bus breaking down on route, and once more the Prince of Wales was in the royal box to see the game. He had come again to see the new 'king'. Little did he know his own destiny over the months to come when, on the death of Edward VII, he too would be crowned.

Kings aside, the real difference between the two games was that here the English forwards were just awful. The Irish pack rushed everywhere, ruling the game. As against Wales, the English line-out was poor, but this time they were beaten about the park as well. For them it was still a learning process and they needed time to work themselves into the game: time they were not allowed. Gent and Adrian were always playing off the back foot as their Welsh counterparts had done. Although John was playing, the ability to turn such defence into attack was minimal. Hayward, winning his first cap, was lost in the awe of it all. Any cohesiveness as a back unit was lost, as was any confidence in each other. The Irish could sense this, and the selectors had abetted them. If the Irish had no game plan beforehand, they had one now: tackle the life out of the only possible source of English invention – Adrian suddenly found two, sometimes three, men on him at every turn. With nowhere to go, and with England's dearth of attacking options elsewhere, their ability to counter was limited. What little they did create came from any yard of space Adrian could conjure up for himself. And when he did manage to break away, he had no support and the move would break down as he was forced to kick to touch. Edgar's only fault as a winger was his tendency to drift away from the wing to be closer to the heart of the action. The few times the ball came over, he was not there.

Half-time: 0-0. Ireland had been on equal terms and would come out upping the pace still further.

Much of the second half was played without Edgar. Following a tackle after twelve minutes he was concussed and was led from the pitch by

Adrian. Edgar had always had a tendency to stay in the thick of it, so injuries to him were not uncommon. With no substitutes in those days, Edgar would never let the boys down. For Mobbs a match was never over until the final whistle blew. He recovered enough to come back on after receiving treatment. A short while later he went down again. At Adrian's insistence he stayed off for the remainder of the game. With fourteen men, the captain's strategy was now only concerned with organising his defence, something not readily attributed to his game.

The 0–0 final score did little for either side, except to partially dampen the fires that had burnt so bright after the Welsh game. This time the varied press were less generous in their reviews: 'A great game drawn. Stoop robbed of his game'; 'A great reputation undone'; 'Shackled by men who knew how to tackle'; 'The Harlequin bubble has been pricked today'. This last was slightly unbelievable given that there were only two Harlequins on the field, but England's fortunes were seen as wholly concomitant with Adrian's. With a castle in place, any slight cracks are all too easily blamed on the builder.

The critics were suddenly divided on Stoop. Great behind a pack of winning forwards, but with no taste for defence. This was an interesting viewpoint given that England had organised themselves sufficiently well to at least keep the Irish out. The public debates raged, opinions divided between two schools of thought: attack and defence. The relative merits of the players that had been on display were, however, not at the heart of the debate. What were fundamental to the issue were the developments that had taken place in the game of rugby itself. In the one corner, old-fashioned rugby conservatism, when rugby was soccer and games (not least England's) were poor: '… daring forward play is every bit as good as the handball that some deem rugger… the fallacy of handball has been exposed.' In the other corner, the revolutionary pioneers of new rugby, Adrian and his merry men – ball in hand, tactical manoeuvres, flowing play. They played a game that was not a replica, not a copy of what the traditionalists held dear, but a game that was fundamentally different in both its art and construct. It provided value for money as a spectator sport. And the point missed by most was that their counter-attacks were in their own right a form of defence. Wales had been beaten by Stoop's ability to keep them guessing. Ireland could have been beaten if the tools had been there.

To add insult to injury, the Harlequins lost their first game of the season a week later, on 19 February, after seventeen matches unbeaten. Ironically, this 12–5 reverse was to a Poulton-inspired Oxford University. There were those who almost seemed to welcome the end of their sequence of victories, suggesting that their spectacular tactics could only be employed against sides that could not offer them anything like sturdy opposition.

Their chariot had seemingly run out of steam. Also, Adrian's young protégé, the forgotten man in the selectors' eyes, had made his point.

With the next game against France looming large, anything the selectors did following the Irish game would be problematical. On the back foot, and true to form, they loused up again. The suggestion that a great reputation in that of Stoop had been undone by the Irish forwards, while unfounded, loomed large in their minds.

And so they dithered. How to use the last two games of the season to ensure the season as a whole would be a success, yet not lose the confidence of the public by dropping their man? The next game would be against France and on paper should have been an easy one. The relative strengths and merits of every potential player were called into question (again): Poulton, awesome in attack, shown up by Wales in defence; Mobbs, producing all his old excellences and all his old faults – a daredevil going for the line, but lacking the subtlety of others; Adrian, brilliant behind a winning pack, less so behind a poor one; Coverdale, described as 'safe', bested Adrian in the trials. The papers expressed the thoughts of a nation when the initial team was announced: 'The exclusion of Adrian Stoop. Rugby Union Committee's Strange Act. Is it a joke?' The great promise and momentum that Adrian and his Harlequins had built up had been once more disregarded. Ronnie had been dropped after the first game. Now 'rested', Adrian was not in the side either. Neither, initially, was Edgar. The team consisted of trialists and cast-offs. It was a poor attempt to find the right balance in the scrum between shovers and chasers. It was also a poor attempt to find some fluency in the backs. Injuries, apathy and a Thursday afternoon kick-off subsequently forced a change of direction. Eight of the original selection became unavailable. With an about-face of monumental proportion, the selectors turned to Ronnie among others. No typed-up formal selection letter. Instead a handwritten personal note from Charles Marriott, dated 24 February, received less than a week before the game: 'Dear Poulton, We want you to play v France. I enclose itinerary. Wire me if you are <u>unable</u> to go. You can return Thursday night if necessary.' Given his treatment after the Wales game, Ronnie declined.

The public also read through the selectorial intent. With a win and a draw under the English belt, there was no need to strengthen the side to play a developing French team. Any changes to personnel could only really be experimentation for the final game of the season against Scotland. Amid intense criticism, Edgar was called back, with the promise of captaincy. He had demonstrated the right spirit against Ireland – knock him down, and he just got up again and kept on going.

And so it came to be that England went to France with eight further new caps. They won 11-3, but a good display by France could not disguise a poor English one and the public were not impressed. Unfortunately for Edgar, making him captain for the day was probably also the selectors' way of 'honouring' him, for all his good service. Like Adrian, he had ruffled more than a few feathers with his justifiable, but outspoken, manner. It was to be Edgar's last international. Like so many others, he would represent his country again in the future, but on an altogether different field.

The public shouted loud. The press had a field day. The slightest whiff of controversy makes for good reading, so the critics kept on writing. It was left to the *Daily Telegraph* to sum up the mood:

We have been waiting in the wilderness for years and Stoop showed us the way to get out of it. He was the author of a definite plan and he trained a special body of men to assist him to carry it out. We began that hopeful march with Stoop and his pioneers in front – that is to say behind. We made splendid progress at first. Then we came to a check and we wavered in our faith. We had an artificer in chief of our own deliberate appointment and then we began to meddle with his special tool basket.

What next? The international problem was getting worse instead of better with every game, but as it did so the interest naturally became more absorbing. There seemed to be no alternatives and no plans. The old selection methods, with caps being awarded on individual merit, regardless of better combinations, were creeping back. With the early demise of Wales, Scotland were the team to beat that season. They had held the Calcutta Cup for three years and were building up a good array of performances against England. With Edgar having been 'retired' by the selectors, yet another captain was required. The logical choice would have been Adrian, the call to include him again proving too loud to avoid. But people still carried their wounds, and the only acceptable compromise seemed to be to have John instead.

A Light Shines

Adrian was reinstated at fly half. The Scotland game was to be played at Inverleith on 19 March 1910, five years to the day since Adrian had entered the international arena. The opponents were the same, although Pat Munro had gone. Bert Solomon was again asked to play at centre, but stood his Cornish ground and reiterated that enough was enough. Then finally some sense: if one and one lesson only had been learned during the season, it was the need for a playmaking centre to support the guile of Adrian and the force of John. With Ronnie out of favour, Freek was duly selected at the eleventh hour for his first international. Brothers in arms for the first time. The season that had started out so brightly, but which had descended into selectorial farce, had suddenly come full circle, with three Harlequins forming the nucleus of the backs.

Sensing a Scottish championship victory, 30,000 people, the largest for a match in Scotland, came to watch. It was a grey and typical day until just before the game, when the sun came out to play on the squad of aged and youthful pipers. Scotsmen bristled with patriotism while there was a nervous feeling of uncertainty among the few Englishmen present.

The game started apace. Scotland pressed early, their pack disrupting England's at every opportunity. Once the English forwards started to come together as something close to a unit, they started to gain parity in the set pieces. Adrian, this time served well by Gotley, unnerved the Scots by being – predictable. Every time he received the ball he passed it on: nothing funny, no tricks, definitely not what they were expecting from Adrian.

Strong tackling, bringing John down as he tried to power through, spoilt the few chances England had. Freek dropped the ball once and the English supporters became increasingly pessimistic, not least when Macpherson collected the ball out wide and wriggled through several tackles to open the scoring for Scotland with a try that was subsequently converted. How the crowd roared. England were behind for the first time this championship. Minutes later, Macpherson nearly repeated the feat, somehow ending in touch when the line seemed easier.

Minutes before half-time the English forwards heeled quickly. Gotley passed to Adrian who, sensing the moment, passed on to Freek. Freek's pace took him yards on before he fed John, who swept over the line to score. This too was converted.

Half-time, scores even. The wind in the first half had been against Scotland, and they had still had marginally the better of play. Even so, it seemed evident to all that, despite having had most of the possession, the Scottish backs lacked any genius to carry through. There was a gradual realisation that England had a chance. Freek, however, had taken some big tackles, as had John, who nursed a gashed cheek. Would they last the game?

The second half started like the first, fast and open. The early skirmishes went in Scotland's favour as they sought to regain the initiative, but the ground, the conditions and the streaming sun remained ideal for open running rugby of the Stoop kind. And with three Harlequins playing together the questions that had been posed of them as a unit were about to be defiantly answered. Adrian started to make openings for his backs with quick passing. Seeing the standard raised once more, the English forwards remembered the Welsh game.

Clockwise from top left:

1 Frederick Cornelius Stoop.

2 Agnes MacFarlane Stoop (née Clark).

3 Cornelius Francis Stoop.

4 West Hall, view from the river moorings.

5 West Hall, dining room.

6 West Hall, tennis lawns.

7 West Hall, Dutch gardens.

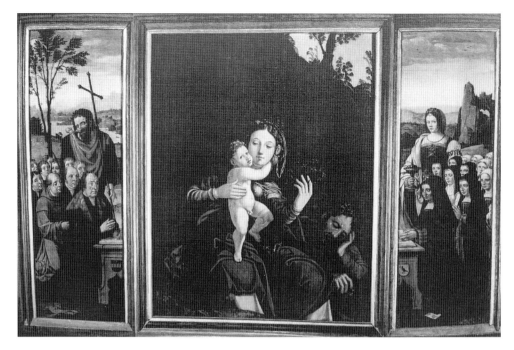

8 The Stoop Triptych.

9 Frederick's children, 1894: Nelly, Freek, Cora, Adrian, Nesta, Janey (Khe was not born until 1898).

10 Lockers Park School cricket team. Freek is third from left, middle row, Adrian is third from right, middle row.

11 Harlequins, 1902. Adrian is centre, front row, Cartwright is second from left, middle row, Curly Hammond is centre, middle row.

12 The Stoop family.

13 (above) Oxford Varsity team, 1904. Pat Munro is third from left, middle row, Adrian is centre, middle row, Harry Cartwright is third from right, middle row, John Raphael is second from right, middle row.

14 (below left) Varsity programme of Adrian's captaincy.

15 (below right) Letter from the RFU notifying Adrian of his first international.

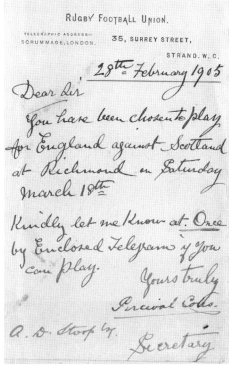

16 Twickenham, mid-1900s.

17 England v. Scotland 1905, Adrian is second from right, on the ground.

18 England trials, late 1905. Adrian, against all instincts, falls at a forward's feet.

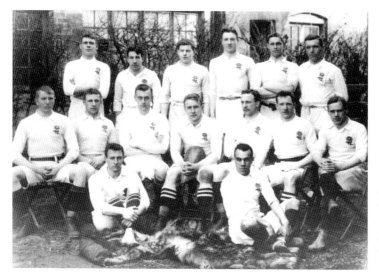

19 England *v.* Scotland 1906. Adrian is front left, James Peters is front right, John Birkett is third from right, back row. Hammond, Raphael and Cartwright are second, third and fourth from left, middle row.

20 Harlequins, 1907. From left to right, middle row: Sibree, Lambert, Adrian, W.A. Smith (president), Birkett. Roc Ward is in the back row, behind Smith.

21 The camera captures an informal moment at Twickenham's first game, Harlequins *v.* Richmond 1909. Freek sits in front of Adrian. Ronald Poulton is far right, middle row.

22 (above left) *The Bystander*, selecting the team against South Africa 1906.

23 (above right) The Harlequins: peerless.

24 (below) Harlequins *v.* Northampton 1909, a one-horse race.

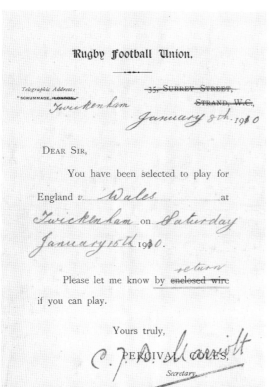

25 (left) Ronald Poulton's ticket to the big game, Twickenham's first-ever international.

26 (below) The Prince of Wales, soon to be George V, seated right, checks the form.

England + Wales.   January 1910.

27 A line drawing of England v. Wales 1910.

28 Adrian as captain for England v. Ireland, 1910. Alongside him to the right are two other England captains for that season, John Birkett and Edgar Mobbs.

Opposite page, clockwise from top:

29 England *v.* France 1911. Adrian is third from left, middle row, between Danny Lambert and John Birkett (with ball).

30 One of Adrian's prized mementos from England *v.* Scotland, 1911.

31 Freek to Adrian against France, 1911, which Adrian considered 'the greatest game I ever played in'.

32 Adrian's try against France, 1911.

This page, from left to right:

33 (above left) Dispensing advice to the English team, 1911.

34 (above centre) Dancing on air.

35 (above right) Dispensing advice to the referee, 1911.

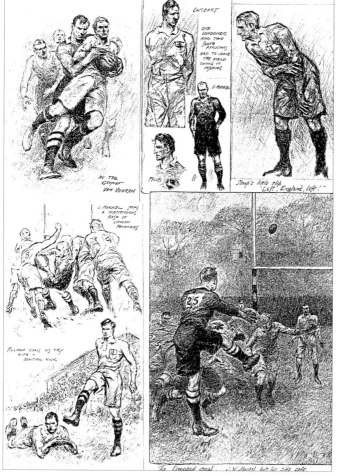

36 (above) England *v.* Scotland 1912. John Birkett and Adrian either side of captain Dibble. Ronald Poulton, back in English colours, is far right, middle row.

37 (left) A line drawing of London *v.* South Africa, 1912.

Opposite page, clockwise from top left:

38 A final dash for the line, Scottish defenders being left all ends up.

39 A Dutch affair, Adrian and sisters, 1913.

40 Central District representation at the RFU, Adrian standing fifth from right.

41 A new England *v.* South Africa, 1913.

42 Harlequins in the mist, 1913. From left to right (players): John Birkett, Herbert Sibree, Roc Ward, Adrian and G. Elmslie.

43 Immortal Harlequins, 1913. From left to right, middle row: Lambert, Poulton, Birkett, Adrian, Roc Ward, Sibree. Wakelam is left front.

44 The Poulton swerve, leaving Irish defenders all ends up, 1914.

Seven minutes after the break, England found themselves in their own half, winning the ball at a scrum. Again it came out to Adrian who shaped to pass once more, as he had done all game.

Except for the first time he didn't.

A glorious feint and he was off. With one of his pulsating runs he raced over the halfway line leaving a panicked opposition far behind him. The English in the crowd rose as one. They had paid good money, but would have paid ten times more for a glimpse of Adrian Dura Stoop in full flow. As time momentarily stood still, Adrian ascended to some altogether higher, more ethereal plain.

Having read his mind, Freek and John were not far behind. Both knew that anyone could score a try if they backed up and backed up close enough. At the right time, Adrian drew the remaining cover and fed his brother, who then unleashed the unstoppable John for his second try.

The pivotal moment had come a little later than against Wales, but at the critical point the game was once again all but over. Hope, confidence and good ball play immediately deserted the Scots. Time and again the Scottish forwards lost the ball, and on the occasions when they won it, it was painfully slow. English forward dominance ruled and as the game went on they secured two further tries.

The Scots despairingly tried to claw back England's lead towards the end of the game. Johnston, the English full-back was led off the field in the last few minutes. Shades of Ireland? Not this time. England continued to attack with a confidence born of success, going on to win 14-5, four tries to one.

The papers had their headlines once more: 'Great English victory: Scotland outplayed. The Stoops' success.' If Adrian was Man of the Match, his brother was not far behind.

England had won the Calcutta Cup for the first time in four seasons, but more significantly the championship for the first time in eighteen years. Adrian Stoop, with a little help from his friends, had at last delivered it and the pains of the great split with rugby league had been put to rest. Vindication for England, vindication for Adrian, and vindication for the Harlequins who had run the show in the last game. Harlequinism had been the chief factor in achieving what no one else had been able to achieve in the best part of two decades. While some of the selections during the season might have been considered unsatisfactory, the three great friends, Adrian, John and Edgar had all captained the side. Ronnie had been sacrificed, but he was young and his time would come, magnificently, again.

Adrian had started the season in spectacular fashion, and finished it imperiously. Again the press responded in kind, with appreciations of Adrian many. 'The Season' was recounted thus:

Ye Rugger stalwarts, hail! Hooray!
Hail, champions of the ball!
The croaking critics of your play
Are feeling, so I'm told today
Considerably small.

To you the Leek concedes renown,
And halves the Shamrock goes
And now, your energies to crown,
The Scottish thistle topples down
Before the English Rose.

It may have taken him five years from his first cap, but the building he had started then was now mostly complete.

The Harlequins too finished their season equally imperiously, losing only by a try to the great Newport, reckoned by most adjudicators to be well after time. The defeat stemmed from what Adrian considered his worst decision ever as captain, sacrificing a forward to the backs to allow his team to sit back and defend their twelve-point half-time lead. Even the great were fallible at times. The Harlequins record for the season in their 23 games read won 18, lost 4, drawn 1. They had crossed the line 132 times against 38, registering 541 points for to 147 against. Only Gallaher's men of five years previous could come close in terms of one-sided attacking brilliance. Hamish Stuart of the press corps wrote:

The Harlequin bubble, which was supposed to have been pricked once and for all in the final trial of 8 January, (though unlike most bubbles it received a second probing on February 12) has shown a Phoenix-like facility of recovery and growth… In two successive Saturdays the alleged bubble has, so to speak, become a strong-sided balloon capable of long and sustained flight.

It had taken five years since the early promise of 1905 to change the course of English rugby and its history once and for all. Sports lovers puffed out their chests again.

And so, 1910 proved to be a coming together of collective glories. English rugby was to the fore once more. The Harlequins had finally found their home. Rugby School basked in the glory of some of its favoured sons. The Stoops' celebrated in style at West Hall. The pains of the past now exorcised, life for Adrian was indeed full of roses.

THE CABBAGE PATCH
1911-1914

*Those were enchanted days, when you saw London, Lords and Marie
Lloyd, all for the first time; days when you might be excusably senti-
mental, especially about your first glimpse of the immortal Harlequins.*

(A. A. Thomson, *Rugger My Pleasure*)

In 1910 the selectors had made a lucky dip into their country's future
and everything about England had changed, as if by magic. Success
breeds success, but it was early days for new England. While the eyes of the
rugby world were on Adrian, he knew no one man could have carried out
so dramatic a change. He had needed, and had found, fourteen others to
do it with him. The opening of Twickenham no doubt acted as an inspiration, but the new spirit of attack was built on Corinthian foundations.
More specifically, improved handling, combination and tactics that set out
to seize the initiative had been at the root of what England had achieved.
The press likened the dramatic change in English fortunes to 'the touch of
a physician'. They also knew a standard had been set.

Two key points needed to be addressed going into the new season: it was
vital to maintain the momentum and to ensure consistency of selection. In
the past, selection methods had meant that the men playing for England
were by no means representative of the best talent in the country. At last
brilliance was being allowed to shine through. The trials might have been
a reasonable idea, but what was almost as important, if not more so, was to
allow the players some opportunity to play together, to train beforehand.
For the internationals of early 1909, thirty-three players had been selected,
of whom only five had been reselected for the games just gone. Of those,
only two had played more than one game, with both Poulton and Mobbs
playing just once. Only four players had played in all four games of this
season's championship.

Notwithstanding statistics, if there had been an individual success of the
season it was Adrian, the guiding spirit of both the Harlequins and, gloriously once again, England. The try he had conjured up against Wales had
sparked a revolution, inspiring the players and giving them the confidence
they lacked. *The Admirable* cut to the chase:

Will Shakespeare wrote some plays which meet
With pretty general praise.
Few authors, critics say, can write
So neatly nowadays.
But if the Muse he chose to woo,
Stoop could write 'Lear' and 'Hamlet' too,
(Such is his universal skill).
Better by far than poor old Bill.

Napoleon, when he went to war,
Was always on the spot.
His tactics on the battlefield
Were noticeably hot.
He gave his adversaries fits
In Egypt and at Austerlitz.
If Stoop had had his job to do
The French had won at Waterloo.

Lloyd George has an ingenious mind.
As puzzle editor
On 'Snick-Snacks' he'd be just the man.
('Twas he who wrote Form Four)
But yet he'll often spin and reel
When he steps in banana peel –
But Stoop – mark this with care my friend –
He conquers but he does not bend.

Adrian was clearly enjoying his rugby again. Everyone wanted him. As chairman of the Aldenham Institute Rugby Football Club he showed how important his early school memories were to him. The sportsmen of Aldenham, near Hemel Hempstead, were not alone in benefitting from the best. He was on the committee with the Barbarians and back on his beloved tours with them, this time as captain. With him for Easter 1910 were John, Freek and Danny. The Barbarians had always seen the games in Wales as an opportunity to duel with the best. In Wales, however, the tourists had often been spoken of in less than praiseworthy terms, having traditionally failed to do their abilities justice. They had suffered some heavy losses in previous seasons, one recently by ten tries to nil. This made for good public entertainment, but while the Barbarians contained self-sufficient individuals, there was some regret amongst the top Welsh sides that they did not provide stronger opposition. That line of thought was abruptly brought to a halt.

In one of the finest games seen in Cardiff, the Barbarians won 16-5, the outstanding feature of the game being the running and pace of the Harlequin backs. Cardiff were completely outplayed in what was described as 'a day out for Adrian Stoop'. He was at his happiest, with his friends, in his element. And the public could not get enough of him.

On the domestic front the Harlequins had been peerless. The new players coming into the club were much as the old. Henry Brougham, a footballer at heart, was recruited by Adrian after another visit to Wellington School. Adrian saw in him the same qualities that he saw in his earlier recruits: adaptability, a desire to learn and a desire to mix in. Besides, Henry's eyebrows sloped one way and Danny Lambert's the other, so at least the wings would be perfectly balanced. Henry Blythe Thornhill (Teddy) Wakelam joined from Marlborough, and by his own accounts he certainly brought a great deal to the social side of the club.

The Harlequins', and England's, successes were about to have a major impact on the direction of the game in England. Sibree, A. Stoop, Birkett, Poulton, F. Stoop, Lambert – these were all brilliant individuals, but collectively they were even better, combining as if one. A.A. Thompson suggests his ideal player to have been 'the legs of Poulton, the body and arms of Birkett, and the head and brains of Stoop'. The lessons that rugby learned were best summed up by a *Times* critic of the day:

To consider what the Harlequins have done. At first glance, one is inclined to think that they have invented a whole new set of principles of the Rugby game, and developed therefrom an entirely novel system of play. But if we look into the matter carefully, we see that this is not by any means the case… In all other directions they have but made new applications of old principles – people talk scornfully of 'handball' winning at what should be 'football' until one wonders if passing is a patented invention by Mr Adrian Stoop.

Much of the play of the Harlequins backs is merely the result of an extension of the relatively old principle of passing, an extension which finds its expression in the reverse pass, the pass which misses out the man, and the cross kick, which after all is really a form of the pass.

In the individual – Stoop has actually returned to a forgotten principle, at the correct application of which, never previously perceived, he has arrived by the use of his wonderful genius for the game. Other 'novelties' are based on no more recent and original principles than such 'dicta' as 'take the ball in your stride', 'run straight', 'make an opening if possible before passing'. It is by concentration on these last-mentioned points that other clubs have achieved their immediate improvement, which is such a remarkable feature of the present season.

They could not hope, and they wisely did not attempt, to reproduce in a moment the more subtle and intimate of Harlequin methods; they did not have a

*Stoop to instruct them, nor in most cases the equals in ability of Stoop's colleagues
to carry out his plans.*

*But they could, and they did, quickly learn to improve their own natural game
at the many points where improvement was the inevitable outcome of Stoop's
teaching. Such is the real explanation of the levelling-up process which has taken
place, and is still going on – the finest thing that could possibly have happened to
Rugby football.*

The cross kick was owed to Mobbs; the series of codes that heralded
many of the mesmeric passing moves was pure Adrian. The 'Stoop
System', as it had become known, was much copied, never equalled. By
raising the bar, by increasing the qualifying standard, Adrian was asking
questions of all others. They too would have to jump higher and run
faster just to maintain parity. The significance to the standard of English
rugby in all classes was immense.

The champagne rugby flowed. And the champagne flowed at the
parties Frederick and Agnes continued to throw at West Hall. Ever the
generous hosts, Frederick was happy that his sons were continuing the
Stoop legacy, albeit in an altogether different field. And how they entertained. Adrian was the master of the singing, *The One Fish Ball* being his
signature:

> *A man was walking up and down,*
> *To find a place where he could dine in town;*
>
> *He found himself a fancy place,*
> *And entered in with fancy grace…*

After the celebrations it was back to normality of sorts for the architects
of Twickenham's most famous victories. Freek went back to Imber
Cottage, close to West Hall, and the daily grind of stockbroking at Stoop
& Co., John went to his land agency and Ronnie, still up at Oxford, to
complete his studies.

The new season was a hangover for everyone.

24 September 1910, and it was the first game for the Harlequins, against
Old Merchant Taylor's. The bikes, the motors, the bath chairs and 1,500
people came. Freek broke down early on and the Harlequins were headed
for the morning-after feeling until Adrian stepped in. A punt over the top,
a chase and try reversed the deficit and the fourteen-man Harlequins went
on to win 11-5. Normal service had been resumed.

In October the *Pall Mall Gazette* intimated that the general standard of
play in the country had been limited 'except for a few brilliant excep-

tions' who 'were not afraid of the ball in possession' and 'were almost as likely to score from their own line'. Notable in their efforts were a higher order of heeling and passing and 'a diminution in the number of breathers being taken'.

A month later, 6,500 came to see the Harlequins play Poulton's Oxford. The crowd knew a pleaser and came again in their hordes to see their young hero in December's Varsity. As a casual reminder to the selectors, Ronnie provided the difference once more, scoring two of his team's five tries.

Despite all the adulation coming the way of his protégés, Adrian knew the progress had only just started. In December, he discussed the terms of a new lease with the RFU. By January 1911 they had all but reached agreement on another three years, the only sticking point being restrictions on the number of matches to be played on the ground.

Before the ink had dried, the rugby world was turned upside down again with the French beating the Scots at the turn of the year. The French had unlocked from their armoury two very fast wing forwards, who successfully bottled up the Scottish three-quarters, and then matched this with a solid defence. The French press went wild with excitement, devoting a leading article to the result. The next game for the French would be the English at Twickenham. Fresh in their triumph, and after the close-run game of the previous season, the French fancied their chances.

First, England had to meet Wales. The English side in the trials for the season had featured various combinations of Adrian, Ronnie, John and Freek. The team initially selected for 21 January 1911 was an absolute first, containing as it did Adrian, John, Freek, Danny and Ronnie. In the end injuries prevented Freek and Ronnie from playing and Wales gained their revenge in a classic, crossing the line four times to England's three. Despite the English backs being altogether faster and technically superior to their Welsh counterparts, the decisive score came when an adventurous break by Adrian from the twenty-five resulted in John dropping the ball, and Wales profited.

On the back of this defeat in the first game, the French match suddenly took on a different dimension. The game itself saw a backline of John, Danny and both Stoops back to terrorise France as it had done in England's inaugural game against them in 1906. With John as captain, England entered the game with but a single tactic. Pass the ball, without any attempt at making an opening, to the wings, then kick back to centre or further on being confronted by either wing forward, forcing him to turn and chase back. And that was all they did. Heel, pass, kick. Heel, pass, kick. After twenty minutes the French were effectively reduced to thirteen men, such had been the chasing efforts of their hapless wing forwards. The half-time score read just 8-0, but by the close of play it was

37-0. Danny Lambert had notched up twenty-two points from two tries, five conversions and two penalties, an English points-scoring record.

Neither the papers nor the crowd knew what to make of the first half, accusing the English of not taking the game seriously. Little were they aware of the master plan, or that all but the English wings had suffered sprained wrists from all the passing.

Puzzlement and questioning apart, the success of the game and the functioning of the Harlequins as an international unit had several by-products. Adrian forever considered this game to be the most brilliant display of football by an English team in his experience. It was not surprising that six of the English side had been or were to be English captains. The experience of such a game and its preparations would serve them well.

The next game, against Ireland, saw Adrian, Freek, John and Danny again in the side. As in the previous year, the game was dominated by the forwards. The little the backs saw of the ball came from chasing the relieving kicks to touch. This time the game was won late on when a poor kick to touch from Freek resulted in a try for Ireland and the only points of the game.

Despite the narrow losses to Wales and Ireland, for once the selectors kept a degree of faith in their directional consistency, and the public's appetite. For the Scotland game, Adrian and John kept their places while Freek lost out to Ronnie. Bizarrely after his French exploits, Danny was also replaced. This would be difficult for Adrian: Ronnie was in for Freek, and the captaincy would pass from John to Gotley.

As it was, 18 March saw rain and a greasy ball. Scotland scored first, but almost immediately Adrian and John conjured up a try for Wodehouse. Continuing, they then set up Ronnie to let in Lawrie just before half-time. The start of the second half saw one of the great tries, a flowing move involving most of the English side and resulting in John going in under the posts. In keeping with the spirit of the game, Scotland responded with a try of their own. With barely a score in it the scene was set for a grand-stand finish. Those that had witnessed the shirt being ripped from John's back barely a year before could not believe what happened next. In to the final minutes of the game, Cunningham, the Scottish centre, went through with only the English full-back to beat. He only partially succeeded, his shorts – and modesty – all but being ripped from him. With but ten yards to go to the line he decided discretion to be the better part of valour and decided to sit down to cover the embarrassment. Scotland's last chance of drawing the game gone, England came away victorious and with two wins out of four matches for the season.

While the international season had resulted in something of an anti-climax for England, Wales and Ireland both gaining revenge by the odd try, the last by-product of the season's games was to be of far greater significance. That last international had come with the news all rugby fans had awaited: Poulton's name back on England's team sheet. Surrounding him were Adrian and his fellow Harlequins, who had once again dominated the domestic season. Their committee then, and for the next few seasons, contained Adrian, Ronnie, Herbert, Holly, Roc and Danny, as treasurer (replaced in 1912 by Holly when it became apparent finances were not Danny's strong point). The Harlequins' profit at the end of 1910/11 was £423, reflecting the ever-growing interest the public had in seeing them.

In May 1911 Adrian picked up the first of his administrative roles within the RFU, becoming a Central District selector. The name Stoop had become synonymous with all that was good about English rugby. Now he had his first exposure to the science of selection that he had done so much to challenge. His was now the reputation that all looked up to. After the Surrey v. Kent game that year, the novice young Kent standoff W.J.A. 'Dave' Davies said:

I was offered a shilling for every time I tackled Stoop. No money passed. Whether due to his illusiveness, my reluctance to tackle, or my friend's financial instability, I do not remember.

Fredrick Stoop did see money change hands. Being engaged in heavy competition with Royal Dutch was one thing, taking on the now-merged Royal Dutch/Shell Group, was another, even with Samuel's goodwill. His Dordtsche merged into the larger company during the course of the year.

When Evening Comes

As he reached his thirties, Adrian's marble mine and the backing of his father allowed sport in all quarters to consume his time. He joined the Corinthians, as a member of their board, to promote relations with them and to further sport in general. 'The Outcasts', a social side formed predominantly from the more recognised sporting stars of the day, took on Westminster School at football. Playing as a forward alongside Danny, Freek and Teddy Wakelam, Adrian played his part in the ten goals they scored. The Harlequins then took on the Corinthians in an unheralded display of cross-code sport. The Corinthians won the rugby, the Harlequins the football 5-4.

The internationals of early 1912 saw the balance of power return, England sharing the championship after winning three out of four games. England had at last established a brand of rugby to which it was best suited, utilising the best of the talents it had at its disposal. The heralding in of a new order, however, inevitably meant the passing of the old.

The prelude was again the Varsity. Having scored five tries two years beforehand, and having created or scored all five the previous season, this year Ronnie excelled even himself, scoring before Cambridge had drawn breath. He had a hand in the next two before having to leave the field through injury in the first half. He returned in the second, although clearly in pain. The five times Oxford crossed the line in total would have been significantly more had he played to his fullest. A *Times* correspondent could only liken him to a hypnotist: 'swinging the ball from side to side as if he was rhapsodising on a concertina, compelling the defence to follow him spellbound.' Ronald Poulton was now the first name on the English team sheet. In the scrap for the other places the England trialists against the South contained Adrian, John, Herbert and Danny. On the South side were Henry Brougham and Edgar. Henry excelled and was duly picked for the Wales game, his first in his country's colours.

The game in itself was notable only as an extension to the list of those featuring Harlequins backs over the two seasons and a further example of Adrian's unfailing ability to pick out a gem. What was most amusing however, was Adrian's abject treatment of an object thrown from the crowd as the teams were about to be photographed. Coins and bottles may be the violent weapons of choice these days. In 1912 it was a leek. The offending vegetable was picked up by Adrian, who then took his time in solemnly burying it. Wales were also buried. Henry joined Adrian, Ronnie and John and marked his winning debut by scoring one of his side's two tries.

Adrian missed the next game, against Ireland, but John, Henry and Ronnie scored a try each in England's five-try demolition. The scene was set for the Calcutta Cup match against Scotland on 16 March, and England's potential triple crown. Almost seven years to the day since he had started out on a long and eventful path, the opponents were the same. Unfortunately, so too was the result. Reduced by injury to fourteen men for the whole of the second half, England were always up against it. Trying to push the game on, Adrian made several uncharacteristic errors and any hope his side had of staying in it was lost. Only Ronnie added to his reputation, making the best of the sloppy passes that came his way. The English were at least able to see off France to end the season and secure a share of the championship. Adrian was not selected, but had the consolation of seeing John and Henry score a try apiece. It was also an opportunity to see the Cambridge forward J.E. 'Jenny' Greenwood in action. Ronnie's reports suggested he was one for Harlequins' future.

As a postscript to the season, a cricket match was played at Twickenham in April, between two of the biggest names in sport: the Harlequins and the

Outcasts. Losing one's place in either side paled against a catastrophe of altogether more gigantic proportions – the sinking of the Titanic. Adrian's rugby revolution had symbolised the progress to which the game in the twentieth century was heading, yet also the fear of the unknown that that progress inspired. The great ship symbolised equally the progress and the fear of a revolution of an altogether different kind: the industrial age. As the most recognised side of the day, Adrian's Harlequins played that game of cricket in aid of the Titanic Fund, in honour of those who lost their lives. Adrian played wicketkeeper and was bowled for two ducks. With Danny, Henry, John, Holly and Roc playing, he was mercilessly ribbed for this. By the end of 1911/12 the club had won 22 of 26 games, the highlight being a 32-0 thrashing of Edgar's Northampton . With a profit of £299, the club and the players had never been in better health.

Having finished at Oxford, Ronnie moved to 16 Portland Place, Reading, where he continued his engineering apprenticeship at Huntley & Palmer, the firm owned by his uncle, the Right Honourable G.W. Palmer MP. Rugby became but one of his loves. On 14 April he joined the 4th Battalion, Royal Berkshire Regiment, as well as becoming captain of the Reading Athletics Club and continuing his interest in the local boys clubs.

Adrian, who had always had an interest in military history, also joined the Queen's West Surrey Territorials, as they had become. Formed six years earlier under the Haldene scheme of army reorganisation, C and D companies were stationed at Guildford, within easy reach of Byfleet.

Apart from a gap in 1909/10, Adrian had been on the Barbarians committee since 1907. Previously it had only been possible to elect up to fifteen new members each season as vacancies arose. Following a change in membership policy, the upsurge in English rugby and with it the desire to blood younger recruits, competition for tour places was strong. Not being offered a playing berth in 1912 caused Adrian to leave office. Unlike Edgar who, after twenty-three county games, two trials and seven internationals, had just announced his playing retirement and who had just arrived on the committee, Adrian had not yet realised that it was time to let the new generation through. Adrian loved the tours, being as they were a general wind-down at the end of season. If he could not play against the best in Wales with the Barbarians, then he would do so with the Harlequins. And so the annual Harlequin Easter tour to Wales was born.

On 1 May the Harlequins camped at the Langland Bay Hotel for their first Easter tour. The tours would remain a great curtain call to the season, but under Adrian the games lost none of their seriousness. Players playing the next day were expected to not drink, to observe a curfew and to be in bed by eleven. In Adrian's eyes it was a crime for a player playing the next day to abuse his duty by being out all night. The public were paying to be entertained and Adrian's standards were such that his men would honour that. Freek was one of the first to pay the price, staying out late one night only to find himself running the line the next day. Or rather paddling it – a deluge had left the Swansea pitch calf-deep in water. A consultation between Adrian and his opposite captain agreed on the game going ahead – after all the public had paid good money.

The 1905 All Blacks had been the first to bring in a 'rover' – a loose forward whose job it was to disrupt attacks. Billy Williams whistled him off the park. With the rapid development of half-back play, however, and acceptance of 'fly half' as a position in its own right, the rover's role became more defined and accepted. The fly half would inevitably be top of the hit list; Adrian, and those that played like him, became marked men. The Welsh and specifically the Irish had tried to do it en masse in 1910, with varying degrees of success. Adrian was then quite literally one step ahead. Now it was the turn of the rovers. Not being as quick as he had once been would eventually catch up with him.

The next tourists to arrive in late 1912 were the South Africans. They came to England with a fearsome reputation, having dispatched Wales, Scotland and Ireland by an aggregate score of 57-0. In Douglas Morkel, they had a place-kicker who, with the wind, could kick points from anywhere up to the halfway line, and even beyond.

As part of the tourists' sequence of games against the counties, two London divisional games were played, arranged for November. Game one featured Herbert, Adrian, Freek and Danny. With the Londoners down 8-0, Adrian eventually pulled them back to evens, before eventually losing 12-8.

The other game featured Freek, Ronnie, Herbert, Henry and, at fly half, 'Dave' Davies, the new kid in town. Having been tested and bested the year before at the counties, nonetheless, like Poulton, Davies was straight out of the Stoop new school. In the absence of Adrian and John, both of whom were injured, everyone expected the Londoners to be routed. However, finding himself completely at home with Herbert's tried and trusted methods, Davies ended up playing an ace to Stoop's king. They won by two goals to one and a penalty and the press commented: 'he did all that a great player could do. Not as we see Adrian Stoop do, perhaps, but in a way that was great nevertheless.'

Further evidence of strength in English clubs and of an increasing focus on wing forwards, if any were necessary, came with the December Harlequins *v.* Blackheath game. The Harlequins featured seven past and present internationals in their famed backs while the Blackheath forwards were virtually all those who had represented the winning London side of a few weeks earlier. The backs were unable to make any headway, forcing a change in strategy during the game. The Harlequins would have to wear down the opposing pack. That they were eventually successful relied in no small part on the fact that they were now playing forty-minute halves, not thirty-five as had been the case in club rugby until a few seasons before.

The international trials saw much of the winning London side representing the Probables. For the first international game of the season, against the tourists, Davies got the fly half berth. Wodehouse was the England captain, Ronnie the leader of the backs. Adrian had lost his international place for the last time.

Ironically, it was the game against Scotland to close the 1911/12 season that had been his last in England's colours. He finished where he had started, although this time there was no cold to blame. He was off the pace. Of the internationals he had played in, the best were those where he was in the company of his beloved club teammates. John played in all of Adrian's matches bar the first. Adrian was on the winning side for three of the four he played with Ronnie, the single loss coming when they only had fourteen men. He had played in all three of the games that Freek had played to date, but while he had had great games with Peters, Gent and Gotley, injury ensured he never got an England game with Herbert Sibree.

Notwithstanding his own achievements, if he had passed on the position of stand-off half to Dave Davies, the role of crowd favourite had long been happily ceded to Ronnie. If by 1910 Adrian had become the more mature finished article, so too now, in late 1912, had Ronnie.

A New Order

The selected South African eight were known to be very heavy; the English eight were fast but light. In discussion with Adrian, Ronnie had come to the conclusion that the English forwards would be able to set up attacks in the first half, but would be worn down by superior weight in the second, and compelled to give ground. With Morkel in the tourists' ranks, it was essential that any South African kicks be taken either against the wind or beyond the range of goal. In Ronnie's mind it was imperative that England play against the wind on winning the toss, and more pertinently that South Africa play against it in the second half.

As the crowd gathered, waiting impatiently for the start, a weary, careworn Englishman made his way to the ground. Little did they know his story of the night before. The wish of a dying boy in Notting Hill had been to see his hero, the enigmatic Poulton. Ronnie had received a call and, totally in character, responded immediately. The young lad had had his wish granted, Ronnie staying with him long into the early morning until he passed away.

Once at the changing rooms, Ronnie quietly got on with his pre-match preparations. Wodehouse came in, announcing the winning of the toss, and proposed playing with the wind in the first half. Lost in his thoughts Ronnie nodded without hearing what had been said.

As the kick-off approached, the record crowd of 30,000 plus were not to know they were about to see another classic. Like the inaugural game at Twickenham, they had barely got themselves settled when, once more, the outrageous happened. Poulton emulated Stoop by scoring before breath had been drawn, this time starting and finishing a move with a length-of-the-pitch solo run almost from the off.

The conversion was missed. South Africa responded with a try of their own, also unconverted. Ronnie, however, was playing like a man possessed. The crowd thought they had seen the try to end all tries with his first effort, but before the dust had settled he was off again, running the length of the pitch, arms out, head back, dummying and swerving through all and sundry. This time, however, the covering South African full-back just caught him in the corner, and he was brought down a yard short of the line. Had Ronnie looked to his left, he would have seen Freek alongside, ever alert and quick enough to keep up with him. Had either scored, England would surely have won.

As it was, Douglas Morkel was to kick two of Twickenham's longest ever penalties in the second half, when the weight of the South Africans had started to tell. Wind and choice of ends did, as predicted, prove decisive. The South Africans won an exciting but close game, England's first defeat at their hallowed ground. *The Sportsman* of 6 January made a singular comment: 'Poulton immortalised himself as the only man who has scored against the South Africans in an international.'

After 1910, the established facts were many: the need for consistency of selection generally; the need for consistency at half-back; and the need for training as a team. Also, that a captain's head counts for as much as his hands and feet together. The 1913 South African game revealed further what was already known: that even the best set of backs can't survive without a strong pack to work from. At least the newfound spirit was built on surer foundations. Poulton and Davies were there to take up the baton. England won all four internationals in early 1913, including the first defeat of Wales in Cardiff for eighteen years, to take the championship outright. Twickenham's good fairy celebrated further success.

Rugby in its native country had been fully restored to its place at the top of the pile. For the Stoops it was time for another party. Every year they had held lavish garden parties on the lawns of West Hall in the summer. With the Dordsche incorporated into Royal Dutch and Shell, their garden party of June 1913 was a Dutch fair, in which all the guests turned up in Dutch costumes: 'It was like fairyland, with fairy lights in all the trees. How they did it all I don't know, because it was before the days of electric lights.' The Stoops had seemingly pulled off yet another miracle.

With the championship success of the season just gone, everyone yearned for more. Adrian's Harlequin monster had without doubt become an England one. Everyone still listened to what he had to say, not least in his classic essay on the game called – after the poem – 'On Passing'. First published in the *Rugby Football Annual* of 1913/14, it became the standard by which others were taught:

When a three-quarter who is known to have a safe pair of hands misses the majority of passes he receives in a particular match, the invariable criticism of the onlookers is that he is 'off his game', whereas in nine cases out of ten the fault lies in the manner in which the ball is passed to him. Then, the better the player he is, the greater is his inability to hold the ball.

A simple experiment will illustrate my meaning. Try to pass a ball in the direction to which you are facing and you will find that in order to obtain any command over its direction it will be necessary to pass the ball in such a way that it rises considerably on leaving the hands. Now when the passer and receiver are converging this is what happens, and the result is that the ball usually strikes the latter in the face or on the shoulder with its relative velocity increased by the convergence of the players and probably spinning end over end at the same time. It is in the nature of such a pass that it is delivered at short range and this almost expands the difficulty of accepting it into an impossibility. The better the player, the less he will allow himself to be crowded into touch. When his inexpert colleague runs with the ball across the field, the less the former gives way the more difficult it will be for him to accept the pass.

As the receiver is seldom able to give his whole attention to the ball but usually is largely occupied with watching his opponent, it is essential that a pass should be made so that it is easy to take. And to ensure this, three points should be borne in mind. (1) The passer and receiver must be running on parallel, if not diverging, lines. (2) The ball must travel in a horizontal direction and (3) it must fly without spin and with one end pointing towards the receiver.

It is quite a simple matter to prevent the ball from spinning. It should be held with both hands at one end, with the other pointing away from the body. But to obtain the force necessary to make the ball travel horizontally and at the same time keep control over its direction is by no means easy and it is an art, which in most cases requires considerable practice.

The force is obtained from the muscles of the back, while the arms are used merely to control the direction. As an illustration, let us suppose the pass is to be given to the left. The action of the body is the same as if we are throwing some object, which is held between the teeth, over the left shoulder with the greatest possible force.

It takes the form of a swing from the right hip, using the muscles down the right side of the back, finishing up with a hollow back and the chin pointing towards the left, while the shoulders have been swung through an angle of about 45 degrees. The arms should be held straight, though not necessarily rigid, and the only conscious movement of them should be raised towards the end of the swing; at the commencement they are merely used to connect the ball with the shoulders. At the end of the swing, we are looking in the direction in which the ball is to travel, and the direction of the ball will be that in which the arms are pointing when the ball is released.

The same considerations apply to a pass given by a scrum-half, but as in his particular case every fraction of a second is of the greatest importance… there should be no picking up or swinging back the ball; it should be swept straight off the ground to the stand-off half in one movement. It is by practice and by practice alone that it (such a pass off the ground) is attained, for in no other way are the muscles of the back and sides strengthened in the manner which the pass demands.

The teacher had spoken, and rugby players old and young were listening – except for those smart enough to have paid attention before, who were already practising what had been preached. Particularly Dave Davies, now a naval officer, who came across Stoop once more:

At the beginning of the 1913/14 season, playing for the United Services against Harlequins at Portsmouth I, quite inadvertently by the use of the referee as a screen, dodged past my famous adversary. When I was eventually hauled down, the game was stopped momentarily to allow the players and spectators to hear the true version of the episode from Adrian.

Burgeoning reputation or not, no one was spared further words of wisdom.

Thus 1913 turned out to be a pivotal year. Those who had done so much for the cause were in the twilights of their careers. Edgar had realised for himself that times had changed. Discarded by the selectors in 1910, the knocks had become too great and he knew his club playing days were also coming to a close. He had done his bit for England. For his retirement party, the town of Northampton turned out en masse to see off its favourite son.

Adrian had signed off internationally, but he still had his beloved Harlequins. His last acts as 1913 closed were for the club: firstly, an attempt to secure Twickenham for another five years; secondly, setting up a committee of himself, Roc and Holly to find and buy a new ground for the 'A' team. Smile he could, as all England could. He had built the fortress, and had protected it. He had never lost in any of his internationals there. The public had come to see, and would come again, for the future of England was to be in safe hands.

Since the resumption of his international career, Ronnie had never looked back. He never needed to: for the internationals of early 1914, he was the new England captain. Having to travel from Liverpool, where he was spending the year completing his engineering studies, his main problem was having too little time for the things that mattered most in his life, principally how best to help those less fortunate. Captaincy of his country was but an aside to the psychological gifts he bestowed on others.

To some concern among Harlequin first-team fringe players, Adrian would still find a place for him on the odd occasions Ronnie might be available. For Adrian, Ronnie was the future of the club.

The first three games, against Wales, Ireland and Scotland resulted in close wins for Ronnie's England. The singular characteristic of each was a relative superiority of the opposing forwards, more than offset by the pace and panache of the English backs generally, and Ronald Poulton specifically. If the opposition ever looked to be getting on top, Ronnie would have them back on the defensive with one of his mesmeric, swerving runs. After the Welsh opener, which Ronnie had effectively won by his own brilliance, Clem Lewis wrote:

He has such a funny way of running – it is no use looking at his head or his body, for they seem to be going in opposite directions to what his legs are… the man who discovers the secret of his running will do great things.

He closed the last of those three games with a typical 'as-only-Poulton-could' try. The public came from all walks of life to see the good become great. King George V seized the moment to return to watch the game he both loved and was president of, for the first time since 1910.

The scene was set for the final game against France and a potential unparalleled second consecutive outright championship. Before Ronnie could get into his famed stride, however, came the news of his uncle's death. Being the closest relative and having spent much of his time at the Huntley & Palmer plant in Reading, Ronnie was always seen as the likely heir and successor. And so it proved when his uncle's will came through. Ronnie would be the beneficiary of a vast fortune, on the condition that he adopt the name Palmer. This vexed him greatly, not for the fact he was to become known evermore as Poulton-Palmer, but for how best to utilise his newfound wealth for the benefit of others.

His most immediate task was the last international of the season in Paris, on 13 April 1914. The French loved a dashing hero, and Poulton was their man almost as much as he was England's. The crossing took the English over to Boulogne. Garlanded with flowers on reaching the port, and again on going into the game, never before had one man captured the spirit of the time so eloquently yet so modestly. England won the game by a landslide, crossing the line nine times. Ronnie obliged everyone by scoring four of them. The definitive captain's innings. To all and sundry he had become simply the greatest sportsman living, to some one of the greatest of all time.

Adrian smiled the same contented smile that Donkin had many years before. Back then, in 1900, they saw sufficient to lay a stone tablet in tribute to the great game of rugby that had been invented at and by the school. There were no tributes grand enough to recognise Poulton's indelible mark on it.

Some tried. In early 1914 the historian B.H. Liddell Hart brought together a collection of some of rugby's greatest names, most prominently the Welsh legend Rees Gabe, to draw up a list of rugby's greatest ever. The single forwards list contained Curly Hammond and Lump Cartwright. The backs were split by position into 'Immortals' and 'Classics'. The half-dozen 'immortal' half-backs contained Rotherham, the two Dickies, Owen and Jones, Pat Munro and Adrian. Of the three-quarters, Gwyn Nicholls, Arthur Gould, Morgan and Ronnie Poulton were 'immortal' while MacLear, Trew, Gabe and John Birkett were the 'classics'.

Two of those immortals, and one of the classics, had paved the way for England's greatest ever period. From 1910 to 1914, the English lost only one game at fortress Twickenham, and that to the 1913 South African tourists. In the space of eight years they had gone from the seven-game losing sequence at the end of 1906 to the eight wins on the bounce to close April 1914. Relative prosperity was felt by immortals and mortals alike. The Harlequins wrapped up their year against the United Services. Fifty cars, one bath chair and 2,500 people were there. The club's profit for the season was £417.

Everyone set off to enjoy the close season. In July Adrian went on a fishing holiday to Gairloch. Freek was at Wakelam's in Charmouth with his fiancée. Ronnie was set at Huntley & Palmer's in accordance with his uncle's wishes. In August, war was declared. The serenity was shattered and lives were to be changed forever.

nine

THE TURNIP FIELD
1914-1919

In that rich earth a richer dust concealed.
(Rupert Brooke, 'The Soldier')

Nine days after the outbreak of the First World War, the RFU issued a circular advising all players to join the forces. There were calls for all forms of rugby to be discontinued, and virtually all forms duly stopped, except at school level. Rugby men enlisted in their droves.

In 1913 Britain had acquired the Persian oil field of Abadan. With the advent of the war, chief concerns were to protect both the oil fields and the route to India. On 26 July 1914, Second Lieutenant Stoop marched from Bordon to attend camp at Salisbury Plain with the 5th Battalion of the Queens (Royal West Surrey) Regiment. The Queens were soon returned to their Guildford drill hall in preparation for mobilisation. On 5 August they moved to Strood, near Chatham, to join the 4th and 6th Queens for training at Maidstone. From the delights of West Hall to the billets, blankets, tents, and wooden cut-out rifles of training camp. A month later they were moved to Canterbury, with orders to proceed immediately to India.

By the end of September they were at Southampton ready for the off. Confusion delayed their progress, but on 29 October the SS *Alaunia* departed English shores. A stop in Suez allowed them to take on fresh supplies: apples, figs, oranges, dates and priceless Turkish Delight – Fatty Cobb the cook found himself in great demand. Onward progress was initially halted by the threat of German cruisers. To pass the time, sports competitions were held on the deck: boxing, tug-of-war, obstacle races and pillow fighting over makeshift baths. Eventually arriving in Bombay on 1 December, they were then sent by train to Lucknow, where they became reorganised as the 1/5th Queens. The final two-mile march to their barracks, in the blazing sun, would be but the start of their journeying. In the space of a few months, Adrian had left behind the green fields of south-west London for the heat and dust of much further east. Instead of preparing for the start of a new season, Adrian was getting ready for battles of a different kind. Gone were the multi-coloured Harlequin jerseys, scrumcaps, diamond socks and Gilbert boots. In came the khaki drill uniform and shorts, pith hats, topees and spine pads.

Back in England, others were also preparing for action: Ronnie was already a Second Lieutenant in the 4th Battalion Princess Charlotte of Wales Royal Berkshires, a roll forward from his Territorial days; John became a Lieutenant in the Royal Artillery; Danny was a Lieutenant in the 6th Battalion of the East Kents (The Buffs); Freek was in the 7th East Kents. All were to be stationed in France. Keen to go early, Kenneth Powell paid to join the Honourable Artillery Company and was dispatched almost immediately. Edgar was refused officership, being just over the age limit of thirty-two. But as in rugby, nothing would prevent him from playing his part, and he enlisted as a private. It was somehow difficult to see a one-time captain of his country in with the rank and file. Recognising that his leadership qualities far surpassed those of a mere private, he was quickly promoted through the ranks.

As 1914 drew to a close, everyone had steeled themselves for kick-off. Final preparations were made. Danny married his childhood sweetheart Joyce on 17 December at West Brompton, almost as the news of Powell's death came through.

In India, the early part of 1915 remained quiet, the 1/5th Queen's activities consisting mainly of garrison duties. Lucknow was both dry and uneventful, the only source of amusement being the post, when it arrived, with letters from the Bombay ladies who lunched, and news from home: stories of those who were preparing to go, of those who had already fallen, and of the early madness that was the Western Front. They were stories punctuated only with small illuminations, such as 'the Christmas Truce' and its legendary game of football on a turnip field somewhere in southwest Belgium. His own inactivity would not have amused Adrian, needing as he did to keep his mind and body active. With him in India were several Old Rugbeians, including Captain Ashby, Lieutenant Spens, Second Lieutenant Bushell, Second Lieutenants G.C. and O.S. Cleverly and Private Morris-Davies. There is, however, only so much time you can spend reminiscing about the old days.

Edgar's tales were becoming legendary. Not only was he moving up the ranks almost week by week, but he had already recruited, by his name alone, a 'Sportsmen's Battalion', principally comprising rugby players from around the East Midlands area to fight over in France. Not content with raising men for active service, he also offered up the services of the Barbarians for a series of games against service teams, to raise morale and funds for war relief and help recruitment. Games were played against his Shoreham camp, Leicester, and RAMC Crookham between December and March 1915.

As Edgar kept active, Ronnie's battalion remained static, much of his time being spent on trench-build training, in preparation for the mud of Flanders. They left for France early in April. The Berkshires' crossing took them over the route that Ronnie's England team had followed for that glorious finale to the end of the previous international season, exactly a year before. Déjà vu. Only this time the white of England was transposed to services khaki.

On 7 April Ronnie arrived with his men near the front line at Ploegsteert in Belgium. Before the war, Ploegsteert had been a small rural village, with a few small stores, a café and a church, not unlike Twickenham before Billy Williams' influence. During 1914 it had been a relatively quiet sector of the front, but by now it had entered sporting legend. It was Ploegsteert's turnip field, at Anton's Farm, that was the site of that greatest of all sports stories, the Christmas Day football game of four months before.

The Berkshires' first job, in early April, was to prepare their own cemetery for the event of casualty. The rest of Ronnie's month would be spent on engineering works, real trench fortification and extensions. With the Royal Engineers becoming involved in their development, trenches were becoming more sophisticated and professional. In those early days at Ploegsteert, they were little more than holes in the ground. And with no structured communication trenches, men could not move about during the daylight hours – most of the work was carried out at night.

On 14 April Ronnie was able to fit in a game of rugby, captaining a divisional team at Pont de Dieppe. The morning of the 17th saw him set out from the school next to the church, where he was stationed. He wrote:

A beautiful morning… it is a beautiful walk to the farm where the headquarters are, through the wood, blooming with cowslips and bluebells, past two or three beautifully kept graves.

Written as if he was a world away from the chaos around him. His old school playing colleague, Rupert Brooke, could not have described the scene more poetically.

The 17th also saw Edgar's last game before he left for active service. Another Barbarians XV played Wales at Cardiff in the biggest game of the lot. Oh, for Ronnie not to have left two weeks earlier. Down a player as they left Paddington, John Birkett was found to be on the train. Edgar would take no more pleasure than to play alongside his old adversary for perhaps a final time, the first since Ireland in 1910. During the game, the two played with such great form and ran so hard and straight that Adrian would have wished to have been there. The result of the match produced one of the greatest surprises, 'England' winning 26-10. No one had expected the scratch Barbarian side to stand any chance against a Wales side containing thirteen internationals, nine of whom had narrowly lost to Poulton's team the year before. England's golden heroes were still alive and kicking.

In the weeks that followed, the news of the game would have been of great interest to Ronnie – a reminder of different days, when representing your country extended to eighty minutes on a Saturday afternoon.

The night of 4/5 May was exceptionally dark, the moon not having risen, and there was a slight fog. Ronnie was on the last of four nights supervising trench works near Anton's Farm. Here was the rugby legend of cabbage patch days, gracing a turnip field of football legend. Soccer and rugger represented gloriously once more together on the same pitch again. The irony was not lost on him.

At twenty past midnight a single shot rang out. Ronnie slumped into the arms of his Sergeant. Death was instantaneous.

Ronnie's expression in death 'was peaceful and happy'. His was only the second grave on his regiment's plot, a simple wooden cross marking the spot. Lieutenant C.R.M.F. Crutwell wrote:

Those of us who have known him for a long while, and loved him, can enter just a little into the grief of his own people. You will have heard the details of his death. It is a great consolation to know that he died painlessly for England, beloved by every one in his Regiment. When I went round his old Company as they stood to at dawn, almost every man was crying. He will always be an inspiration to those of us that remain. He will be laid in the wood this afternoon in soil which is already consecrated to the memory of many brave soldiers. The oak trees are just coming out, and the spring flowers; and the place would remind you much of the woods around Oxford.

His loss was felt by all, not only in his battalion, but also to a shocked country and rugby's cognoscenti. People wrote of their deep admiration for him.

The news shattered his old school, still reeling from the death of Rupert Brooke that same week. It was a real end to innocence, with the almost simultaneous loss of two of its most revered sons. Their paths had taken them different ways, yet their young lives had been intimately shared by their public. Brooke, in his last years, had been deeply troubled – tortured by jealousy and showing degrees of stupidity and self-centredness in his private life, he found expression in the fluidity of his writing. As a person Poulton could not have contrasted more, being the richer in means and in spirit. His chief anxiety lay in how best to use his wealth for the benefit of those less fortunate. He had £1 0s 6d on him when he died. The army deducted £11s 9s 6d from his final pay due to overpayment, leaving a service balance of £42s 15s 0d as part of his will. This was a far cry from the fortune that had come his way, which others had been sure he would have used to best effect. He never got the chance. By formal will dated 10 March 1914 he left £22,310 and his books in memoriam.

The headmaster of Rugby School, the Reverend A.A. David, conducted a memorial service on Sunday, two days later. The paths of Poulton and Brooke were to come together for a final time. Brothers in arms for the 1905 school playing season, they started out as equals. It was left to David, ten years later, to sum up their short lives in his moving sermon that Sunday morning. Called simply 'Counting the Cost' he said:

We have indeed given of our best. If we were asked to describe what highest kind of manhood rugby helps to make, I think we should have [Ronnie] in mind as we spoke of it.

God had endowed him with a rare combination of graces, and given him an influence among men such as very few in one generation can possess. What had we hoped would come of it.

There are those in Notting Dale, in Oxford, in Reading and in his Battalion who will be the better men all their lives, and do better work, because he was their friend, is their friend.

Strong and tender and true, he lived for others and died for others.

Rugby players then or after referred to him as simply the greatest. The *Meteor* said:

After Kenneth Powell, Ronald Poulton; and his place can never be filled; for to his friends (and they were many) he did, in quite a peculiar way, sum up a generation and realise an ideal… for the secret of his charm and of his influence lay in the ready and ever-widening sympathy which impelled him, without a touch of affectation or condescension, to share his own happiness and strength with all who needed a friend.

To Adrian he was, quite simply, the greatest. The news soon reached Lucknow. Adrian thoughts were with Ronald's family, as much as with others he knew that had already gone over. In a letter to Ronald's sister on 13 May he wrote:

So many of the best men have gone under that one feels that the most satisfactory thing would be to follow their example. The gaps among one's friends will be too awful when the war is over. The Harlequins also have Tom Allen and Kenneth Powell to avenge, and I do not think we shall forget when the time comes.

The time would.

The war to date had already thrown up too many an instance of individual senselessness. Poulton's death brought it home. The following month came Gallipoli, and the first real representation of collective senselessness. Among those that fell was Dave Gallaher. In June 1915, Hilaire Belloc, the noted travel writer and poet, delivered a lecture at Rugby School on 'The War'. The main thrust of his speech was that it was too early to estimate how far the madness would carry. Likening the war to a game of rugby, defence and attack on both sides in those early days were seemingly equally represented, either by weight of men or weight of munitions. Any advantage in the results of key campaigns, whether on the eastern or western fronts, owed little to strategy and more to some other advanced technology. Gallipoli, the Dardanelles and the taking of their twelve miles of the narrow straights could have been key, and would have supported the work that submarines had done in blocking the free access of the Turks to the Sea of Mamara beyond.

And to Adrian's marble mines.

A Change of Scenery

For the present, India offered little in the way of activity. Adrian was very much on the bench again. No green fields, no cabbage patches, no turnip fields. Cholera and other diseases were rife and his tremendous fitness probably saved him from being laid up on a more permanent basis. He was the lucky one.

The best part of a year of inactivity was interrupted when news came through of the death of Danny Lambert. Killed at Loos on 13 October 1915, the day before his birthday, Danny was to have no known grave, being one of the faceless names to be commemorated on the eventual Loos Memorial. His sparse belongings were sent home and contained his map case and a bundle of letters and postcards. Less than two months later his wife Joyce gave birth to the son he was never to see.

The grief would have been immense for all. First Poulton, now Lambert. The greater powers were taking Adrian's tools away again. Here was a man who was starting to lose the very parts that had made him whole, the very parts that allowed him to function. It had nothing to do with the selectors this time. Adrian would need something to close the void that was rapidly being created.

Closure of a different kind would soon be at hand.

Audrey Needham was nearing her twentieth birthday. Born in India on New Year's Eve 1895, she had seen little if anything of her parents in her relatively short life. Her father, William Frederick Needham, was straight out of the old school of ex-pats. The youngest of fifteen children, by the age of seven he had met Ada Geraldine Paget. At the age of fourteen he had her initials tattooed on his arm. Having announced that one day he would marry her, when he was old enough he did just that. Camped out in India, he had earned his living as an indigo planter. Generally he prospered and the locals looked up to him; as a result he was able to manipulate his position for the better. Asked to manage a large estate in Jaidebpur, East Bengal, his only problem there was the great heat, which particularly did not suit his young daughter. The five-year-old girl was sent to England to await her parents' eventual return. Unfortunately, William's new job kept him stationed on the estate for the years to follow.

Audrey had arrived in England in 1900. There she lived the life of anyone growing up in an alien land. This was particularly difficult in a land struggling for its identity, coming out of the Victorian era as it was. Leaving again eleven years later, the headlines made by the national rugby team a year beforehand would have been of as much interest to her as any impressionable teenager.

Arriving back in Jaidebpur was as difficult as when she had left. She hardly knew her parents and once more she suffered in the intense heat. Almost immediately she was sent up to Missouri with a chaperone. Once there, they booked into The Charleyville Hotel to see out the hot, dry spell.

Idle time for the Queens was all too frequent. Leave, for what it was worth, was at least a chance to escape the endless monotony. Adrian and some colleagues decided to go up to Missouri, if only for a change of view. Once there they at last found time to relax. For Adrian it was a chance to forget the personal traumas that had gone before. To the local girls, having English soldiers in town was both a novelty and a chance not to be missed. Almost immediately the men found themselves being invited to a dance at The Charleyville.

On arriving, Adrian found himself drawn to a young lady who seemed to know as much of his homeland as he. The two lost souls clicked almost immediately, danced the night away, and forgot the cares of their separate worlds, despite the close attentions of a chaperone who made life difficult for all. Undeterred, the soldiers arranged to meet the girls for a picnic up in the hills the following day.

When it came, it was perfect. The servants went on ahead while the girls were transported up on sedans carried by the coolies. Adrian and his friends followed on behind, blessing their good fortune. The rest of the guys back at camp would never believe what they had missed out on.

The two new friends found themselves kindred spirits, Audrey telling of the nursing course she was undertaking, Adrian talking of the good old days, of Ronnie, of Danny, names she was almost familiar with. The break was welcome for all concerned, but like all good things it had to end. Adrian returned to his regiment, Audrey to her chaperone.

Then on 27 October 1915 the news the Queens had hoped for: 'The 1/5th Royal West Surreys will mobilise at Lucknow as strong as possible. Field service clothing winter scale and field service scale of tentage.' This was followed up on 5 November when the Chief of General Staff wrote to confirm that mobilisation was only a precautionary measure. It was back to training, route marches and blisters from boots that were too hard in the hot weather. Until, finally, on 25 November: 'Please be prepared to move the 1/5th from Lucknow to Bombay at few hours notice.'

They left almost immediately and the band played them out to 'Auld Lang Syne'. Arriving at Bombay at 2 p.m. on 1 December, the officers stayed over at the Taj Mahal hotel, in preparation for embarkation to Mesopotamia with the Expeditionary Force. On 7 December their ship, HMT *Elephanta*, anchored at Basra. The troops were then transported in barges, towed by tugs, up the Euphrates and then on forty-one mahaillas to Nasariyah. For the final stretch the Queens travelled up the river on steamers. The rough waters caused supplies and four men to fall overboard, two of them losing their rifles in the process. To save the men from loss of face, Adrian used the skills he had learnt at West Hall to put on a diving exhibition. He recovered one rifle while one of the locals found the other.

As they travelled, much was happening in Mesopotamia. In early December the British forward column had been forced to retreat at Kut. With limited supplies and only 10,000 men, their situation was becoming desperate. The Turkish commander had started to blockade the roads to stop any relieving force and held strong positions alongside impenetrable marshes.

Arriving on 15 December, the Queens' thoughts of action were dulled by their initial assignment to construct a road to 'Ur of the Chaldees', with further digging of redoubts and other defensive works. Adrian continued training on the Lewis machine guns. Camp conditions were basic, the men having to collect their own food and wood for fires. Nonetheless, Christmas Day saw a dinner of cold beef, hot chicken, plum duff and standard rum issue, with the first mail since they had left Lucknow arriving late at night. The next day it was back to the routine and the guarding of the Turkish prison camp.

The period of relative inactivity that had been 1915 came to an abrupt end for the Queens in January.

The troops were suddenly moved to assist the Kut relief force after the original force was trampled on by the Turks. Leaving a small garrison at Nasariyah the Queens' advance was not easy. Rain had turned their road to a quagmire and sixty camels had to be hired. Twelve miles from Kut, they laid a diversion that would allow a retreat. They marched seven miles along the Suwaij road without incident, and took a defensive position on an irrigation canal 900 yards from Suwaij village. As they lined the canal, firing broke out from Arabs to the north. Outnumbered and outflanked, the Queens were forced to retire by alternate companies and platoons. Their progress was delayed by the time needed to rescue their wounded. In their first five serious hours of action, they had lost one dead and one missing, with fourteen wounded. Not a great result in their first taste of conflict.

The Queens stayed at Butaniyeh and the warring fractions backed off as the subsequent weather turned cold and wet, turning to snow on occasions. Long range firing came in from the Arab picquets, but otherwise routine continued.

February saw Adrian escort a convoy of the sick to Nasariyah, being sniped at along the way. Then it was more of the same: lessons in loading camels, trench improvements and so on, but waters flooding the camps and cholera outbreaks led to the city being made out of bounds. On 30 May 1916, Adrian was promoted to Lieutenant (Acting Captain). In June he escorted a party downriver to mark the graves of those that had already fallen. It was time also, perhaps, to reflect on memories of others that had fallen elsewhere.

The summer of 1916 initially brought more heavy rain, followed by intense heat – 124° at times, 105° in the shade, and there was precious little of that. Disease and illness were again rife: cholera, heatstroke, asthma, and colitis. The coffee shop run by the Indians was closed due to an outbreak of dysentery. As it was too hot to eat at 1600hrs, eating times were changed to 1930hrs. Little did the men realise that the discomfort of their lives was nothing at all compared to the horrors that made up the Western Front.

Both Roc and Freek had suffered gunshot wounds, Roc to his left thigh and back, Freek to his left shoulder and hand. Freek's had been serious. Hit on 18 March at Mauecourt, some of the metal shrapnel had gone through his scapula and reached the surface of his left lung. Operated on three days later, he was not discharged from hospital until 9 April. Leave followed in May 1916, and while by August the wound had healed, he had still not fully recovered the movement in his shoulder. He remained on extended sick leave until the end of the year.

Edgar's war had been one of personal attrition. In his rugby-playing days, the manner in which he played attracted injury. War was never going to be any different. One of his many wounds kept him away from the

Somme on that darkest of days. But, knock him down and up he got again.
By the end of 1916 he had distinguished himself by earning the DSO.

September 1916 saw the Queens' tedium increase as they built roads out
from Nasariyah. This time, however, the Arabs moved up close again and a
column was sent to repulse them. They were charged by 7,000 Arabs. Some
degree of confusion reigned, there being no guns in support. Forced to
retire again, the Arabs followed them back along the road. Adrian's men
reinforced the rearguard and they made it relatively unscathed back to
camp. This was their best three-quarters of an hour of action since kick-off.

Technology was about to take over the Middle East, the rest of the year
being taken up with courses in the Lewis machine guns and more general
training. Further ill-health yielded on average sixty hospital admissions a
day. Following the dropping of bombs on the troops' football pitch, more
'interesting' competitions were engaged in: tree climbing, trench digging,
and range finding.

By the end of the year, Adrian and his men had become fully conver-
sant, and indeed efficient with, the Lewis guns, which would prove of great
significance in the year to come. 1917 was to be pivotal for many reasons.
On 10 January, Freek had resumed service, this time at the Machine Gun
Training Centre, joining as he did the Motorised Division of the Machine
Gun Corps. On 26 January Roc joined D Battalion, Tank Corps, of the
6th Battalion, The East Kents (Buffs).

27 March 1917 saw orders for the Queens to move to Baghdad. They
proceeded in four trains to Basra, then up the Tigris on steamers to
Hinaidi. Once there, yet another quiet period allowed Adrian to take his
first leave since December 1915. Circumstances conspired to allow him to
meet Audrey again. They had not seen each other for over a year, but
somehow, through their many letters, they felt they had known each other
all their lives. This time they got engaged.

He returned to the men on 17 June and was transferred to the command
of 'D' company. On 1 July they arrived at Baghdad. The general lack of
information abounding signalled two things. Firstly, something was up:
there were too many promotions, as well as new officers arriving and new
recruits without training; there were two moves in a month. Secondly, there
was confusion: they were not expected and no camps had been readied for
them. The frustration was really beginning to show, and it increased further
when a captain criticised Adrian's machine guns. Matters got worse. There
was sandfly fever, and with no supplies, water or fatigues, training was
restricted to specialist areas: machine guns, signals, and stretchers.

In July of the previous year the British had carried out operations on
the flood control station at Ramadi, where the Turks had significant
entrenched positions covering the town from the east and south-east.

Meeting great heat and a well-organised defence, those operations were abandoned. The Turks had taken advantage and driven the troops back and formed further defensive lines.

The preparations, or decided lack of them now, at Baghdad, fuelled the argument that a major offensive was about to occur. The British now had a column of adequate size to remount an offensive on Ramadi. Those expected to pull the strings had little clue as to what to do about it.

The Final Whistle

While Adrian steeled himself for action, his old friends were now having to dig deep. They too were readying themselves for their biggest game; they had already had the sternest of trials.

Freek found himself posted to Mesopotamia. Roc went on leave between 16 and 30 June 1917, returning an acting major. By July Edgar had been made a colonel.

Edgar had given everything. For him there was nothing left to give. Like when playing Ireland six years beforehand, and like the previous two years of the war, the team came first. He kept getting knocked down, kept getting back up. In the glory season of 1910, Edgar's last international was as captain, in France. As then, he was to be in charge of his countrymen one more time. His time was over. On 31 July, he led his men on an attack to wipe out two machine-gun nests deep in woods just a few miles along the road from Ploegsteert's turnip field. Colonels did not lead over the top. But this was no ordinary campaigner, this was Mobbs. England's Edgar died from a bullet to the neck, leading a charge to obtain the position of one of the enemy machine-gun posts. Falling in to a shell hole as he was shot, he died whispering the guns' co-ordinates. Like Danny Lambert, his rugby opponent of many a season, his body was never found, lost in the Flanders soil, commemorated forever on the Menin Gate Memorial.

The news filtered through to Mesopotamia, despite press censorship over the deaths of leading figures. Many a rugby player had fallen; most were familiar to Adrian and he them. There were just a few he would have had real time for: his Harlequin backs who represented what he stood for; Ronnie, his star pupil, who he hoped would have been the future of the club for years to come; and Edgar, his peer, fellow club captain and fellow sportsman. Although outside the esteemed inner circle, Edgar's views, his passion, his pride and loyalty for those that served him were ideals similar to Adrian. He too had now gone.

Barely two months later, the Queens left Baghdad and marched to within eight miles of the Turks at Ramadi. They bivouacked on the banks of the Euphrates, awaiting orders. On 14 September those orders came. The Turks held a semi-circular position one mile outside Ramadi. Their eastern front ran along and behind the Euphrates valley canal, their south front across the bare sandy downs from the valley canal to the Aziziyeh canal. The British intention was to attack from the south, hemming the enemy in by both cavalry and infantry movements.

The Queens set out in the dark, the heavy Lewis guns loaded on mules. Adversity followed them: deep sand frustrated them; tents, when eventually pitched, became stuck in a huge sandstorm; arriving on the 19th, their supplies consisted of only porridge, bacon and biscuits. With a sense of irony, some lambs, the emblem of both the Queens and the Barbarians, were purchased from a local farmer, fate perhaps dictating some bizarre final ritual.

On the 23rd, news came through of the enemy on the move. The Brigade immediately sought to secure several tactical locations, including the dam across the Euphrates valley canal. At 1925hrs on the 27th, the Queens were ordered to dig in. At 1230hrs the next day, 'B' company went over the exposed flank to dig in on two lines to the north-west side of Rayan Knoll, midway between the south end of Ramadi Bridge and the Aziziya ridge. The Turks withdrew their advanced positions and, believing an attack would come across the Mushaid Ridge, continued to shell the positions they had left.

At 1800hrs the next day the Queens received orders to dig in again on the knoll. A second night's hard digging was accompanied this time by a sense that the next day would somehow be different. Having been idle for so long, Adrian had much to occupy his mind, much to catch up on, many scores to settle. Three years in the wilderness of the war provided a reminder of days long gone. The coming morning would bring his greatest test: the troops were inexperienced, with no real action behind them. His Waterloo all over again. But whereas against Wales in 1910 he had covered all quarters, and again against Ireland the following game, this time he had no plan B. There was no Birkett and no Poulton.

At 0500 on the 29th the Allied brigades commenced their attacks on the three important ridges at the southern end of Ramadi. To the left of the Turkish lines, an infantry column advanced and consolidated its position. To the right, the infantry strategically withdrew under cover of a separate attack and moved behind and around their colleagues on the left to attack the Aziziya ridge. The Punjabis took it, 'C' and 'D' company of the Queens taking Double Hill. Adrian was involved from early on, in an attack on Faraja ridge. Commanding the Lewis guns, he was in the thick of the action from the start.

He had always been good at masking his emotions, just like his play. Now was just the time for a cool head as the battle commenced. Now, however, the emotions spilled out: the anger, the despair, the grief for lost friends, for Ronnie, for Danny, for Edgar, for the lost years. Adrenaline and raw emotion. As the battle waged, Adrian would not have heard the shot that rang out. He would have felt the piercing pain. He had been hit. Unlike Ronnie who had been hit in the heart and killed instantaneously, the shot that caught Adrian was a slow burner. His medical records did not need to go into any great detail, merely recording: 'Shot in the scrotum of the testes.'

The wound bled profusely. He had to dig deep once more, as unconsciousness would surely come. He also had his men to consider. He kept up the firing until he too finally had nothing else left to give and darkness clouded over.

With the final advances on Ramadi successful, the Turks surrendering en masse, and the town held, at 1500hrs Lieutenants Bell and Gillot searched for the dead and buried them. Adrian was lucky: despite a heavy loss of blood from his groin, he was to survive.

It took him two months to recover. Letters from Audrey kept his spirits high. On 25 November, Adrian returned to his men a Captain, happy for his own survival. The first news that greeted him was the death of Roc Ward five days earlier, leading a tank attack. Roc was buried at Metz-en-Couture cemetery, Pas de Calais and Adrian mourned the loss of another dear friend.

The winter months saw defensive fortifications at Ramadi. For Adrian, an opportunity to exorcise the ghosts. He was able to clear the mental scars by revisiting the scene. Testing out Lewis guns mounted on Ford cars, more road-making and hockey were the limit of activity. On 12 February the troops left for Fallujah, arriving on 5 March. Preparations were made for a major offensive on Hit. Almost before they had begun, the Turks withdrew.

The war had been long, and for all anyone knew still had some way to go. Having fully recovered, and because of his sporting reputation and training abilities, Adrian was put in charge of the boxing and the football teams that, not unexpectedly, won the regions cup.

As a reminder, however, of the frailty of life, on top of his recovery from wounding, Adrian soon suffered a bad attack of malaria. Eventually taking leave on 30 April he made his way to Bangalore with but one motive. On 8 May 1918 he was married to Audrey at St Mark's church, and they honeymooned up in the hills.

Elsewhere, those that had survived the war in Europe were returning home. Holly Ward had been injured, captured and spent much of his time making a nuisance of himself as a prisoner of war, devising all manner and means of escape attempts. John, whose campaigns had taken him through France to Italy, was injured and mentioned in dispatches on 30 May. He was awarded the Order of the Crown of Italy, 5th class.

In Mesopotamia the glorious first of June was celebrated with a cricket game between the officers and sergeants. On the 16th the battalion was notified of medals for the Ramadi campaign: Captain Berry, Lieutenants Spencer and Stoop. The *London Gazette* recorded Adrian's Military Cross thus:

For conspicuous gallantry and devotion to duty in action. He commanded the Lewis guns of his Battalion with great skill and daring under heavy fire, rendering invaluable assistance, and only desisted on being severely wounded. He has previously done good work as Lewis gun officer.

From here on in, the Queens' scale of operations started to diminish. By October they had moved to Najaf. 1 November 1918 saw an armistice with the Turks and the war out in Mesopotamia was over. In January 1919, Adrian was sent with a draft to join the 1/5 East Surreys, while the remainder of the Queens returned home. Adrian stayed in Lucknow for the rest of year, knowing his wife was expecting their first child. His next statement of intent was to draw up a will, leaving everything, his personal chattels, the money he had accumulated, his marble mines, to Audrey.

On 16 November 1919 Adrian and Audrey sailed for home, bringing with them their son, Adrian (Bunny).

45 Adrian with officers of the 1/5 Queen's Royal West Surreys, Mesopotamia, 1915.

46 1/5 Queen's receive briefing beside the River Tigris at Hinaidi, near Baghdad, July 1917.

47 (above) Adrian, Mesopotamia, 1917.

48 (below left) Adrian and Audrey on honeymoon, 1918.

49 (below right) Adrian, back on Civvy Street, 1919.

50 (opposite above) The Stoops 1919. From second left, back row: Adrian, Freek, Agnes, Khe, Frederick. In front of Adrian are Audrey and Bunny.

51 (opposite below) The Harlequins at Twickenham, 1919. Adrian, as president, is centre, middle row, next to John Birkett (with ball).

SOUVENIR PROGRAMME, 2d.   Published by Authority.

EAST MIDLANDS RUGBY UNION

𝔉ranklin's 𝔊ardens, 𝔑orthampton.

Thursday, February 10th, 1921.

𝔐obbs 𝔐emorial 𝔐atch :

East Midlands

v.

The Barbarians

Kick-off at 3 p.m.

PROCEEDS FOR THE

Promotion of Rugby Football in the District.

Printed & Published by Billingham & Son, Bridge St.

52 Final remembrances: the Mobbs Memorial match, 1921.

THURSDAY, FEBRUARY 10th, 1921.

East Midlands

The Barbarians

East Midlands	The Barbarians
Back :	*Back :*
1 J. MORTON (Coventry)	16 R. H. KING (Quins.)
Three-quarters :	*Threequarters :*
2 W. P. SHIRLEY (Quins) (Right)	17 R. H. HAMILTON-WICKES (Left) (Cambridge)
3 E. C. COOK (Northampton)	18 A. M. DAVID (Old Alleynians)
4 H. JONES (Richmond)	19 V. H. PRICE (Oxford)
5 G. A. KILBEY (Northampton) (Left)	20 B. L. JACOT (Oxford) (Right)
Halves :	*Halves :*
6 J. ELTON (Coventry)	21 H. J. PEMBERTON (Coventry)
7 A. TOWNELL (Edgware) (Scrum)	22 E. CAMPBELL (Oxford) (Scrum
Forwards :	*Forwards*
8 A. G. BULL (Northampton)	23 A. W. L. ROW (Blackheath)
9 H. F. NAILER ,,	24 V. GRENNING ,,
10 A. E. LUCK ,,	25 A. B. BLAKE ,,
11 H. GRIFFIN ,,	26 F. SPRIGGS ,,
12 C. P. TEBBITT ,,	27 A. B. P. ROBERTS ,,
13 S. D. KITCHENER ,,	28 H. B. T. WAKELAM (Quins)
14 T. RAWBONE (Rugby)	29 G. R. ROUGIER
15 S. BONES (Coventry)	30 H. L. PRICE (Oxford)

Referee—A. D. STOOP, Esq.   Kick-off at 3.0.

53 Adrian's final duties for a great friend.

54 Harlequins past *v.* present, 1923. From left, front row: Freek, Gracie, Birkett, Wakelam, Adrian. Holly Ward is in the striped shirt. Wakefield is behind Adrian. Sibree is second from left, third row back.

55 Harlequins 1924/25. From second left, middle row: Hamilton-Wickes, Adrian, Wakefield, V.G. Davies, Dave Davies. Far left, back row, is William 'Horsey' Brown.

56 The Grange, from the rear.

57 The Grange's gardens.

58 (above left) Adrian, late 1920s.

59 (above right) Audrey, late 1920s.

60 (right) Agnes and Frederick on their golden
wedding anniversary, 1932.

61 (left) Adrian, president of the RFU 1932/33.

62 (below) After-match reception, England v. Wales, 1933. Adrian, as president, is standing.

Quieter moments. Clockwise from above left:

63 Adrian, fishing.

64 Adrian and Audrey on holiday.

65 Adrian with Bunny, Billy, Michael and Dicky.

66-69 Adrian with Tinny Dean, teaching the legless Douglas Bader how to play golf.

70 (above left) Adrian with Bunny.

71 (above right) A man in grief. Adrian with S.F. Copper in 1936 after Billy's death.

72 (below) Billy's window. A small boy, far right, with all that Christmas day had to offer, including England's ship set fair.

Kitty Lloyd's paintings. Clockwise from top left:

73 Dicky.

74 Bunny.

75 Michael, heading off to war.

76 Adrian and the Harlequins, 1945.

77 Harlequin dinner 1947, Adrian is centre right, turning towards the camera.

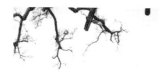

78 An old English oak.

79 Adrian with Tubby Clayton.

80 RFU duties, 1950s, Adrian is third from right, front row.

81 Four friends, Harlequins, England captains and presidents. From left: Cartwright, Adrian, 'Jenny' Greenwood, Wakefield.

82 Subject for D.Q. Fildes portrait hanging at the Stoop Memorial Ground.

ST. MARTIN-IN-THE-FIELDS

A SERVICE OF
THANKSGIVING

for the life of

ADRIAN DURA STOOP, M.C.

born March 27th, 1883, died November 27th, 1957

I HAVE fought a good fight, I have finished my course, I have kept
the faith: Henceforth there is laid up for me a crown of righteousness.
2 *Timothy* 4 : 7.

SUNT lachrymae rerum, et mentem mortalia tangunt.
Virgil, Aeneid 1 : 462.

LORD, I have loved the habitation of thy house, and the place where
thine honour dwelleth.
Psalm 26 : 8.

12 Noon

MONDAY, 9th DECEMBER, 1957

83 'I have fought a good fight, I have finished my course, I have kept the faith.'

ten

A FAMILY AFFAIR
1920-1929

The only really satisfactory aim in life is to reach an unattainable ideal.
(*The Young Idea*, Adrian Stoop)

As the war had progressed, Frederick Stoop kept himself busy, awaiting news of his sons and hoping against the worst. Having leased twelve acres of land from the Byfleet United Charities, his latest plan was to provide a recreation ground for Byfleet. This was delayed and the land was used as a market garden in its own right to provide food supplies. In 1917, after a problem in hiring horses for the local fire engine, he placed his own newly purchased lorry at the disposal of the fire brigade. Of greatest concern, however, was the safe return of his two sons. As the war came to its conclusion and his sons started to return, by way of thanks he donated £5,000 to form a pension fund for the poor of the parish. He was to take a personal interest in the administration of the fund, of which he was chairman. In further recognising a need to regroup and support in the aftermath of the war, he started and financially supported another boat club for the less well-off villagers, using craft no longer required by the original boat club.

On 28 September 1919 Freek arrived at Crystal Palace, ready for ordinary life again. Frederick grew more anxious as he awaited the arrival of his eldest and the days went on. His anxiety showed.

At the annual meeting of the Byfleet council Frederick was nominated chairman. A colleague said he would second the nomination on the condition Frederick stated his view on the proposed local housing question. Standing by his principles, he refused to accept the position if it was to be conditional on a pledged course of action. He would not be drawn into the politics surrounding the issue and would only accept if he were elected unanimously. A long and heated discussion was concluded by Frederick leaving the meeting saying he could not now accept the chairmanship or continue to be a member of the council. In his absence the council nominated and unanimously approved his election as president and, further, his representation on four committees. Attempts were made to persuade him to return, but his mind was both made up and elsewhere.

Adrian and his new family arrived at Purfleet on 23 December. It was the first time in five years that he had set foot on English soil. It was a very different England. In that time much had changed: the good had gone over the top and the lives of others had changed beyond recall.

One of the greatest reflections on the loss of life came with Edward Poulton's book, titled simply *Ronald Poulton*. The forward told of the loss of his most famous son, but also of greater tragedies. The loss as well of his daughters Emily in 1917 and Janet in 1919 would have broken many a man. This one sought solace in publishing a book of personal letters to and from Ronnie that showed his family in its truest light. Coverage in the *Meteor* took a complete page:

They were always looking for some outward and visible sign of an inward and spiritual pride, in vain because the inward pride did not exist. Not of course that he did not love football. Nobody, probably, has ever enjoyed it as much as he enjoyed it; and, through his enjoyment, he helped, at a critical moment in the history of the game to save it from becoming dull.

His portrait found a place on many a greasy wall, and still, I know, is hidden in many a grubby pocket, and in many a boyish heart.

The War Graves Commission started the long process of replacing the original makeshift wooden crosses on the battlefields of France with white marble headstones. It was Frederick who came up with the idea of, and carried out, the transportation of the wooden crosses of those who had lived in his Byfleet, so that they might be hung as a lasting tribute and memorial on the west wall of the local church. The rough wooden cross that formed the corner of a foreign cemetery and belonged to Ronald Poulton-Palmer was moved to adorn the wall of St Cross church in Oxford. His grave and those around him were replaced with, and became resplendent in, white marble.

On 21 February 1921 King George V laid a tablet at Twickenham after the Ireland game: 'In proud and grateful memory of rugby football players who gave their lives in the Great War.'

There were other, more personal, tributes to be paid. Edgar Mobbs had *been* Northampton. The town unveiled their war memorial in the town centre in 1921, and in tribute to his standing as a soldier his bust sat beneath it. As a tribute to his standing as a rugby footballer, the inaugural Mobbs Memorial match was held in the same year, between his great loves the Barbarians and the East Midlands club. Adrian refereed the game, a personal tribute to his peer, fellow captain and great friend. Their paths crossed for the final time. The minute's silence, Adrian having blown his whistle, was all the more poignant. An eerie reminder of those going over the top? Or back to the days of 1910, and the ghosts of yesteryear? Strangely, Adrian was to blow his whistle again after only sixty-eight minutes of play. A sense of irony, that the game was cut short, just as Edgar's life had been. Dai Gent reported:

The men rapidly made their way to the dressing rooms and it was not until the spectators on the unreserved stands began to protest, that Mr Stoop realised anything was wrong.

Mr Stoop would be damned if the tribute to his old friend would not go the distance:

Much perturbed, he immediately requested the players to take the field again and although Luck, the Saints' forward, was already in the bath and others were stripped and about to join him, they readily assented.

They had never found Edgar's body, but his spirit lived on.

1921 kept Adrian busy, bringing as it did a general strike and civil disturbances. He was called back up to the Army to help deal with matters between 11 April and 4 July. Four days later, after peace was resumed, he received his Military Cross.

Tributes had been paid and remembrances and memorial ceremonies were over. When friends have gone, you re-evaluate your own life and its priorities. And with your own days of youth gone, you seek other challenges. Adrian knew the past would always be there to be remembered, but he had to move forward. And he had to rebuild.

Teddy Wakelam, Holly and John had taken over the running of the Harlequins, waiting the day when the club's keeper would return. Now he was back and ready to take the helm again. Wakelam would soon move towards a career in radio. John had a family to look after. Almost immediately, Adrian took on board the club presidency and secretaryship. Holly remained as treasurer alongside him. Adrian's call to arms was simple: it was up to each one of the players to get fit and to stay fit – to play the game for their club, and as a team. As he had demonstrated once before, it was team spirit that would be at the heart of any renaissance.

New 'pupils' were found. Courtesy of Maxwell-Dove, who had noticed his rugby skills when out in the Rhine, Bill Gracie, as fine a Scottish rugby player as any, came on board. Gracie was an all-round athlete, but being foremost a sprinter, his speed was tremendous. Adrian knew another star had been found. Like Ronald Poulton, Gracie's methods were unorthodox, but as Adrian was often to say, he did everything wrong, but did it so quickly that nobody could catch up with him. With Gracie alongside Eric Liddell, Scottish rugby had never had a faster set of backs. The young pilot Wavell Wakefield found himself posted at Uxbridge, and was originally to join Blackheath. He had a reputation as a tremendous all-round athlete, being 440-yards champion for the RAF, an MCC cricketer, a top-class skier and waterskier and a sub-aqua diver. Adrian's attention was drawn to him very quickly. The last player to exhibit such all round sporting prowess had, all too fleetingly, become one of English rugby's greatest. As Cartwright had before to him, so Adrian talked the young officer into joining the Harlequins, and a lifelong friendship began.

Recognising the need, like so many in the post-war years, to be guided through its aftermath, others turned to Adrian. Surrey also made him president and so successful was his two-year tenure that they changed their rules to allow him to stay on indefinitely. They knew only too well that having elected the best available, it could only be in their interests to keep him.

Club and county were back on track. England continued almost where they had left off in 1914. Their first game back after the war on 17 January 1920 was, inevitably, against Wales. Wakefield got his first cap, and 'Jenny' Greenwood, finishing off at Cambridge, was captain. With a largely experimental pack, and a wet and muddy pitch, England lost 19-5. 'Dave' Davies was back for the next game and played throughout the rest of the season. They did not lose, and took a share in the championship. 'Dave' was captain for the next season and England won all their games.

Rugby had forever been Adrian's passion, and those parts he had loved most, the Harlequins and England, were set fair again. Now, however, he had a new perspective. A brother to Bunny, James Richard (Dicky) was born in July 1920. Having spent the best years of his life at West Hall, an ever-burgeoning family would require a place of its own. Adrian had a new mission in life.

Home from Home

Ideally any house would need to be within striking distance of West Hall and within easy access of London, and more importantly Twickenham. Trying to find a suitable place became a fruitless task. Adrian and Audrey spent many a day searching the Hampshire and Surrey villages looking at houses that were either too small or nowhere near a main road. Early in 1921 they were directed to Hartley Wintney. Pulling off the busy A30, they could not have failed to notice the golf club and the pretty cricket green, surrounded by neat little cottages and with the Cricketer's Inn almost at square leg. A short drive later, they rolled up to The Grange. The buying particulars sent to them gave a location a mile and a quarter from the nearest station, and of a thirty-acre freehold estate comprising a Tudor mansion, in well-wooded parkland, charming pleasure grounds, stabling and three cottages. The sale, by auction, would also include a fifty-eight acre working farm, several other smaller residences and fifty-seven acres of grassland.

Unsurprisingly, The Grange was the largest house in Hartley Wintney, and had a history. With parts dating back to the late seventeenth or early eighteenth centuries, the house had endured a succession of wealthy owners, each adding more features and more rooms. From 1817 to 1833, the owner had been Captain Dillon Massey, late of the 37th (North Hants) Regiment at the time of the battle of Waterloo. With a mixture of styles, the largest, most recent addition, was the east wing built in 1869 in mock Jacobean style for a wealthy Scottish banker, William Walkinshaw. The house had passed on to his son, Frank, whose wife had been the daughter of the then Lord Basing. His family lived there, playing the part of village squires, the house being of a size where it needed upwards of nine servants to keep it running. Walkinshaw supported much of what went on in the village, holding such positions as chairman of the parish council and president of the golf club.

The Stoops were greeted by the gardener-cum-caretaker. He showed them around the house, which had been empty for over twenty years and inside which nothing had been cared for since. Cobwebs and darkened rooms gave it a ghostly feel. The fifteen bedrooms, five bathrooms, morning room, dining room, sitting rooms, kitchens and staff quarters made it more than just an ordinary house. The walled kitchen garden was enormous. Outbuildings and the attached farm seemed lost in the general acreage that surrounded. Audrey was taken from the first step. Adrian knew the road outside led directly to Twickenham. The gardener did not know who the couple were, but having shown many around already, he fully expected the disappointment when the huge reserve price was mentioned.

The speculative journey that day was to change their lives forever. Later that evening back at West Hall, Frederick knew his son had seen the house he wanted to bring his family up in. He also knew they could not afford it. He did however offer to visit it the next day. Agnes was unmoved. She had spent many a year before the war trying to set her son up with a wife, yet he had waited until India to find one. She had also hoped he would find a house closer by.

The next day Frederick and Agnes saw how much the house could mean to their son and his wife. Frederick dropped by the auction at St James Place in the summer and paid for the house as a belated wedding present.

Once in, Adrian and Audrey set to readying the house. Planting enough fruit and vegetables to keep the house going, flowers and plants for the house were grown in the many greenhouses. A cook, kitchen maid, housemaid, parlour maid, chauffeur, butler, houseboy, nanny, and nursery maid were hired for the inside. For outside, they found gardeners, a carpenter, a painter and decorator. The farm was let out and the cottages for the chauffeur and head gardener were readied. Almost before they had time to move in and settle, another son, Michael, was born in 1922.

The sudden activity up at the big house caught the attention of the local villagers. Before long Adrian and Audrey had got to meet most of them. Edward Lloyd in particular had many a tale to tell. Being an Old Rugbeian, he had lived in the village since well before the turn of the century. Excelling at cricket, he was the president of the local cricket club, a sport that Adrian still maintained more than a passing interest in. In Edward's daughter Kitty, a keen local artist, tennis player and beekeeper, Adrian found a good friend.

Friends old and new joined in the April 1922 Harlequins 'past *v.* present' game, played, appropriately, at Twickenham. Among the past players were Herbert, Adrian (once more as captain), Freek, John, Holly and G.D. Roberts. On Wakelam's present team were Wakefield, Gracie, Gibbs, Hamilton-Wickes and V.G. Davies. Fitness counted against the 'old boys', but they showed enough of the skills for which they had once been famed, and avoided any trips to the King Edward's Hospital to which the proceeds went. 1922 closed with Captain Stoop being transferred to the reserve list on 22 December. His army days were all but over and other, more painful memories were laid to rest. The following year memories of a different kind were celebrated.

The centenary game at Rugby School saw England and Wales taking on Scotland and Ireland. It was also the golden anniversary of Frederick's landing in England. To mark the occasion, a copy of the Stoop Family Triptych was given to him. The painting adorned the entrance hall of West Hall, a proud reminder of a great family history, alongside the Stoop coat of arms. Unsurprisingly, the occasion became an excuse, as if they needed one, for a family party at the great old house. As part of the festivities, the family posed for photographs representing up-to-date wings to the triptych. Where this one differed, happily, was in the complete representation of all the sons and daughters before it was finished. No need for crosses above the departed this time. To complete everyone's happiness, Adrian and Audrey's youngest and last son, William Francis (Billy), was born on 25 December. Being the last, 'exceptionally sweet' and born on Christmas Day, he became popular with everyone. The family was now complete, and Christmases were to be the happiest of occasions. With four sons in four years, Adrian had not only overcome his personal injuries – he was well on the way to producing his own team.

Adrian's life continued apace. He still played on occasions for the Harlequin firsts. During a game against Leicester the London referee unfairly penalised Leicester, and Adrian deliberately put the free kick to touch to restore Leicester's advantage. A little later, a Leicester player was sent off, again unjustly. Adrian sent off one of his own to even things up. It was good to be playing again. And although his involvement on the international playing front had ended before the war, his reputation was about to earn him a succession of roles in the RFU. As well as still being the Central District representative, he became a member of the International Board in 1923. He was being given the opportunity to divest his rugby knowledge yet further for the good of the game.

At the Harlequins, new players were about to start out on long careers, knowing that they would be schooled yet further by one of the greats. 'Horsey' Browne was one such player. The great Irish forward of the bullet head, squat face and flattened nose would have held his own in any dispute. His genial nature, however, was one that saw him get on in any company, and he was never too proud to learn. Horsey was a reminder to Adrian of the golden days, a fellow after his own heart. Still going on his beloved tours, Adrian joked around with some other residents of their Welsh hotel. Demonstrating to a youngster how to fall on the ball, Horsey quickly suggested the boy kick him when he was down. So rarely was he found there, no one else had ever had the chance! Adrian reminded the boy that a fly half on his feet was worth ten on the ground. Everyone knew that Horsey would forever be the life and soul, taking over from Wakelam as court jester.

1924 saw the Paris Olympics. One of the first events was to be the rugby. Rugby had been included a few times since the inaugural games. Indeed, in 1920, a team from America had beaten France 8-0 in the games, these being only the two teams entered. In April 1924, Adrian asked the RFU committee for approval to play a Californian team en route to the Olympics. All he could add was that there was little information about them, except that Valentine was an Oxford Blue. The American team was made up mostly of college students from Stanford, inexperienced in the finer arts of the game. They were to play a series of warm-up games in England first. The first two they won.

The last, against the Harlequins, was won by the home side: little surprise, containing as it did, among others, Horsey and Dave Davies, who at Adrian's behest was seeing out the end of his career with his great friend and one-time sparring partner. The young Americans had learnt first hand what no amount of amateur practice could give them – any side coached by Adrian Stoop was a tough prospect. Impressed enough by the fixture with the Harlequins and the reputation of their president, Adrian was asked to train and coach the Americans in their run-up to the Olympic tournament. He did so. The Games themselves consisted of only three teams. The Americans duly beat Romania and then France in a savage final distinguished only by the inspired passing and running display put on by the Americans. Gold medallists, they had learnt well.

1925 was very much a year for forward planning. First up, on 3 January, was the game that everyone wanted to see: England against the visiting, once again undefeated, All Blacks. The 60,000 crowd that crammed into the recently extended Twickenham was the greatest ever for a rugby game. Those sitting in the new North Stand had a perfect view of the angles of running and positional sense. To Adrian, this was a game he could have wished for twenty years prior. His Harlequins, Gibbs, Hamilton-Wickes, Kitterminster and V.G. Davies made up the lion's share of the backs, Wakefield was captain in the forwards. Shades of yesteryear. England came into the game having won every game they had played since 1921 bar a loss to Wales and a draw to France. The championship of 1923, with Dave Davies' last international game, was won outright, as was that of 1924 under Wakefield's captaincy.

With Brownlie sent off after just ten minutes, the fourteen-man All Blacks went on to win a classic. An injury to Gibbs evened up the sides, but uppermost was the performance of the Harlequins. Proud as ever, Adrian updated his own view of England's greatest ever:

This [England *v*. France 1911] *was probably the most brilliant team of the century, perhaps sharing the distinction with Wavell's team against the All Blacks, when the Harlequins again supplied the fly half and three three-quarters.*

The year progressed with Adrian becoming more immersed in the administration of the game, and putting his strongly held views about. An early-April meeting of the RFU was held to consider the length of term the president should be in office for. The meeting was opened with a letter of protest from Mr Wray against a remark made by Adrian at the previous meeting. Few normally escaped Adrian's demanding nature. Adrian apologised and withdrew the remark complained of. His increasing series of responsibilities saw him focus on the laws, finance and ground sub-committees. Taking both the latter roles seriously, he effectively put in a letter to himself complaining on behalf of the Harlequins about their leasing arrangements, considering fifteen per cent of gross receipts to a minimum of £35 (including parking) to be too high a minimum.

With an expanded Twickenham, the next big development phase for his club involved the continued search for a new ground for the 'A' team.

Adrian became trustee of Harlequin Estates. Four and five per cent debentures were issued, the principle subscribers Frederick, Adrian, Freek and John. A site was purchased for £2,125 in Fairfax Road, Teddington, with another £3,700 being spent on a pavilion.

1926 saw Ireland win their first game against England since 1911. Wakefield's last games as captain saw a mixed season. The next season Adrian became an international selector, giving him plenty of opportunity to air his thoughts on players once more. His task was made all the more difficult with the selection in January of Hamilton-Wickes and Gibbs as wings, Worton at scrum-half, and his new boy, Laird, as fly half. The four-strong Harlequin representation in the backs meant Adrian would have to go some to avoid a charge of favouritism. The youngest player to play for England, at a few months over eighteen years, Laird at fly half had a huge legacy to fulfil. England won and the pressure was off. Or should have been. Another mixed season came and went. With Dave Davies as a fellow selector the following year, Adrian had a like mind. With the two in tandem, nobody would have bet against a good year for England. They won the Championship, and beat an Australian touring side – five matches won in a season for the first time ever.

Others too were starting to bask in the rosy glow. For the 1928/29 season, Lump was president of the RFU. Adrian was one of his vice-presidents. Wakefield, whose own stock had risen immeasurably, inscribed in a copy of his co-written book *Rugger*:

Adrian

Whatever merits this book may have are due in no uncertain measure to your help in the past few years.

With our very best wishes,

W.W. Wakefield, H. Marshall

Adrian too contributed to his sport's literary heritage, going back to Rugby School to help write and publish its footballing records. There was probably no-one better placed to do so. The time he spent there gave him an opportunity to see how the school had moved on, ready for when his sons would be sent their after their initial education at Rottingdean. The seeds of his next writings were all but sown.

The Young Idea contained all facets of the game as Adrian believed it should be played, using the school education system as source:

I am a great believer in the game as an educative force if it is played as a game, but not if it is learned as a lesson… the best way to learn is by making mistakes, as long as they are your own and you do not blame others for your own.

At the heart of this discourse was the notion that people did not go to school for the teaching, merely the educative values. Any school should establish a sound tradition, based on sound principles, and let the pupils work out the rest. The pupils should also learn by their mistakes. Moreover, it was they who were the guardians of those traditions. The masters were but paid servants of the school. Traditions undermined their authority. The master should subordinate all his personal feelings in the interests of the school. Teaching was the duty of encouraging self-reliance and a sense of honour, as apparent in the games system at Rugby School at the turn of the century. The ideal was to produce a team of players who could think for a whole game, under a captain who knew how to lead. Leadership was the product of experience, for which brains could not be put to best use unless one had mastered the absolute basics, for which constant practice was needed. The mechanical details should make no demand on the brain, allowing it to be devoted entirely to the game.

The Young Idea considered the basic principles of tackling, passing, dribbling, kicking and throwing in, and the rudiments of play for the forwards (a second's delay meant a loss of eight yards to backs), half-backs (speed first, accuracy second), fly half (swing and pass out within two strides), three-quarters (make openings for the wings), wings (the main weapon a change of pace) and full-back (ten to touch better than forty not).

Once again a rugby public listened intently.

Frederick had always shown an interest in his sons' young ideas, supporting them to the hilt. And what he cared for now as much as for anything was the visits of his sons, daughters, and now grandchildren. As with Adrian and Freek years before, the youngsters found themselves in a paradise that could only otherwise be dreamt of. Swimming in the river became a highlight of the trips, the challenge being to swim across it for the first time – £5 being the prize for the achievement. Michael earned his money when barely five. When asked what he would do with it, he suggested buying London. He was too young to know that but fifteen years beforehand his father had all but been given the keys to it.

Life had become rich again, a fact reflected in the kind, and indeed lavish, hospitality Adrian and Audrey showed to friends and acquaintances at The Grange. Their staff were equally happy with the kindness that their employers bestowed on them, and tried hard to please. What they became acutely aware of, if they weren't already, was that rugby was Adrian's life. Every weekend he gathered around him friends, players and anyone else who was as sold on the game as he was. The gardeners particularly thought their employer to be quite mad, finding as they did rugby balls flying past them as they worked. Not wishing to leave them out, Adrian got them into the spirit of it by having them join in. The waiting staff found it difficult to keep straight faces as Adrian bowled apples along the great dining table to fielding dinner guests, judging the bounces to left and right perfectly.

Everything about the place seemed idyllic. The Stoops were so relaxed that they cared little for the seemingly odd events that happened in the house: the strange grey light that appeared to Audrey in her bedroom and the ghostly smiling lady who appeared sitting at her dressing table. No one cared until one night Billy awoke from his bed in his parent's room. He complained of a strange man, dressed all in black with a cowl over his head, standing by his bed; of the man bending over him; of the man trying to take him away. Adrian put on a light. No one was there, yet Billy remained terrified. Try as they might, his parents were unable to calm him that night.

The next day the Stoops found out some of the secrets of their house. They were told of the murder of a young girl centuries before and of a monk on a mission. To older inhabitants of the village, it seemed the great house retained some strange link with an altogether ethereal world. The answer was to have the house exorcised. Thereafter, the grey light and the smiling lady remained, but the monk never came back.

Life moved on and, like the greenery at the Grange, remained rosy. Competition among the Stoop households remained as pleasant as ever. West Hall's gardens had a good thirty-five year start on The Grange and Frederick's produce had already started to be noted by the Royal Horticultural Society – his apple 'Byfleet Seedling' being recommended for inclusion in the commercial fruit trials being held at nearby Wisley. Adrian's vying with his father for the best garden would take time.

As the decade closed, Adrian's immediate efforts lay with the Laws committee. In January 1929 he raised the question of referees penalising players for offside merely because they were in front of the ball. The whole issue of offside was of importance, many an international referee administering it differently.

The trials and tribulations of rugby referees came fairly low down on the Richter scale when later that year the American stock market crashed. A world slump was just around the corner. The Harlequins lost £1,600 in investments, Adrian too on some of his own. The letting of his farm, Harlequin debentures and marble mine at least kept his financial portfolio fairly well buffered.

—w—

SEISMIC SHIFTS
1930-1939

Always play with the wind. At half-time it may change around and blow in the opposite direction.

(*Captaincy*, Adrian Stoop)

Going into the 1930s, most of the important areas of Adrian's life were in a settled state. Parts of Twickenham were once more involved in a rebuilding programme, the West Stand gaining an extra tier. If the spring of 1910 had been a pivotal and defining time in Adrian's life and career, February of that year was also the month of Douglas Bader's birth. Now aged twenty-one, Bader was the outstanding athlete of his day, being compared favourably to Poulton before him: 'a strong, beautiful and toned human machine' – the similarities were there for all to see. To Adrian he was the new Poulton. As a cadet at Cranwell, Bader got his Blues for cricket, rugby, hockey and boxing. He played for the RAF at cricket and rugby. And by the late 1920s, he was a Harlequins man, more than holding down the celebrated fly half position of his club president.

Adrian's role as international selector had Bader pencilled in for a likely England slot. Another of Adrian's half-backs of promise, G.J. (Tinny) Dean, had just got into the England team, and after the successful seasons of Wakefield and Gracie and Browne, he had great hopes for his new stars.

Adrian was re-elected vice-president of the RFU, but 1931 was to be a difficult year after the severance of relations with the French RFU due to the unsatisfactory condition of the game in France. Despite an honest 3-0 victory in 1927, France's first ever against the English, professionalism had crept in and their second victory that year was to be the last game between the two for many a season. England lost all four of their games, the first time they had been winless since 1905. Internationally there was clearly much work to be done.

Away from the commercial matters surrounding his rugby offices, money, or rather the keeping of it, was not Adrian's strong point: he had it, it looked after itself and generally got spent for the benefit and further-ance of others. The Grange served as the centre of the Harlequin scene. With so many bedrooms, Adrian had long since realised its potential, not just as a social centre for his rugby friends, but as a training ground as well. With such a grand house and visits from the rich and famous, the Stoops had become the aristocracy of the village, much as the Walkinshaws had been before. But while in some ways they fitted that style of life, being rich enough and well-heeled with it, somehow it rested heavily with them and they were reluctant to fully act the part. Adrian would often be seen running the lanes around the house, kitted up, caring little who saw him. He would often drive down to the postbox at the end of the lane in his drophead coupé, roof down whatever the weather, on the wrong side of the road, just so he could post a letter without exiting the car. He was noted as something of a flamboyant driver, despite having a chauffeur as well. And as his men trained on the lawns, Audrey liked to help out in the hayfields and around the farm. The grounds were often opened up for the village functions. Above all, they became known for their generosity, much as Frederick and Agnes had over at Byfleet.

Another side to Adrian came out, the one that had seen him keep young Cooper in good spirits many a year ago when the boy had broken his leg. The recipient of Adrian's well-being this time was poor Horsey Browne. When in 1931 he was taken ill with cancer, those who knew him could not reconcile the tragic illness with the man they had come to love. Initially put up in a military hospital where the best medical treatment was brought in, when it became obvious that nothing more could be done, Adrian transferred him to The Grange. There he stayed his last few days with his parents, and among friends.

Adrian's association with the Hartley Wintney cricket team led to many a game with them. The cricket club welcomed the influence of their benefactor, who made sure he balanced their books at the end of each year. Wakelam had already organised a Harlequins side to play at Hartley Wintney the weekend after Horsey's death. The mood was sombre and reconciliatory. Nevertheless, all parties got on with it, as Horsey would have wished. Dave Davies came along and was run out by Adrian, keeping wicket, for 40. Wakelam broke his collarbone: business almost as usual. After the game, a gymkhana and sweet treasure hunt was put on for the children. The adults had their own party later, for which there could be but one sad toast.

Less reported, but of relative significance, came the death of Dicky Owen, Adrian's adversary in the 1910 Wales game. Owen had played the game for the love of it, as had Adrian. He was one of Wales' greatest and his death provided a frank reminder to all the greats who live too long on the memories, when the legs and lucky sixpences have gone, along with the adulation. Once a steelworker, now a publican, down on his luck and down to his last few pennies, Owen swallowed his beer and his pride and committed suicide in squalid circumstances, bottle still in hand. Tragedies like this remind one of how fragile one's hold on life can be

Surrounded by his wife and four sons, Adrian's life moved slowly on.

It was not only the Harlequins who benefited from the sessions on the lawn. The maids at the Grange were also all up early, cycling along the lanes before work. Adrian even insisted on an earlier start come late spring, so that they could wash their faces in the dew to keep them fresh! Adrian's sons got used to their father's penchant for fitness: the runs, the cold baths and, strangest of all, a unique method of running with a rugby ball – head back, arms outstretched, waving side to side, legs crossing over mystifyingly. It seemed strange to the young boys, but to have mastered the technique would have been to become the master. If his sons could do one thing to make Adrian happy, it would be to emulate the skill that had disappeared in 1915.

Poulton's memory lived on long in Adrian's mind. Michael showed real promise as a rugby player, but young Billy's interest knew no bounds. Adrian had hopes that one or the other would follow in their father's exalted footsteps. The sons loved their father's indulgence when time could be found. Often he would be seen in the North Stand of Twickenham, behind the posts, alongside one of his sons, pointing out the better aspects of the game afore them. Sitting behind the north goalposts allowed a north-south perspective to see how the backs lined themselves up and, most of all, to see if they ran straight.

Every Christmas the local 'Mummers' came around, three or four of the local lads, dressed up, and carrying sticks and lanterns. Invited into the hall at The Grange, they play-acted fights with their wooden swords and 'performed acts of the devil', lying dead on the floor at the end, all in exchange for a few drinks. The celebrations were but a small prelude to the main event – Billy's birthday on Christmas Day.

Gradually the boys took on personalities of their own. Bunny was the quieter and more studious one, Michael the more mischievous. Speed and the spirit of adventure was Dicky's attraction. He was greatly interested in motor cars and spent many a day cycling off to Brooklands with Michael to see the racing cars. Billy remained the cute one. He was adored by his parents, his brothers and the staff. A governess was employed to ready each son for school: first Rottingdean and then Rugby. They adored their home and they adored their parents, who had the knack of continually surprising them: trips to London to see all the exciting things the capital had to offer; their first bicycles and cameras; Adrian, whom they hero worshipped, showing them the delights of rugby and cricket; at weekends a day out on the village green watching their father captaining the local side; sometimes even a trip up to Twickenham to see an international. They knew they were lucky to have the parents they did. As far as they were concerned that would never change. The family enjoyed their lives to the full, even if to some they appeared as mad as hatters.

Hospital Pass

As far as fitness went, the qualities that made Bader an exceptional athlete also made him an exceptional pilot. He was one of the team of two selected to perform the star aerobatics turn of the RAF display at Hendon. However, he had other things on his mind. The Springboks had arrived from South Africa for a series of tests, and with the goal of getting into the England side in front of him he was training harder than ever before. As November 1931 rolled on, he was aware that the international selectors would be watching him, but was dismayed that he was over-trained and had not been playing well. One of South Africa's early tour games was to be against the Combined Services. As last season's England fly half also played for the Navy, were Bader to be chosen for the Services in preference to him, he would probably be in for England.

Adrian hoped that his latest protégé had crossed the mark. As much influence as he might have had, ultimately the responsibility for selection was the selection committee's. Besides, he had other matters to attend to. Bader's international career would happen one day, if not just now. Frederick, however, was hospitalised and undergoing a major operation. The hospitals were kind to the man who had benefited them most. Whether the local Pyrford or other Surrey hospitals, Frederick was always a generous subscriber to a rebuild or an extension project. Just recently he had donated £500 to the building fund of the Weybridge hospital.

At the end of November Bader's wait was over. He was selected to play at fly half for the Combined Services.

In the game itself Bader played with a dashing, high-geared vigour. Those old enough and lucky enough to have seen the young Poulton saw something they remembered fondly. Just after half-time, Bader flung himself at a giant Springbok forward just as he made for the line. In halting him, and stopping a certain try in the process, he sustained a broken nose. The only thing on his mind was the England game in less than three weeks. There was too much at stake to worry about it, too much yearning for that first cap. He played on.

The following weekend, on 12 December, he played again for the Harlequins, 'not even bothering to strap his nose first. He tried his hardest, but kept fumbling passes and spent the rest of the weekend worrying about his uneven form.'

On the morning of Monday the 14th, Bader was up early in his Bulldog, practising aerobatics. Seeing some colleagues flying over to Woodley aerodrome near Reading, he tacked on to make a threesome. On landing he regaled the young pilots there in the theory of aerobatics. One suggested a demonstration. Realising he was off limits, and having been reprimanded for such before, he declined. The goading, however, got too much. Bader could not resist the challenge. Up he went in the Bulldog and turned, slanting down to make a low run of the field. The Bulldog, however, was not the normal aerobatics Gamecock. Being heavier, it was more difficult to manoeuvre. A left wing tip hit the ground, pulling down the nose down sharply. The plane somersaulted into a crumpled mess. Dazed, Bader tried to make sense of his predicament. His knees felt funny and his right leg jutted out at an impossible angle. He could not see his left. Blood spurted on to his white overalls. He knew he wouldn't be playing rugby on Saturday.

He was taken straight to the Royal Berkshire Hospital, where both his legs were amputated. He would have died but for Adrian's intervention.

Hospitals seemed to be a way of life for Adrian at the time. First Horsey, then his father, now Bader. Adrian paid for the top surgeons and medics available in the hope Bader might be returned to reasonable health, pulling as many strings in the hospitals as could be afforded.

Adrian and Audrey kept visiting as the recovery slowly continued. Several times they drove him to The Grange for tea. Being in acres of lawn and parkland, surrounded by friendliness and away from prying eyes would aid the recovery yet further.

Eventually Bader would have to leave the hospital to be administered to by the RAF. Adrian's continued hospitality knew no bounds. During this time Bader was to stay many a night at The Grange, becoming almost permanently housed there. One morning he scared the life out of a maid by bouncing down the stairs on his backside and hands, because he couldn't be bothered to put his legs on to go and pick up something trivial. The recuperation of Bader took place while Adrian had other, weightier, matters to contend with.

Frederick had recovered enough to celebrate his golden wedding anniversary. The most lavish of all their parties was held in its celebration, to which the whole parish was invited. The residents of Byfleet seized the opportunity to express their own gratitude and affection. A tablet, placed in the village hall was unveiled:

On 1 June 1932, the golden wedding anniversary of Mr and Mrs F.C. Stoop of West Hall, this brass is put up by their neighbours to the end that their many acts of kindness and gifts for the public good may ever be had in remembrance. During their 38 years residence in the parish they have ever been foremost in everything which made for the welfare of the people of Byfleet, whose esteem and affection they have won by their personal service and thoughtful care for others.

1932 was the year that the worldwide depression reached its nadir. An opportunity arose to purchase a further twenty-eight acres of ground to provide greater car-parking and training facilities at Twickenham. Given the economic climate, the RFU decided against the further commitment. Later that year, Adrian's long and distinguished Central District representation came to an end and he was made the 32nd president of the RFU. Of all the positions he had held, this was the one that meant the most. His father, proud of all his sons' achievements, knew Adrian had fulfilled his greatest promise. His involvement in rugby had taken him from his early school days to the presidency of the RFU. It was a journey of incredible highs and lows, dramatic and at times intense. There had been moments of gloom and moments of glory. He had given the nation so much. Now it had returned the favour.

In his presidential year, a number of challenges were presented for adjudication. Rugby football by floodlight at paid-for games was deemed not in the best interests of the game. On a serious but seemingly lighter note came the curious case of the 8ft 5in New South Wales outback player who, with a height of 10ft-plus with outstretched hands, could deflect penalties from crossing the post. As the rules implied that defending players should remain passive when kicks were taken, the action of raising the arms was deemed contrary to this. So too the subject of replacements for injuries. A request had come from New Zealand for dispensation against the prohibition of this. Adrian, in response to a letter from their union, replied:

The letter of October 13th last from your Union on the subject of Law 12 – replacement of injured players, has received long and anxious and not unsympathetic consideration by the Committee of the RFU and the International Board... in the first place we are strongly opposed to the practice of replacement. It is contrary to our traditions, and any alteration in our attitude towards it would be attended by grave risks to the game as played over here. In the second place, the International Board has expressed its opinion that Law 12 does not contemplate replacements. We regard accidents as 'all in the game' and so to speak, 'a rub of the green'. The practice of replacement of injured players does not prevail in any other Rugby playing country, and we consider it to be a matter of vital importance that the British Commonwealth of Nations should show a united front as regards the rules and conduct of the game. For these reasons we urge you most earnestly to do your utmost to keep in line with us.

All in a days work. Laws were one thing, selecting a team, however, was another.

The first international of his presidential year took place on 21 January 1933, the opponents, appropriately, Wales. Right from that inaugural Twickenham game of 1910, Wales, like the Irish, had continually found the English ground a graveyard to their own fortunes. For this game, however, Wales came with seven new caps, and ironically a strong Varsities component. Under the inspired leadership of their captain, the young Welsh back division carried the day. England lost a player through injury. Controversy ran to the end: having been leading 4-3, Wales scored a try to take the score to 7-3. Amid the crowd's frenzy, no one, not even the score-keeper, knew whether Wales had converted the try. Had the kick been given, England would have to score a converted try themselves to take the game. There was outrage when at the end of the game the referee indicated that he had not given the conversion, whence a drop at goal would have sufficed to save the game. Regardless, the books recorded a Welsh victory, and the Stoop-inspired millstone against them had been finally been consigned to the history books. It had taken twenty-two years to wrest back the laurels. To rub it in, England lost 0-3 to Scotland and 16-17 to Ireland.

On 27 March 1933 a letter came through stating that as of 1 April Adrian had reached the Army age limit and would have to relinquish his commission. A reminder, if any were needed, that age catches up with us all. Loss of records and titles pale in significance, however, to the loss of friends. As his presidency year continued, death removed a number of outstanding figures from the English game, including Ernest Prescott the treasurer.

Personal grief followed when on 10 July 1933 Frederick Stoop died in his sleep. He had never fully recovered from his operation of sixteen months earlier, and his health had steadily declined thereafter. Having just returned from a trip to the South of France, his illness had taken a serious turn, and his death was not unexpected. The funeral was held three days later. The Netherlands minister attended and flags at all the local clubs and schools were flown at half mast. All of his sons and daughters were there except Nellie, her ill health keeping her away.

Byfleet mourned with the Stoops. Frederick was held in universal esteem. For forty years his interest in the well-being of the village and its inhabitants was both personal and practical, his generosity unbounded. Whether it had been the provision of sewerage facilities or surface-water drainage schemes, he had always been prompt to further any scheme that would be of benefit to the local inhabitants. Always in mind of his roots and the community around him, his will bequeathed a number of assets for the good of others, including the old boathouse and its fleet of boats to the parish council.

On 16 September *Country Life* carried an advertisement: 'To be sold freehold, an important residential estate of one hundred acres.' The virtues of the West Hall estate were extolled, including the magnificent accommodation, the garage and stabling facilities, and the grounds. A chapter in local history was over.

The Stoops' bequests continued with the death of Frederick's brother Cornelius in the same year. His private art collection was bequeathed to the Tate. Among his collection were several Van Goghs, including 1890's *Farmhouse near Auvers*, as well as works by Braques, Cézanne, Degas, Matisse, Rousseau, Modigliani and Laurencin. Also, Picasso's *Femme avec Chemise (Madeleine)*, *Horse with a Youth in Blue*, and *Seated Woman in a Chemise*.

The death of his father and uncle hit hard. Further loss occurred with the early death of his sister Nellie in 1934. The grief was only partially abated with the birth of Audrey's sister's son at the 'hospital' that had become The Grange.

Bader's recovery process was slow, but Adrian was determined that with so much sadness around, one of his own would come through. Gradually he and Audrey introduced Bader to their other friends, that he might slowly rebuild his confidence in public situations as his new legs became more familiar to him. Over time people merely assumed him to be a young man with a bad limp. One night they took him to a nearby party where someone put on a gramophone and couples started dancing. Not to be outdone a new challenge, Bader asked a young girl to dance. As they started he caught his toe, falling over and nearly taking the girl with him. As he got clumsily up, she proclaimed him drunk and left. She later found out the truth. Bader's next victim was to be Adrian's testy wire-haired terrier dog, Worry. At dinner times, Worry would amuse himself under the table by partaking of a victim's leg should they have the misfortune to place it in his reserved spot. The poor animal met his match when trying to feast on Bader's tin leg. He ran off, hairs bristling, tail between his legs.

Using Adrian's influence and contacts, Bader landed a clerical job with Shell, long-standing favours between the Stoop family and the oil company being returned in kind. Around this time, with Adrian's gentle persuasion and using his never-ending stream of contacts, Bader started flying again. Soon there was little the instructors could teach him. Legs or no legs, he mastered the art again with little trouble. His renewed confidence knew no bounds. Soon he was to meet his wife, Thelma, at his regular haunt, Pantiles, a tea shop in Bagshot. They got on from the start. Almost immediately she was taken to The Grange to meet the people who had made him almost whole again. Drawing from their own personal experience they approved wholeheartedly.

Adrian believed, based on his own experiences, that Bader would never be complete again unless he returned to the grounds that they had both once graced. The game he chose to take him back to Twickenham to see was one that meant much to Adrian too. Harlequins *v.* Richmond, the game that had kick-started his own resurrection so many years before. Bader was very excited leading up to the game, a sense of belonging again, perhaps held in check by the raw emotion and nerves he felt. Shortly after kick-off the Harlequins set up their wing for a dazzling try. It was just like the old days for both men. But Bader suddenly became quiet and did not speak for the rest of the game. Adrian knew almost immediately the try was scored that he had made a mistake, but that it would be an even worse one to suggest that they leave. In that hour Bader felt more bitterly than ever before the loss of his legs. All his old friends were playing and it hurt. On the way back to The Grange, the conversation was of other things. Bader later told Thelma he would never watch another game of rugby, and he never did.

Undeterred, Adrian resorted to plan B. Along with Tinny Dean, they took Bader out to a nine-hole golf course nearby, suggesting he see them hit off, and maybe walk the first couple of holes with them. Bader said he would hang around and wait for them to return. Adrian gave him a seven iron and a ball and told him to mess around while the two played. After they had gone off, and away from any scrutiny, Bader placed the ball and took a swipe. He fell over. Again he tried. Again he fell. Try as he might he made no contact. Another challenge. Eventually he connected. Lying on his back he could see the ball soar through the air. He kept on trying.

The next day he took the seven iron out on to the lawns at the Grange. This time Adrian coached him. On occasions he connected, but each time he fell. The next challenge was to hit the ball and remain standing. He succeeded. Gradually Adrian helped him to find the right stance. Bader was fortunate, for he could not have had a better tutor. The next weekend he continued. Determination gave way to obsession. Adrian knew Bader had got the bug. He would now be able to play sport again on even terms with the world again. Golf was to be the drug that made his life complete. From that moment he took on any challenge that came his way. Tennis was next, the courts at the Grange having as fine a surface as any, and many a welcome visitor. Kitty Lloyd was as fierce an opponent as any, possessing an underarm serve to test the finest, legs or no legs.

Where Bader did not succeed too well was in keeping his MG sports car free from scrapes. At Virginia Water, coming over a hill while returning to London, Bader and Thelma were involved in an accident with a motorbike and sidecar, Thelma sustaining a cut nose and black eye in the process. A few months later, on the way to Rugby, following another bump, this time with a Rolls, Bader's co-passenger received the same injuries. They were lucky to have received such relatively slight injuries. Bader had made great strides to get himself reinstated in the RAF, and was soon to find himself alone in a plane again for the first time since his accident.

As Bader continued his rehabilitation, Adrian was in the autumn of his life, trying to enjoy his final playing days, and the twilight of his career.

Land Slip

1935 was not to be a good year.

It was the year of the King's Silver Jubilee, and celebrations were many and varied. The Barbarians played London in an exhibition game. In Hartley Wintney a huge fête was held with all the usual rides and attractions. Adrian was in fine form. The highlight for the parishioners was the penny-farthing: five bob to the oldest man and woman who could complete a circuit of the field on it. The local bobby had not endeared himself recently by penalising one of the locals for showing the whites of his car tyres. Now off duty, he was unceremoniously tipped off the bike almost as soon as he had started. Adrian completed the circuit like a two-year-old.

Congratulations were also due to Wakefield on being made an MP, but that was as far as the happiness went.

On 4 January the island of Mamara suffered an earthquake. To the west the foghorn building was demolished and the cape part of the island broke off and disappeared into the sea. A tidal wave followed. Production from the marble mines was suspended. In the relative scheme of things it potentially meant a while out of production and loss of earnings. Of greater concern to Adrian, however, was the health of others: his uncle Adriaan, but more importantly, his mother Agnes, who had been unwell for a while.

On the night of Thursday 28 June Agnes became seriously ill. The following morning, such was her concern for others, on realising she had a few hours to live, she calmly dictated her parting wishes and remembrances – thinking of others to the very end. She lapsed into unconsciousness and died shortly afterwards. Again, the public of Byfleet mourned the passing of a cherished neighbour, one who like Frederick had given her all to the village. She had been president of the sports club, having taken over the presidency on the death of Frederick. Adrian too mourned the death of his mother, as she lay in the Upper Chamber of the as yet unsold West Hall in her last sleep.

The funeral service took place the following Tuesday at St Mary's church, prior to interment at Brookwood Cemetery. The mourners were

many, including close members of the Dutch side of the family, representatives of all the parish services, clubs and hospitals and all the West Hall
staff. John Birkett supported his friend to the end.

1935 came to a sad close with news of his uncle Adriaan's death. Where
the years to 1932 had been triumphant, the years from 1933 to 1935 had
recorded such sadness that 1936 must surely stand still to allow time for
the grieving process. It started with the death, on 20 January 1936, of King
George V, patron of the RFU and spectator of many a great game at
Twickenham.

18 April 1936 was a fine spring day. Adrian decided that a trip to Bath
to see the game that day should be a family outing. However, the day being
so fine, Michael and Dicky wished to see the racing at Brooklands and set
off early on their cycles. Adrian left with Audrey, Bunny and Billy in the
car to see the game. They took a picnic and stopped at a picturesque village
on the way. Setting off again in good spirits, they failed to see, and collided
with, a lorry coming up the same hill that they were going down. Billy,
who had been sitting on his mothers lap, was thrown through the wind-
screen. As Adrian and Audrey got out of the car, they saw their young son
lying unconscious, bleeding profusely from his head. They were unable to
stem the initial flow. The nearest hospital was miles away. Eventually they
got him there where he was admitted for an operation.

The Stoops waited for what seemed an eternity before the surgeon
stepped out to see them. His face gave away the news. Their youngest son
was dead.

They took him home, where he stayed in his bed until his funeral. No
one had closed his eyes, so while he stayed there he looked as if his spirit
was still with him. The family were shattered, their lives changed forever.
Losing Billy left a terrible mark on Adrian and he felt he would never be
the same again. Adrian had reckoned himself to be a bit of a faith healer.
He needed to pull himself around again. He had been through many a
period of mental and physical pain, and had always come out the other
side. But this was a different situation altogether. During the First World
War, Audrey had been a great source of strength, their relationship drawing
on the emotive losses elsewhere. She knew that, again, life had to go on.

Grief stricken as she was, Audrey had to shake Adrian out of his terrible
depression. They booked a quiet holiday away from it all at their house in
Saalbach in Austria. Up in the mountains, they could cut themselves off
from the world and try to come to terms with this latest tragedy.

The Stoops paid to have a great memorial stained-glass window fitted
in St John's church in Hartley Wintney, in tribute to their lost son. Instead
of religious deities and great saints, the magnificent windows depicted
Billy and but one saint, Nicolas, with all his associations with Christmas

and their son's birthday of 25 December. For the Stoops the window would be a permanent reminder of how happy Christmases past had been. Christmas would never be the same again.

Adrian's grief and sadness was magnified by a strain this tragedy was to place on his marriage. Audrey was twelve years younger than Adrian and in her earlier years had learned to adapt away from a family set-up. Adrian's life had always been one of loving attention. The two dealt with their loss in their own ways, but somehow they lost a part of themselves along the way. Despite the internal problems, The Grange remained an open house for Harlequins, friends and villagers: to the outside world the couple exuded charm and delight, on the inside they were burning up.

A growing interest in spiritualism took on a greater depth. He found Sussex a difficult county, suggesting it to be full of bad spirits. He would readily turn away from a place if he thought there were spirits there. Guests to the house were forever fascinated by the statue of Buddha that sat in the drawing room.

Adrian looked to the simpler pleasures of life as a form of release: his exterior had always been hard to get behind, now inside he was lost. Those that knew him well in the village did their best to support him in his time of crisis. The Hartley Wintney Beekeepers Association, including Kitty Lloyd, played their part trying to act as if life were normal, even though it would never be the same again. In private his fishing allowed him to reflect on how cruel fate can sometimes be: a different road, a different story.

His rugby colleagues could do little to help, except in keeping him busy and moving forward. If Adrian had sometimes come across to others as a little eccentric in his ways, he was about to up the ante. On a visit one day, Audrey's sister and son were tipped out of their motorbike and sidecar along the drive at the Grange, trying to avoid a pheasant. Turning up on the lawns a little scratched and bruised they were surprised to find themselves in the middle of a Harlequins rugby practice session. Good news for Adrian, as he was missing a scrum-half and a wing. Disappearing inside, he returned with a French and a Welsh international shirt from the oak chest in which he kept his collection of swapped shirts and the two ruffled guests found themselves the unlikeliest of internationals.

Those that missed out most were Adrian's three other sons. Michael's greatest regret was not seeing enough of his father. In those pre-war days of the thirties, with boarding school and with Adrian's continuing involvement in rugby circles, opportunities to see him were limited. Limited to an hour at teatime in their holidays, the sons had been cared for by their nanny, sleeping in a different wing of the great house. There were treasured memories of times when Adrian visited school. For Adrian this represented recuperation of sorts, albeit in small measures. Back to school, to Rugby, where it had all started, days of innocence, and days of gym practice.

Still mindful of his status and the esteem in which his name was held, Adrian continued to give something back. In 1936 he took a team to open a new stand at Sutton RFC, the respect people had for him countering the grief he felt. The following year he presented the Hazells, his farm tenants, with four tickets to the Ireland game on the condition that they take his cook and her husband. They never made it to the match due to a bomb scare.

Elsewhere in Europe storm clouds were gathering again. Nowhere was it being felt more keenly than in the Stoop household, what with their Mamara marble mines situated so close to Turkey. Urgently needing both news and governmental support, Adrian engaged the help of Wakefield, now the MP for Swindon. Using his influence, Wakefield wrote to the Commons:

My dear Channon,

Further to my chat with you in the lobby last night, a very old friend of mine – A.D. Stoop and another own a property in the Island of Mamara, in the sea of Mamara, where they have sunk a very substantial sum of money for the obtaining of marble.

They are at the present time in a difficulty due to the fact that the Turkish Government requires this island for defensive purposes. Accordingly, it is necessary for their engineer – Signor Bernieri, of Marina, Carara, Italy – to visit Istanbul at the earliest opportunity to discuss the position.

It would be most helpful if a note could be given to the British Embassy at Istanbul, advising them on behalf of British principals, and could they give him every assistance in the discussions which he will be having with the Turkish Government.

I would very much appreciate it if some such help along the lines indicated, could be given.

Yours,

W.W. Wakefield

Within the week, the Foreign Office had forwarded the plea to the British Embassy in Angora. They alerted the Consulate-General in Istanbul that Bernieri might visit. Their tone was hesitant, as Mamara was within the forbidden military zone of the Dardanelles, where there were now severe restrictions on foreigners.

As foreign matters developed, Adrian started to close the page on another chapter.

Captain of his house and in the XV, Michael was his father's son. With Adrian as a father, and Wakefield as godfather, he had a legacy to live up to on the rugby field. On one visit Adrian took the Harlequins' 'A' team to the school, playing himself at fly half. Opposing him was Michael at centre. The young Rugby School half of the day relished the thought of playing against one of the greats. Adrian might have had a huge reputation some thirty or so years before, but the schoolboy anticipated an easy ride. Adrian had other ideas. The youngster had his education well and truly completed that day, coming off second best to the legend. That was a precursor to Adrian's last hurrah.

On 8 March 1939, partnering Tinny Dean, he played the last of three games of rugby for the 'A' team against Eastbourne. Aged fifty-six, the significance of the timing was not lost on him, being exactly twenty-five years after Poulton and Mobbs had played their last competitive games. The side lost 5-6.

By the end of June, it was clear that Bernieri would not be able to pull any strings. Having failed in Istanbul to get permission to visit the island, the Ministry of Foreign Affairs played the no foreigners card, citing the fact that it was a military zone. Their attention was drawn to letters exchanged between Lord Stanley of the Foreign Office and the Turks at Montreux in August 1936 on the subject: 'The foreigners who are currently landlords can have free access to their property and the right to stay there within the applicable laws.' The Turks had argued that Bernieri was a mere representative, albeit fully empowered, and not therefore an owner. Off the record, the Ministry of Foreign Affairs had verbally stated that with Bernieri being of Italian nationality, unfortunate though it might have been for the owners, they would not feel justified in pressing for a reversal of their Ministry's original decision. Given the Turks' apparent dislike of Bernieri, the Foreign Office could only conclude that Stoop or Cripps would have to apply to visit. If this request were refused by the Turkish Government it might then be possible to call upon the Turks to expropriate the quarries and pay compensation.

Adrian would have to act quickly, not least given the information soon to follow that the Turkish Minister of the Interior had instructed the local authorities to sell the quarries, given that they were not being worked, to meet unpaid taxes. On 1 August the British Embassy received a letter from another local agent:

I think that the information supplied by the Kaymakam of Erdek is probably totally incorrect. The owners supplied me with money in 1936 to the amount of £1,200 odd for the payment of all back taxes to that date. In 1935 the earthquake had occurred and our agent in the Island, Kenan Bey, has told me that he has been endeavouring to obtain exemption from taxes under the special laws made to grant alleviation after the earthquake. In any case I, as the lawful attorney of the owners, have received no tax notice whatsoever. It is, of course possible that our agent did not at the time satisfy the whole of the taxes. I had considerable difficulty in getting receipts out of him but I did eventually see and take copies of certain receipts which I understood to be for the whole of the taxes then due. One of our main difficulties is, of course, that we cannot go to the island and look after our own affairs and have to rely on somewhat unreliable agents. I am endeavouring to get more definitive information from our agent as soon as I can find him and I will then write to you again.

I am aware that litigation has been going on between our agent and the Treasury in connection with a part of the property which we held on lease from Greek owners. This leased property ran along the boundaries of one of our quarries and the actual line of demarcation of that boundary was so vague that there was some doubt whether the entrance to that quarry was on our land or on the leased land. It was for this reason that we contested hotly the attempt of the Treasury to put these leased lands, which had become Government property, up to auction. We contended that long leases granted by the original Greek owners to Messrs Stoop and Cripp were still valid and I understand from our agent that we eventually got a judgement in our favour in the Court of First Instance and later in the Court of Cessation.

If the information sent to you has no connection with this particular case, in other words there really is danger of the property being sold for unpaid taxes (as to which our agent has said nothing), I am at once addressing a letter to the local Treasury officials asking whether there are any unpaid taxes, as I have received no demand note for the same. I am also asking them to suspend any proceedings.

Before any further action could be taken, war was declared. Irrespective of legalistic wrangling, overnight the mines became to all intent and purpose worthless.

Poulton's and Mobbs' playing careers had been ended abruptly by the First World War. The end of Adrian's had coincided with the start of a second. Adrian could only reflect on those that had fallen and those that might still.

twelve

DAD'S ARMY
1940-1955

The basic principle is the same as that of war – victory goes to the side that concentrates an overwhelming force at the critical point.

(*Captaincy*, Adrian Stoop)

Everyone felt the effects of the onset of war. The once-tranquil village of Hartley Wintney saw as much military activity as any, the cricket pitch more than most. As more army lorries arrived it came to resemble more of a car park than its rich history had ever intended. Pillboxes dotted the countryside. The haunting drone of air raid sirens became all too frequent. The only thing the war seemed good for was newspaper sales, people being desperate for news in general and that of loved ones in particular. All too frequently in those early days the news was grim. The mass evacuation at Dunkirk, the Battle of Britain and the Blitz brought the war to home shores as 1940 wore on.

In 1914 Adrian had gone overseas to fight. His war then had been both slow and painful, the long days of training and manoeuvres punctuated only by the sad news of the deaths of friends. His war this time was to be 'fought' on home soil. Joining the Home Guard as a Sergeant, he was back in the 'army'. His 'active' service was an all-too-real reminder of what had gone by once before: training, manoeuvres, weapons training and doing turns at sentry up at the two churches, keeping an eye out for German paratroops. Nights up at the old St Mary's were longer than any Adrian had known. He could not fail to notice his son's grave, those memories still being all too fresh and painful. He also knew that Bunny, now aged twenty-two, Dicky at twenty and Michael at eighteen were all at fighting age and would more than likely be off at some time soon.

Dicky's love of speed also saw him enrolled in the RAF. Shot down over Malta he managed to eject, and was saved by his parachute, although he received bad burns. Recovery time at least kept him away from some of the fiercer fighting to follow.

Michael joined the Grenadier Guards, as part of their armoured division. Tanks had come a long way since the primitive beasts of Roc Ward's day: their sphere of operations, however, was very much the same.

Bunny initially wanted to have no part in the war, and chose to be a conscientious objector. He would, however, do what he could on the home front, even if it meant just driving an ambulance. The bombing of Coventry changed his mind and on 8 March 1943 he joined up with the 10th Royal Hussars (Prince of Wales' Own), Royal Armoured Corps. Their tradition was legendary, going back as it did to the days of Waterloo, their coronet and feathers, together with the rising sun and Red Dragon, and the motto 'Ich Dien' ('I Serve'). His initial posting was an attachment to the main army as a liaison officer.

On 3 September 1943 the Allies invaded Italy, the objective being to draw the German troops from both the Russian front and from France, in advance of D-Day. Progress through southern Italy was rapid and by the end of October the Allies were facing the German winter defensive position, the Gustav line, stretching from the river Garigliano in the west to the Sangro in the east. Initial attempts to breach the western end were unsuccessful. Much of the rest of the month was spent gathering intelligence ready for a significant push in the new year

With their own war won out in the desert, the 10th Royal Hussars were sent to Italy in support of the offensives there, principally to provide relief for the ambulance and rescue fleets. In December 1943 Bunny was posted on to Philipville, but almost immediately found himself seconded to the 9th Battalion of the Royal Fusiliers and off with the rest to Italy.

The new year came in with a snowstorm, and the massed artillery of both sides was used to salute their unseen adversaries. On the evening of 17 January the Allies attempted to cross the swollen waters of the Garigliano, which ran wide and deep. Some divisions crossed with ease, some with difficulty under hostile shelling. Many assault boats were sunk. The Fusiliers met with ill fortune and a strongly entrenched enemy. They lost their Colonel, became disorganised and could make no progress. Someone needed to take charge. Second Lieutenant Adrian (Bunny) Stoop was given the baton, having only arrived that day. How does one spend a night, knowing one has to lead a team with whom one is unacquainted, unsure of their relative strengths and weaknesses? His father had had two pivotal nights, thinking about leading a team of unknowns, many years before. One had been for a game of rugby, the other had been a matter of life or death. For Bunny the night was short. Early on 18 January his men became involved in fierce fighting and he was shot in the stomach. Sent to a field hospital on one of the islands, care of the chaos that he had found himself in on arrival, no one really knew who he was.

The Garigliano was crossed on the 18th and Minturno, some seventy-eight kilometres north of Naples, was taken two days later. The site for a cemetery in Minturno was chosen in late January, but the Germans staged a fightback, some ground was lost and the area came under German small-arms fire. With the German counter-attack, initial reports coming from that sector of fighting were vague. The telegram the Stoops hoped they would never get arrived. Bunny was missing, presumed dead.

In the confusion, no real information came out of Italy. Adrian and Audrey waited and hoped. Perhaps a letter would come through saying he was still alive. The absence of further news left some hope. One morning, some two weeks later, Audrey woke to see that old beam of light parade through her room. She claimed she saw a vision: on one side of the light Billy, on the other Bunny. Whatever the secrets of his house, real or imagined, at that point Adrian knew his eldest son was dead and was with his brother.

Bunny died of his wounds on 9 February. The fighting around Minturno meant the cemetery could not be readily used to bury the dead. It was not until May when the final advance on Rome was launched that the cemetery was deemed safe. Four months of burials took place. While Bunny's war had been as short as Poulton's, the personal impact on Adrian would be even more devastating.

Notwithstanding the senseless loss of life, and friends, that had occurred in the First World War, in the space of a little over ten years the man who had had everything had lost pretty much all that he had held most dear: his parents, an uncle, a sister and two sons.

As the end of the war neared, Adrian kept himself busy, if only to hide the pain. The local branch of the charitable Toc H organised fêtes in aid of the Red Cross at The Grange. Both Italian and German POWs attended. First-aid classes were run and the Stoops helped out wherever they could. Adrian became president of the cricket club in Hartley Wintney, immersing himself in it, and also took on yet more duties with the parish council. Like his father before him, he donated £500 to the Hartley Wintney memorial playing fields, not this time for safe return but for the loss of a son. To lose one son was a devastating blow, to lose two was too much to comprehend. While as equally difficult to get over, somehow a loss during a war is prepared for. The guilt that remained over Billy's death still haunted the family, his loss having been unnecessary. Adrian's will to go on was sorely tested. Once more he had to look deep inside himself.

On exercises one weekend, his fellow members of 'Dad's Army' noticed the first signs of human frailty in a man who had always prided himself on his tremendous fitness and athleticism. After the recent events Adrian was never going to be at his best mentally, but it was clear to all that he was far from his best physically. Arthritis was setting in.

Others' lives continued. In Saalbach, after the tragedy of 1936, Audrey had got on well with two Austrian girls, who had come back to work at the Grange. One of them, Gretyl, had only been supposed to stay a year, but somehow fell in love with the place and the kindness the Stoops showed her. She had stayed on, and fallen for a local lad. Her plans for a grand Austrian family wedding had been scuppered by the war but she was happy to settle for the local registry office. On leaving for the ceremony she was unaware of the running around that the rest of the staff at the Grange were doing. The ceremony seemed all too quick, but on her return, she and her new husband were overjoyed at what they saw. Audrey and Adrian had laid on a feast fit for kings and set up the vicar to perform a special ceremony just for them. For all of the Stoops heart-felt problems, they had not lost their generosity.

Carpe Diem

The war still had some way to go. Michael was still out in the thick of it in northern Europe. Michael had always shown superb mental dexterity; now he was to show his great physical strength. His war efforts were about to overshadow those of his father. He had already gained some notoriety with his tank division, as part of a column which came under heavy fire along one of Belgium's country roads. Ordered to advance (to certain death) along the road, he disobeyed the order, taking his tank off at a tangent, reconnoitring the area ahead, and then dispatching the enemy heavy guns with an attack from the flanks. This unexpected move was one of which his father would have been proud.

On 31 March 1945 Michael did what was expected. His citation for the day told the story:

This officer was leading his troop to attack Aalten. Suddenly, one hundred yards ahead of him, the road bridge over a small river was blown up. Lieutenant Stoop immediately appreciated the importance of finding another bridge over this anti-tank obstacle and, manoeuvring round the right flank, he succeeded in getting up to another bridge which was held by the enemy. Covered by the fire of his troop, he approached the bridge and dispersed most of the enemy. Expecting the bridge to be blown at any moment, he jumped out of his tank and raced to the bridge still under fire. He cut the wires connecting the charges and himself removed the charges. His troop were then able to cross the bridge. The capture of this bridge was vital as it was the only bridge left intact over which the remainder of the Grenadier Group could pass to capture the town.

After the episode of the capture of the bridge, the King's Company of 1 Motor Grenadier Guards were ordered to advance into the town. However, so heavy was the mortar fire and sniping that they suffered very severe casualties and were temporarily held up. Lieutenant Stoop, seeing their difficulties, went forward in his tank and put down smoke to help them reorganise and evacuate their casualties. He personally rescued many wounded while he himself was under heavy fire.

Appreciating it was imperative to push into the town further he found out from a Dutch civilian that there was still one bridge standing at the other end of the town. Thereupon, on his own initiative, he dashed forward with another tank and captured this bridge, holding it successfully until further help came from the remainder of his squadron. During the whole day, this officer performed many acts of initiative and courage, but his capture of the bridges was undoubtedly instrumental in allowing the Battalion to capture the town. His bravery under fire was outstanding.

Cool and calm under the greatest of pressure, he had inherited his father's great qualities. Like his father, Michael earned the Military Cross for his actions under fire. Unlike his father, he had the desire to carry on.

Forced to give up the Home Guard due to the increasing pain of his arthritis, Adrian's thoughts about faith and spirituality became all the stronger. His mind drifted back to the days surrounding the end of the previous war; his near death, his wife, Bunny his son and the war will he had made then. Memorial benches to both Bunny and Billy were bought for Rottingdean. These acted as a reminder but could not ease the pain of Adrian's loss. Still grieving and in some confusion he instructed Lamb, Brooks & Bullock of nearby Odiham to draft a second will, with the intent of revoking the previous one. His initial draft, written on the back of his Twickenham ticket application reminders, reflected the state of mind of a man who had lost pretty much everything he had held most dear. It also made a clear statement of intent as to what he wanted to do with that which he had left:

I bequeath to James Owen Needham and Savill Cator the sum of £2,000 upon trust with power to invest the same or any part thereof in their absolute discretion in investments authorised by law in the case of trust funds and to expend the capital or the income to arise therefrom in such times and in such manner as they shall deem advisable in their absolute discretion for the education, benefit and advancement in the world of Christopher and David Needham and I declare that the residue of the said sum of £2,000 remaining intact and unexpended at the time when the younger or survivor of them shall attain the age of 21 shall be equally divided as to both capital and income between them if they shall both then be living or shall be paid to such survivor absolutely.

I devise and bequeath to Sharkey and William Lane Potter (hereinafter called my Hartley Grange Trustees) my freehold house known as Hartley Grange aforesaid with the kitchen garden, pleasure garden, orchard and land bounded by the Back Drive, Road Ditch, Belswood and Front Lawn with the land up to and including the drive on the west the fence and ditch adjoining the highroad on the south the hedge round Belswood on the east and on the north together with the furniture fittings and ornaments of the drawing room and dining room therein and securities or investments which at the date of my death shall bring in a gross income of £500 p.a. upon trust to hold the said freehold property as a hospital for the use and benefit of such persons as shall in the opinion of my Hartley Grange Trustees be deemed to be natives of Hartley Wintney and I declare that the following conditions shall apply to this devise and bequest:

The furniture, fittings and ornaments of the drawing room and dining room at Hartley Grange aforesaid shall remain in the same positions in the respective rooms as they shall be in at the date of my death and shall be maintained in their present form.

Not more than two patients shall sleep in any one room.

It shall be a condition of admission to the hospital that each patient shall undertake that when (in the opinion of my Hartley Grange Trustees or of a responsible person to be appointed by them for the purpose) he or she is capable of so doing such patient shall write down his or her thoughts so soon as they come to him or her on waking.

The beds of the patients shall be arranged as nearly as possible in a North to South direction.

I bequeath the residue and remainder of my personal chattels as defined by the Statutory Will Forms 1925 to my wife Audrey Deline absolutely.

I bequeath all the residue and remainder of my stocks shares bonds investments and securities and personal estate equally between my said wife and son or sons as shall survive me so that each of them my said wife and son or sons shall take an equal share according to the market value at the date of distribution.

I give devise and bequeath all the rest residue and remainder of my property of whatsoever nature and wheresoever situate unto such of the children or remoter issue of my sister Cora Collin as shall survive me and attain the age of 21 years.

The part The Grange had played in his and others' healing processes would forever be there for all to see. This will highlighted all the things that were important to Adrian: his drawing room and dining room for the memories they held; his belief in an afterlife, based on experiences throughout the house; Twickenham, where he had enjoyed himself most, represented by the north to south arrangement of the beds. To the outside world it appeared he was becoming even more eccentric in his ways. Those that really knew him, knew he was shot to pieces.

After the war, Michael was up at Oxford, along with many others whose careers had been fractured by events. Once more many of the promising youngsters that had gone out in hope were never to return. For those lucky enough to have made it back, the competition for rugby places was huge. Michael would never make the Varsity. Like so many, the circumstances that had passed would never allow them to further their own interests, and their parents' hopes and dreams. Times had changed.

The Stoops had indeed been very rich before the war, but after, running such a huge house with all its outgoings would start to tell. Costs had doubled, even tripled. Adrian kept his male staff, the chauffeur and the gardener, but cutbacks were made on others. Domestic staff were not as readily available and servants were called in as and when needed, on an hourly basis rather than full time. Despite all this he bought a Rolls Royce (second hand) because he thought he ought to have one.

The parties continued, but on a much less lavish scale. Cost cutting apart, to the outside world Adrian and Audrey held out as they always had done, looking out for the interests of the village and the people they came across on the way. Inside The Grange however, they had long since taken to separate bedrooms, in different wings of their house. They had served each others' purpose and privately now lived their own lives. Audrey went so far as to keep a lover in tow.

Adrian had always looked smart in suits, but for the other 340 days of the year he favoured airtex T-shirts, whatever the weather. Going into his sixties he wasn't ready to change. The goose pimples that clearly showed in winter betrayed a man who hankered after the days of his youth. His behaviour became more obsessive. The maids in particular found it difficult to avoid the ritual eleven o'clock sitting on of his knee.

Painful as it might be afterwards, Adrian continued to train the 'A' team and run the line for the Harlequin firsts, but in dispensing his own advice to the club captains, he was found to be interfering with teams more than they would have liked. In 1946 he resigned the Harlequins secretaryship, following a row. He had held the position for forty years but did not wish to seek re-election. Like his father many years before, his mind was set, despite many an attempt to talk him out of it. Wakefield took over.

The time he spent training the Harlequin juniors was more valued. The youngsters were always keen to hear the stories of Poulton, of Lambert, of Birkett and others. Drifting back to the past and those who played with him kept him whole and was a reminder perhaps of the days on the lawns with his sons. So too the games he would watch from high in the North Stand, where he would relay his thoughts to anyone who would listen – girl, boy, lady or gentleman. Most did.

His adoption of a walking stick indicated to all that his arthritis had taken a nasty grip, and his hip was starting to feel the worst of it. In 1949, as Holly resigned his long-standing role as treasurer, Adrian resigned the Harlequins presidency. He needed new interests to occupy his time, most of which he found locally. With vast fields at his disposal, he turned his mind to farming. He spent many a day with Hazell, the lessee of his farm, discussing the merits of ploughing and whether it was a waste of money and energy, or whether going back to nature and building the fertility up was a better answer. Either way, between them they had to work hard to maintain a water supply to the area, particularly in the summer. At least then the cricket pitch was on his doorstep and provided a quiet sanctuary.

For any cricketer, reaching the nineties leaves a painful wait in the path to the big ton. Going into his nineties, Billy Williams knew his 100 years would coincide with fifty of Twickenham. He would not see those celebrations. On 14 April 1951 he died at the age of ninety-one. Tributes were paid to the man whose vision had inspired a lasting legacy. The man who had done most to laud that legacy also received his own tribute. At a dinner held in his name, Wakefield presented Adrian with a portrait, subscribed to by over 300 fellow members. Its significance, marking as it did Adrian's fifty years of Harlequin service, was not lost on those present.

Nor was the significance in 1953 of Dicky being one of the exceptionally lucky 'few' to fly over Buckingham Palace in the fly-past that marked the Coronation celebrations.

The unhappy circumstances in his private life that had set in, starting with the death of Billy, and fuelled further by the death of Bunny were now compounded by his increasing immobility. In 1955 he was asked to retake his driving test. He was never to get his licence back. The man whose great fitness had stood him proud through most of his life was now but a shadow of the man he once was, sad for all to see.

At the same time, Bader's life story and wartime heroics became a book, which in 1956 was made into the film *Reach for the Sky*. Recognising the immense part played by Adrian and Audrey in Bader's recovery, the film-makers saw infinite potential in shooting at The Grange. With so much water having passed under the bridge, the memories that filming would evoke, of the happier days before the deaths of Bunny and even more so of Billy, the Stoops resisted the pleas of the director. A substitute house was found, but the film faithfully recorded the pivotal moment in Bader's recovery, Adrian's teaching him to play golf.

Whereas Bader had recovered from his fateful air crash, Adrian had never really recovered from his own car crash. With Dicky away racing his famed Frazer Nash Sebring at Le Mans and other sports car events, and Michael over in New York, The Grange had lost some of its sparkle. When Adrian needed his friends most, few came. Bader, who lived not far away, was lost in his own newfound celebrity and was never to really pay back the debt he owed. Adrian's faith in his own abilities was dying as a great loneliness descended. He was on his own. Left with the memories, his cuttings and photographs were but a reminder of the good old days.

Into his seventies he was dreadfully unhappy. But he still had his chauffeur and he could still get to Twickenham.

thirteen

A FINAL TERM
1956-1957

*Seize every opportunity to practise while at school. The opportunity may
not present itself again.*

(*The Young Idea*, Adrian Stoop)

Everyone looks forward to the start of a new season and 1957 was as
any other. England had won the championship the season before and
this year had that rosy tint again. Just as Adrian had once helped bring
about the resurrection of the national side, he now decided that he too
would come back strong. His faith was powerful – the walking stick was
discarded as he attempted to put the ails of his body out of his mind. To
all outward appearances he was overcoming his debilitating affliction.

The start of the new season was, as always, busy for the committees.
Adrian attended the full committee on 15 and 20 September. Of considerable note was to be the meeting of the laws committee with the
chairman of the selection committee and the union's representatives on
the international panel of referees. The topics of note were re-examining
the problems of obstruction and other unfair tactics, including late tackling
and over-vigorous play – subjects close to Adrian's heart. The views of the
union were subsequently communicated to the Home Unions committee,
which held an important conference on 4 and 5 October. Present were the
chairmen of the selection committees of each Home Union and all
members of the international panel, and the same issues were discussed
from every angle. The next meeting, scheduled for 29 November, was one
that Adrian would not want to miss.

He died two days beforehand – his heart had gone. At age seventy-four,
the doctors would not have recommended him attempting the headstand
he had. Donkin's ghost would have raised a wry smile at his protégé's
athletic exit.

The villagers who knew the man as serious but immensely kind at heart
were in shock, the local paper proclaiming the passing of a legend in
typically understated fashion: 'Hartley Wintney loses a great sportsman.'
The villagers were not alone in the shock at their loss. The RFU recorded
its own tribute in its minutes at the ensuing committee meeting:

It was written of Adrian Stoop that in the development of attacking rugby, in the technique and act of passing and running, and especially for the part he played in establishing the stand-off half as the vital pivot of the attack, he will stand among the greatest of all time in the history of Rugby Football.

Those who were privileged to serve under him as president and with him upon the Laws Committee, will always cherish memories of a great personality and of a man who lived for the game and the purity of its ethics. Few have had the distinction of election to the captaincy, secretaryship and presidency of their National Union. Few, if any, of us will see his like again.

Few indeed. On behalf of all those that had played with him Dai Gent, his playing partner in perhaps Adrian's finest hour, responded under the header 'A Great Rugby Man':

By the death of Adrian Stoop, Rugby football has lost its very greatest enthusiast. At school [Rugby], at Oxford, with the Harlequins, for Surrey, and, of course, for England as a player, selector, and in his turn president of the Rugby Union, Stoop poured himself, as it were, into this great game.

No longer will he be seen at the back of the West Stand, in the committee rooms, and, when the kick-off was approaching, walking quietly and, for many years now, painfully, for he suffered from rheumatism, to the North Stand where he sat in the middle of the front row, whatever grade of match was on. It was there, he used to say, that the game could be watched most enjoyably.

I knew him well. We were contemporaries, and in the pleasantest, and to me, the greatest match in which I ever played, he and I were the England half-backs. It was England v. Wales, in January 1910 – the first international ever to be played at Twickenham. We had met for the first time a fortnight before, in the final trial on the same ground. On that occasion, I played with him at half-back, but only for half of the game.

He was a beautiful player – good hands, an uncanny sense of where the openings lay, a wonderful timer of the pass, quick off the mark, and a great inspiration to the rest of his side. When our playing days were over, we had endless discussions. I used to suggest that with all this loose forward play nowadays, we should find it difficult to weave our way up the middle of the field. 'Not a bit of it,' he would say, 'I could do it now!'

So I could go on, for memories of his matches, his talks, his infectious enthusiasm, and the drawing up of lists of the greatest players we had seen, will abide with me for a very long time.

The name Adrian Stoop is synonymous with clean, quick, open and joyous Rugby football, though, as I used often to tell him, the game would please me still more if it included more vigorous tackling.

Dave Davies's tribute was more succinct, but reflected a certain austerity that his great friend had: 'Hard to get to know on first acquaintance, scratching below the surface revealed his true character. No kinder heart or truer friend was there.'

Adrian died one of the great but also one of the key players in English rugby history – a force of creative energy in the game to which he had given his soul. He was buried on Monday 2 December following a service at St John the Evangelist's in Hartley Wintney, almost fifty years to the day from when a collarbone injury nearly shattered his career. Snow lay on the ground, a blanket of white against the surrounding countryside, broken only by the primroses. His grave up at St Mary's lay just a few stones along from the final resting place of his youngest son. No Bigside, just a hillside out in the country, looking south over fields. Adrian Stoop had been lain to rest and to dream on in the corner of an English field, surveying the green and pleasant lands around. A great mind at peace forever with all below. The epitaph on his gravestone expressed all that needed to be known about the body within: 'He played the game he loved.'

A memorial service was held in St Martin-in-the-Fields, London on Monday 9 December. Two thousand came to pay their last respects, the number that came to see the first game at the Harlequins' first real home. Among those present were Audrey and their two remaining sons, Michael and Dicky; his brother Freek and John Birkett, survivors of that first game; Wakefield and Bill Gracie, who had done much to continue Adrian's proud Harlequins playing legacy; his old friend, also former England captain and president 'Jenny' Greenwood; Dave Davies, who had inherited and maintained the international legacy; and representatives of all the organisations that Adrian had held dear: the RFU, the Queen's Regiment and Hartley Wintney Cricket Club. Among the hymns was 'He Who Would Valiant Be'.

It was left to Wakefield, his great friend for thirty-odd years, to sum up the real Adrian Stoop in his memorial service eulogy:

We have come together here today to remember Adrian Stoop, and to pay tribute to him, not only as a friend and a colleague, but as a great figure in Rugby Union Football.

When we laid him to rest a week ago on the top of the hill above the village of Hartley Wintney in that beautiful Hampshire countryside, I could not help thinking what a perfect day it was for the playing of the game he loved so well. My mind went back to other great days when at the weekends he walked in the lanes and footpaths or ran about with a ball on the lawn or in the fields with us, his Harlequins, and other Rugby Football friends.

He was a devoted son, a beloved husband and a proud father, who gathered around him his disciples at those much-enjoyed weekends, at first with his parents at West Hall, and then with his wife and family at Hartley Grange. It was on these occasions that we got to know the generous, warm hearted and loyal friend, much different from the brusque and even rather frightening impression sometimes gained by his casual acquaintance.

His name will rank always with the legendary names of those who have made outstanding contributions to the game of Rugby football, and we in the Harlequins are particularly proud to think that it was through our club that his remarkable qualities came to full fruition. Indeed, we might say that Adrian Stoop and the Harlequins are synonymous: certainly it is hard to think of one without the other, and of his profound influence on the club and his mass service to it there can be no doubt whatever. I know that I speak for every Harlequin when I express our deepest gratitude for all he did for us through the years as captain, hon. secretary and president.

Adrian Stoop was a dedicated man. He concentrated the whole force of his strong personality into creative thinking about Rugby football, and this integration of purpose gave him, in this sphere, more than a touch of genius. He sought quality. By deep thought, by continual practice, and by physical fitness, he achieved quality. He demanded quality in others, and not infrequently got it.

Rugby Football was Adrian's life. It gave him great happiness and satisfaction, and what greater gift can God give than this? His happiness came from achievement and he made return in full measure, not only to his club, but as president of Surrey to his county, and as president of the Rugby Union to his country.

His thinking was based upon his own great playing ability, and from the moment he first appeared for Oxford in 1902 in the first of his three Varsity Matches, it was clear that he would make an outstandingly brilliant contribution to the game. Contemporary accounts of his play in the Varsity Match, with their stress on his unorthodox tactics, read like descriptions of the best of modern players in action, which shows how far he was ahead of his time, even in those early days. He was indeed one of the prophets: one of those rare, original minds whose influence can change the whole trend of a game, and as he pioneered for Oxford, joining the Vassalls and the Rotherhams as a great innovator, so he pioneered for England and the Harlequins.

This is not the time or the place to dwell in detail upon his influence upon methods of play or legislation – though his influence was profound. We may, however, properly recall the spirit in which he played himself, and which through his example he passed on to the Harlequins, and to Rugby football as a whole. It was the spirit of attack.

There is no doubt that his influence on the game of Rugby football, which began to be felt fifty years ago, continues to be far reaching. It was through him and those he led that the game became increasingly popular. More and more schools turned to Rugby football and the number of clubs continually increase. The progress of science and the development of industry have created and are creating opportunities for leisure. Because of its tradition, customs and nature, the playing of Rugby football can make an ever-increasing contribution to the happiness and well-being not only to our own countrymen, but of the peoples of many lands.

The strategy discussed, the tactics practised at West Hall and Hartley Grange, and then carried out at Twickenham and elsewhere are now bringing and will continue to bring a reward far wider, far deeper than anyone could have believed.

Like all single-minded men of strong and undeviating character, Adrian clashed at times with his Rugby football colleagues. He was a stormy petrel, and tact was apt to be subordinated to the outcome of his convictions.

This I can say: that whatever the issue might be – and however strongly opinions differed – no one ever doubted that Adrian was following what he passionately believed to be the course best serving the interests of the game he loved so well. This needed courage, which was recognised on other fields, for he was the holder of the Military Cross.

As individuals, those of us who knew him are the richer for his example and friendship. But though our sense of bereavement will be keen, we shall think more of what we have gained than of what we have lost. He will continue to inspire and challenge us for a long time.

I conclude with these words from Isaiah: 'They that wait upon the Lord shall renew their strength. They shall mount up with wings as eagles. They shall run and not be weary. They shall walk and not faint.'

True to form when it came to his own finances, the only will that could be found was the 1918 war will, in which he had left everything to his wife. Adrian's lack of concern over the money, and the increased costs after the war, meant that the fortune that both he and Frederick had accumulated was now mostly gone. The Grange would ultimately have to be sold, never to become the spiritual hospital he had wished for. Freek handled the financial side. Audrey moved to nearby Meadow Lane, but a small plot of her old land was kept back with a view to her perhaps one day building a little house on it. She never did.

An era had ended. The cricket club, the rugby club and the other organisations he had supported so vigorously with his generosity and kindness were left to look out for themselves. All would have to stand tall, but proud, going forward.

Adrian Stoop had put a spirit back into the game. He delivered to the public what they wanted and in that regard did not disappoint. It was left to Audrey to best sum up what life had actually meant to her husband: 'His idea of heaven would be to play in an unending game of rugby, to play in all positions, on both sides, and to referee as well.' He might just have found a space for Ronald Poulton.

—ᴍ—

TEN OUT OF TEN
A LIFETIME'S LEGACY

Education should be judged by what is left after we have forgotten everything
we learned at school.

(*The Young Idea*, Adrian Stoop)

On his death, Adrian was fondly remembered for his friendship, courage, trust, faith and determination to succeed by colleagues and former teammates alike. What they all knew was how much he had transformed the game from its muddied, middling years to the great game that it had become.

Up until Adrian's march, all the major innovators had been from the southern hemisphere. The other home nations had somehow managed to combine their own pursuit of sporting excellence with the demands of day-to-day living. The great game of rugby in England had struggled into the twentieth century with years of little ups and great downs. It had become a faceless sport, and the protection of its amateur status and Corinthian ideals had cost it dear.

Those days are far removed from today. The professionalism of the game as it is now comes a century after the great split of the 1890s. Today, as then, sides have been lost to the game. Richmond's name provides a link between the two ages, being there at the beginning of the union, at Twickenham for its first game, and then one of the first casualties 100 years later due to the demands of the paid game. Now money talks, there is a foundation to the game and England prospers. That did not exist 100 years ago.

1905 was certainly a pivotal year for rugby. England's progress to the all-conquering side of immediately before the First World War had its foundations laid on that sunny September in 1905 when the All Blacks invaded, carrying all before them, and the Harlequins had their trials. Where Adrian was ahead of the game, even then, was that he and Munro had been hand-to-hand passing at Oxford long before Gallaher's men had come to town. For Adrian, the massacre of Stamford Bridge was but an awakening to even greater possibilities. The following battle of the giants, New Zealand *v.* Wales, was keenly dissected by a willing scholar. What was most evident was the stage. Give the public something worth watching and they will come. And so Adrian set about reshaping the game by absorbing the principles set by those two greatest of teams. He revived the open game in England. His own play became full of the unorthodox, dazzling to spectators, bewildering to opponents, who never knew what he would do next. Of the mercurial modern number 10s, the Morgans, the Bennetts, the Johns, he was the father of them all.

Adrian's volume of effort and sacrifice saw him heralded as one of sport's great thinkers and tacticians – a visionary, selfless and shrewd, impressing his skill, personality and enthusiasm on the game. He remains one of the greatest players, but also arguably the greatest character, the greatest personality the game has ever seen, his achievements in the game lasting for over fifty years. Wales might have had Prince Gwyn, but for a period the English had their king, who launched the nation into a period of unequalled prosperity. Without doubt he made modern rugby in this country, transforming perceptions as he went. He showed that if you took the trouble, you could do as Wales had in the 1890s and 1900s, as New Zealand had in 1905, even South Africa in 1913. In their new spirit of attack, England conquered all.

In Adrian's formative years we search for the clues that lead to the unravelling of the mystery of his genius: his family, his education, his early struggles. The languages, the mathematics and the sciences were but mundane side-issues to his real education at school. What he carried away from there was the code of conduct that Arnold had set in stone, and also the ability to pull all the instruments together as one as Percival, the demonic leader of that mythical orchestra, had done. Principles and attention to detail were what mattered most. The simple lessons were the ones that stayed longest in the mind. And those lessons became his career.

How does one define a professional? Rugby School debated but never quite resolved the issue. The dictionary suggests someone who is skilled, has experience, is proficient, has expertise, is learned, trained, able or adept. By being an unrelenting student of the game in an amateur era Adrian could claim to be all of these. He also knew that in order to excel, sacrifices had to be made. There was method to what he did, and what he did he firmly believed to be for the good of the game. More often than not he was right.

Adrian would have been appalled at the excesses of today. He would never be paid for playing the game he loved. That he could pay himself was a luxury, but he would have been no different had he not. The Arthur Gould house testimonial case draws interesting parallels. Giving Gould a house for his services to the game caused a major rift across all the home nations. Adrian too was given a house, albeit by his family, but the only storms that he created where those arising from his refusal to adopt the accepted principles of the day. Everything he had went back into the game. Even the house was shared with his friends. Amateur he may have been, professional only in how he handled himself. Not for him the artificial standards of fitness and performance from drugs. 'On Passing' illustrated the basics of the game simply by 'holding a cushion between your teeth' – this represented the beginnings of sport as a science, written at a time when the rugby world was ready to listen. Quality achieved by deep thought, by continual practice, by physical fitness, replenishing with water, aiding the breathing by smoking less, having the right boots and proper balls. Adrian's strokes of genius lay as much in his attention to detail as in his changing the direction of attack, or his conceptions of planned surprise.

Cornelius Stoop loved his paintings. If Picasso was his artist of choice, Stoop filled this role for others. Two men at the same age, at the same time, challenging perceived best practice. They both had the courage and conviction to do things their own way, letting others decide whether to follow or not. Like Picasso, Adrian was one of those spirits who transcended his own age. Greater than the great because he was always trying to do something more. Condemned by those that could not leave the past, and who were content to assume that what was beyond their limited imagination was utterly bad, they stood tall. Both warranted enormous fame, but that did not mean they were either understood or accepted. And that is exactly what set them apart from the others.

Adrian's greatest opponent, as with all great athletes, was himself – his strong beliefs and his conformity to his own rules. An autocrat he may have been, but such is the way of those that see a job needs doing and set about doing it. An angry man? This reputation stemmed from a caustic tongue needed to drive home the point. He was angry only as much as anyone who has lived a hard life, and lost that which he held most dear along the way. A blistering personality? Not to those who wanted to listen: the players still being developed, the kids, the new students. Nor to those less gifted that he was most sympathetic to. Nor to those to whom he happily extended charity and hospitality. When you give so much to others, it is inevitable there is not so much for yourself.

His forceful personality would always get him noticed. But one man's personality in a strictly amateur game would never have been sufficient to carry the day. A consciousness had to be fostered and standards had to be raised. At the root was little that was new. The principles were those of attack, the ball being passed as soon as possible along the line to the wings. What was different were intelligent and skilful modifications to these basic facets. Whatever his source of inspiration, Adrian added an extra component: a sense of belonging, a pride in oneself and one's team.

Those that advanced his way were not schoolboy stars. He had moved away from the traditional public school ethos. Pick his players he might, but they all belonged. In a sense, Adrian's backs, taken together, formed the complete player. Each could run fast, had good strength, could kick and tackle and had natural football ability, but above that each had something else: Sibree, the perfect pass; Adrian, the brains, tactics and ideas; Birkett, the tackles and ability to bulldoze; Lambert, the direct run; Poulton, the swerving run; Freek, the all-rounder; and the oft-forgotten Maxwell-Dove, just in case extra security was needed behind. Most important of all, Adrian knew they had sporting intelligence. Beyond rugby, they built the complete person. Their strengths and weaknesses as people completed each other, or more specifically, Adrian. The sum of the parts always greater than the whole.

The critics questioned his methods, over and over, suggesting the ball was being thrown about with a freedom bordering on recklessness with some of the more outrageous moves. If they could only realise the intricacy and thought that went behind them. Adrian immersed himself completely in the game. He studied and practised with a fanatical devotion. *Numquam dormio*, never asleep – the Harlequins motto. This was appropriate for a man who spent his nights analysing the opposition in his mind and developing tactics. Adrian was never a dreamer because it was all put into action.

All was based on knowledge and trust. The danger of an attack lies in its variety, and Adrian had conjured up a rare mixture. His knowledge was passed on to those willing to listen. And many did, whether on the Rugby Union laws and ground committees, on the International Board or out on the training ground. Long into his advanced years, the advice and enthusiasm were always there for those that wanted to hear, until he had nothing more to give.

And after the golden days? The memories. And the romanticism. We have television these days to remind ourselves of the greats. You can pick a game out on video and re-run it a thousand times. The 1973 Barbarians, the 1997 Lions, the 2003 World Cup. You can see on film those individual moments of brilliance, from Edwards to Guscott and to Wilkinson, and for the moment you can be there. Thankfully we have Adrian's papers to read, and are lucky enough to be able to find our way back to the earlier days. We can dream about those flying backs who so enchanted the crowds. We rely on the older writers to set the scene: Sewell, Thomson, Marshall and Wakelam all waxing lyrical about what they had seen, struck by the brilliance of it. No individual team today could command so much affection as the Harlequins did then. Little wonder then that Adrian himself drifted back to the days when the names rolled off the tongue: Poulton, Lambert,

Birkett and Sibree. With them, the name Stoop became a part of the language – a byword for the magical, for great trickery and sorcery, never illustrated better than by Dave Davies trying 'to out-stoop Stoop'.

Adrian might not have been the fastest, but he was always way ahead of the game. But for his injuries a different chapter might have been written. He persevered and pulled himself through his darkest days, on and off the pitch, proving on the way that no matter how good you are, your greatest opponent is yourself. From there he took a great interest in the spiritual healing that he so greatly needed in later life.

One can't say he invented the outside half as a position in its own right – it evolved as much through trial and error from others as Adrian's belligerence and determination to see it through. But just as William Webb Ellis was credited with inventing the game of rugby, because his name was indelibly associated with it, so Adrian Stoop is credited with the establishment of fly half as a position, of half-back play and the tactical structures of the modern game, because *his* name is indelibly associated with them.

EPILOGUE
A MAN WHO LIVED FOR RUGBY

Playing days go and we join the ranks of the disinherited. But loyalties,
friendships, memories, the game itself – these remain.
                    (*What Rugger Means to Me*, Howard Marshall)

Adrian's life was lived out almost like a game of two halves. In fact it
was not unlike England's match against Wales in 1910: early period
virtuosity, second-half desperation. But games finish and seasons move on.

After its eventual sale in 1936, West Hall came under the control of the
Swiss bank, thereafter never again to be found under family ownership.
During the Second World War, its underground vaults were strengthened
and used for the safekeeping of gold bullion secreted away from the
Germans. In 1964 it was acquired by the engineering firm Mouchel, and it
remains in their ownership. The great house still reflects some of its old
grandeur. It stands in quiet tranquillity with its immaculately kept lawns and
age-old trees, a reflection of an age gone by.

In 1958, the year after Adrian's death, the Tate Gallery received another
magnanimous donation from the Stoop family. Anne Kessler, Adrian's
cousin, had been born in Holland, but had lived for much of her life in
England. Cornelius Stoop had encouraged his niece to buy paintings in
the late 1920s and, by deed of gift, fourteen works, including Renoirs,
several Duffys and Picasso's *Circus Artist with Child*, were made over to the
gallery, eventually coming to reside there on her death in 1983.

In September 1959 the Harlequins held a memorial game against
the Wolfhounds (the Irish Barbarians), fifty years after the first game at
Twickenham. Its purpose was to aid a fund that would perpetuate the
name of Adrian Stoop, the object of which would be to enlarge and re-equip
the Harlequins' ground at Teddington. Two full-size pitches, additional
changing rooms and bath facilities were built on the ground normally used
by the junior sides, where Adrian had coached, watched and played. The
most appropriate memorial could only concern the ground where he
watched and coached the junior sides, and played late on in his life.

The following month, Twickenham celebrated that half-century with its
own jubilee game: England and Wales against Ireland and Scotland,

refereed by a Frenchman. On Boxing Day of the same year, the Harlequins played Richmond, watched by fourteen of the fifteen survivors of the inaugural match. Among them was John Birkett, with many a memory held dear.

Audrey became the honorary president of Hartley Wintney's cricket club after Adrian's death until hers in 1981. The Harlequins continued to play their end of May bank holiday cricket game there. Audrey entertained the players at The Grange until she eventually had to sell it. Once sold, it was converted into several smaller residences, Kitty Lloyd being one of the first to buy and move in. Audrey's better memories of the idyll that was Hartley Wintney were published in a book on the village. Douglas Bader turned up to sign copies at The Lamb Hotel, just along the main street.

Dicky Stoop's fascination with Brooklands and motor racing continued. He died in 1968 from a heart attack, like his father before him, only this time at the wheel of his racing car up at Aintree.

Michael fondly recalls the great painting collections of his uncle and Anne Kessler, swimming the river of his grandfather's great house, and sitting up in Twickenham's North Stand with his father. Above all he remembers running around the lawns of The Grange being taught to 'do the Poulton'.

But for unimaginative selection and injuries, Adrian's fragmented international appearances would have been more. However, the players that Adrian helped along the way have records that have stood the test of time. Ronald Poulton's five scores in one Varsity, and four from centre, as captain against France in 1914, will probably never be beaten. Danny Lambert's five tries against France in 1911 have been equalled but never bettered. His individual points tally of twenty-two in a single game lasted for nigh on eighty years until 1990.

The Stoop family left many a legacy for the nation, whether donations to the Tate or to local charities. Adrian's legacies, while intangible, were as great as any of them. His greatest legacy still stands. Whatever the politics, whatever the issues, to this day rugby and its history continues to fascinate. When England was in crisis, one man came to the game he loved, and to a corner of south-west London that is forever England. Billy Williams would have been proud of his ground, and of the man who cemented its reputation. A stone's throw away, just over the main road, sits 'The Stoop Memorial Ground', where the Harlequins have played since 1963, in the shadow of the larger ground he helped to promote.

Twickenham is as much in the news today as it was 100 years ago. Ask any New Zealander today and they will immediately be able to recount the travesty of 1905. Memories live long. In the depths of Twickenham's stands memories live longer. A library, filled with stories of the greats, and the irony of two sets of personal memories: Adrian's and Ronnie's scrapbooks. Often the same cuttings, and the same shared brilliance.

Master and pupil. Top-drawer stuff.

PLAN OF CAMPAIGNS

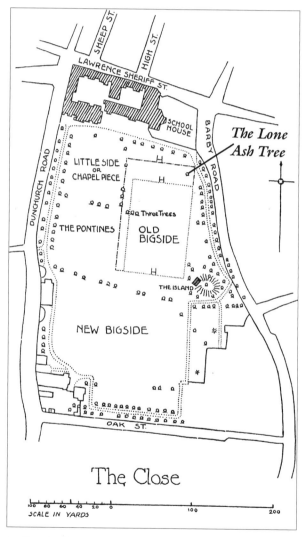

Rugby School in the late nineteenth century, the 'three trees' still standing. (Rugby School)

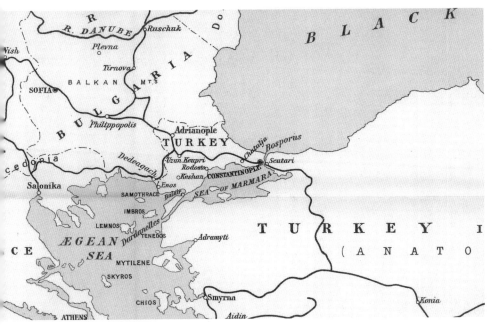

Marmara island, just up from the Dardanelles. (The Naval & Military Press)

Twickenham site, mid-1900s. (Museum of Rugby, Twickenham)

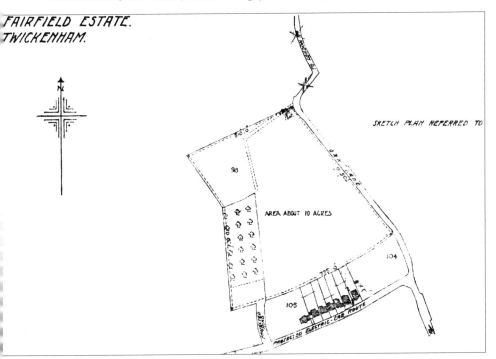

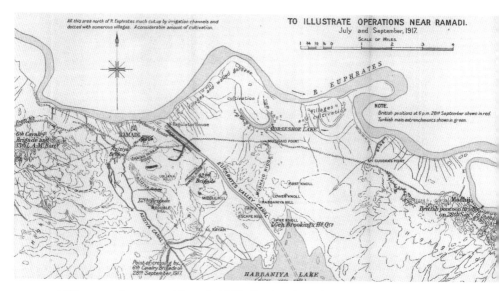

Military operations around Ramadi, 1917. (The Naval & Military Press)

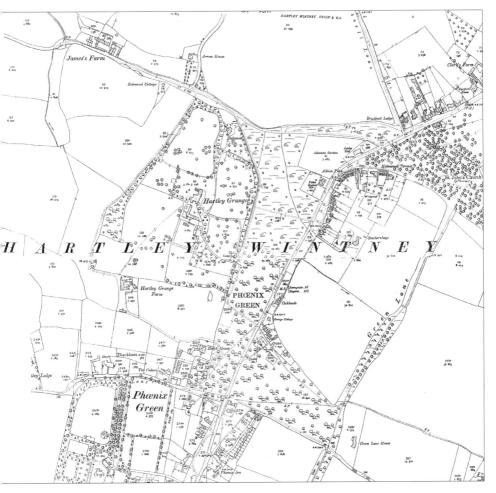

The Grange, Hartley Wintney c. 1920. (Hampshire Records Office)

THE ENGLAND 'MOUNTAIN'

This graphic representation of England results shows an easy climb in the years from the first international of 1871, rarely losing – two defeats on the trot being unheard of – up to the 'Great Split' of 1895. Then came professionalism, sucking out the bed of talent, and with it a rapid decline, England barely winning one game, let alone two back to back. The descent continued until 1906, when, for the first time in ten years, England managed a result in four consecutive games. This was not entirely unconnected with Adrian's reappearance a year after his first cap. Dropped and injured, England's descent continued until 1909/10 when the seeds were sown again. Adrian was back and England were scaling the heights once more.

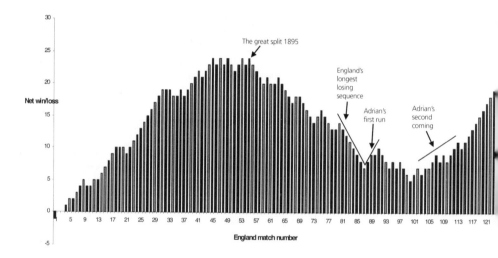

STOOP'S FIXTURE CARD

MATCH FACTS

	First Game	Last Game	Matches	Tries	Drop	Conversions
Rugby School XV	1900	1901	9	3	0	0
Oxford University	1901	1904	43	6	0	0
Harlequins	1901	1939	276	86	4	1
England	1905	1912	15	2	0	0
Barbarians	1905	1910	9	0	0	0
Surrey/Middlesex	1906	1912	9	0	0	0
			361	**97**	**4**	**1**

RUGBY SCHOOL XV, FOREIGN SCHOOL MATCHES

9 Dec 1899	Cheltenham	The Close	W	9-0
24 Nov 1900	Uppingham	The Close	W	58-0
8 Dec 1900	Cheltenham	Cheltenham	W	29-8

OXFORD UNIVERSITY, VARSITIES

13 Dec 1902	Cambridge	Queens Club	D	8-8
15 Dec 1903	Cambridge	Queens Club	W	18-13
13 Dec 1904	Cambridge (C)	Queens Club	L	10-15 (Try)

ENGLAND

18 Mar 1905	Scotland	Richmond	L	0-8
17 Mar 1906	Scotland	Inverleith	W	9-3
22 Mar 1906	France	Parc des Princes	W	35-8 (Try)
8 Dec 1906	South Africa	Crystal Palace	D	3-3
5 Jan 1907	France	Richmond	W	41-13
12 Jan 1907	Wales	Swansea	L	0-22
15 Jan 1910	Wales (C)	Twickenham	W	11-6
12 Feb 1910	Ireland (C)	Twickenham	D	0-0
19 Mar 1910	Scotland	Inverleith	W	14-5
21 Jan 1911	Wales	Swansea	L	11-15
28 Jan 1911	France	Twickenham	W	37-0 (Try)
11 Feb 1911	Ireland	Dublin	L	0-3
18 Mar 1911	Scotland	Twickenham	W	13-8
20 Jan 1912	Wales	Twickenham	W	8-0
16 Mar 1912	Scotland	Inverleith	L	3-8

BARBARIANS

22 Apr 1905	Swansea	L	6-26
24 Apr 1905	Cardiff	W	8-5
25 Apr 1905	Devonport Albion	L	3-11
14 Apr 1906	Cardiff	L	0-15
29 Mar 1907	Penarth (C)	W	8-5
30 Mar 1907	Cardiff	L	0-3
1 Apr 1907	Devonport Albion	W	9-0
26 Mar 1910	Cardiff (C)	W	16-5
28 Mar 1910	Swansea (C)	L	0-11

(C) denotes games in which Adrian was captain

RESPONSIBILITIES

OXFORD UNIVERSITY

Secretary	1902–1904
Captain	1904

HARLEQUINS

Captain	1906–1914
Secretary	1905–1914, 1920–1938, 1945
President	1920–1949

SURREY

President	1920–1948

ENGLAND

Captain	1910
Central District Representative	1911–1933
Member of International Board	1923
International Selector	1927–1931
Junior Vice-President	1928–1929
Senior Vice-President	1929–1932
President	1932–1933

BARBARIANS

Captain	1910
Committee	1907 –1909, 1910–1913

ARMY

Lieutenant	1911 (Territorials)
Lieutenant	1914
Captain	1918 (Military Cross 1918)

OTHER

Hartley Wintney Parish Council	
Hartley Wintney Cricket Club President	1944–1957

appendix five

THE OTHER HALF

In the five seasons from January 1905–April 1909 England played 22 games, using 17 different combinations at half-back – 53 backs in total. No half-back pairing was used for more than two games in a row. They won 7, drew 1 and lost 14.

In the five seasons from January 1910–April 1914 they played 21 games, using 8 different combinations at half-back – 33 backs in total. Stoop and Gotley had the longest half-back run, of five games. They won 16, drew 1 and lost 4.

THE BIG GAMES

Team		Half	Inside Centre		Other Harlequin back
Oxford 1902	D	Lyle	Fisher		
Oxford 1903	W	Munro	Sandford		
Oxford 1904	L	Munro	Nesbitt		
England 1905	L	Butcher	Brettagh		
Barbarians 1905	L	Munro	Hearson		
Barbarians 1905	W	Munro	Brettagh		
Barbarians 1905	L	Munro	Brettagh		
England 1906	W	Peters	Birkett		
England 1906	W	Peters	Birkett		
Barbarians 1906	L	Wade	McKeand		Lambert
England 1906	D	Jago	Birkett		
England 1906	W	Wedge	Birkett		Lambert
England 1907	L	Jago	Birkett		
Barbarians 1907	W	Flemmer	Vassall		Lambert
Barbarians 1907	L	Flemmer	McEvedy		Lambert
Barbarians 1907	W	Flemmer	Vassall		Lambert
England 1910	W	Gent	Birkett		Poulton
England 1910	D	Gent	Birkett		
England 1910	W	Gotley	Birkett	Stoop	
Barbarians 1910	W	Lindsay	Birkett	Stoop	Lambert
Barbarians 1910	L	Lindsay	Birkett	Stoop	Lambert
England 1911	L	Gotley	Birkett		Lambert
England 1911	W	Gotley	Birkett	Stoop	Lambert
England 1911	L	Gotley	Birkett	Stoop	Lambert
England 1911	W	Gotley	Birkett		Poulton
England 1912	W	Pym	Birkett	Poulton	Brougham
England 1912	L	Pym	Birkett	Poulton	Brougham

BIBLIOGRAPHY

A Rugby Compendium, Jenkins (The British Library, 1998)
A Walk Around Plugstreet, Spagnoly/Smith (Leo Cooper, 1977)
Barbarian Records: A Complete Record of the Barbarian Football Club, E. De Lissa (Nicholson & Watson, 1933)
Centenary History of the Rugby Football Union, Titley/McWhirter (RFU)
Christmas Truce, Brown/Seaton (Leo Cooper, 1984)
England: The Official RFU History, Jason Woolgar (Virgin Books, 1999)
Football Records of Rugby School 1823-1929 (George Over, 1930)
From Webb Ellis to World Cup, David Ray (Rugby School, 1991)
Great Rugger Players, 1900-1954, J.B.G. Thomas (Stanley Paul, 1955)
Half-time: 'The Mike and Me', H.B.T. Wakelam (Thomas Nelson & Sons, 1938)
Harlequin Story: The History of Harlequin Football Club, H.B.T. Wakelam (Phoenix House 1954)
History of the Queen's Royal Regiment Vol. VII, H.C. Wylly (Gale & Polden)
Marcus Samuel: Founder of Shell, Robert Henriques (Barrie & Rockliff, 1960)
Modern Rugby Football, C.B.J. Marriot (Bell, 1924)
Oxford v. Cambridge: The Story of the University Rugby Match, Howard Marshall (Clerke & Corkeran, 1951)
Reach for the Sky, Paul Brickhill (Collins, 1954)
Rugby Football, W.J.A. Davies (Websters Publications, 1923)
Rugby Remembered, David Parry-Jones (Partridge Press, 1988)
Rugby Since Arnold, J.B. Hope Simpson (MacMillan & Company, 1967)
Rugger: My Pleasure, A.A. Thomson (Museum Press, 1955)
Surrey Rugby: 100 Years, John Reed (Regency Press, 1978)
The Barbarians, A. Wemyss (Playfair Books, 1956)
The Barbarians: The Official History of the Barbarian Football Club, Nigel Starmer-Smith (MacDonald and Jane's, 1977)
The Book of English International Rugby: 1871-1982, John Griffiths (Willow Books, 1982)
The Game Goes On, H.B.T. Wakelam (The Sportsmans Book Club, 1954)
The Great Number Tens, Frank Keating (Partridge, 1993)
The Harlequins: 125 years of Rugby Football, Philip Warner (Breedon, 1991)
The History of the Rugby Football Union, O.L. Owen (Playfair Books, 1955)
The Life of Ronald Poulton, E.B. Poulton (Sidgwick & Jackson, 1919)
The Meteor (Rugby School, 1896-1919)
The Mobbs' Own: The 7th Battalion, the Northamptonshire Regiment, D. Woodall (Spratton 1994)
The Origins and Early Days of Rugby Football: How The Game Began, Eddy Rawlins (1989)
The Rugby Internationals Roll of Honour, E.H.D. Sewell (T.C. & E.C. Jack, 1919)
Twickenham: The Story of a Rugby Ground, Wallace Reyburn (Allen and Unwin, 1976)

PICTURE ACKNOWLEDGEMENTS

Byfleet Heritage Society: 1-9, 50, 60
Harlequins RFC: 10, 11, 20, 21, 30, **31**, 36, 42, 43, 51, 55, **71**, 76, 77, **81**
Michael Stoop: 12, 47, 49, 63, 73-75
Museum of Rugby, Twickenham (*italics* denotes private diaries of Adrian Stoop, held at the museum, **Bold** denotes publications unknown): 13, 14, *15*, 16, **17**, **18**, 19, **23**, **24**, 25, 26, **27**, 28, 29, **33**, **34**, **35**, **37**, **38**, *39*, 40, **41**, 44 (*The Tatler*), *45*, *48*, 52, 53, *54*, *56*, *57*, *58*, *59*, 61, 62, *64*, *65*, *66*, *67*, *68*, *69*, 70, 78, *79*, 80, *82*, *83*.
The Bystander: 22
Illustrated London News: 32
Queens Royal Surrey Regiment: 46
St John the Evangelist's, Hartley Wintney: 72

REFERENCE ACKNOWLEDGEMENTS

The National Archives:
— service records of Adrian Stoop (WO374/65838)
— service records of Ronald Poulton (WO374/52025)
— Foreign Office correspondence, Mamara (FO371/23299)
— citation for Military Cross, Adrian Stoop (*London Gazette* 11.01.19)
— citation for Military Cross, Michael Stoop (WO373/54)

INDEX